THE OCCULT LIFE OF THINGS

THE OCCULT LIFE OF
THINGS

Native Amazonian Theories of Materiality and Personhood

EDITED BY Fernando Santos-Granero

The University of Arizona Press   Tucson

The University of Arizona Press
© 2009 The Arizona Board of Regents
All rights reserved

www.uapress.arizona.edu

Library of Congress Cataloging-in-Publication Data
The occult life of things : native Amazonian theories of materiality and personhood
/ edited by Fernando Santos-Granero.
    p. cm.
    Includes bibliographical references and index.
    ISBN 978-0-8165-2874-5 (cloth : alk. paper)
    1. Indians of South America—Material culture—Amazon River Region.
2. Indians of South America—Amazon River Region—Rites and ceremonies.
3. Indian cosmology—Amazon River Region. 4. Material culture—Amazon
River Region. 5. Ceremonial objects—Amazon River Region. I. Santos-Granero,
Fernando, 1955–
    F2519.1.A6O33 2009
    299.8'9811—dc22   2009014537

Publication of this book is made possible in part by the proceeds of a permanent
endowment created with the assistance of a Challenge Grant from the National
Endowment for the Humanities, a federal agency.

14   13   12   11   10   09   6   5   4   3   2   1

Contents

Illustrations

Figures

Tables

THE OCCULT LIFE OF THINGS

Introduction

Amerindian Constructional Views of the World

Fernando Santos-Granero

With a few notable exceptions (Wilbert 1975; Ribeiro 1980, 1987, 1988; Reichel-Dolmatoff 1988; Whitten and Whitten 1988, 1993; Guss 1990; Pollock 1995; Rival 1996), in the past decades anthropologists have shown scant interest in the material culture of native Amazonian peoples. This contrasts with the work done on other ethnographic regions, such as Africa, where since the 1980s there has been a renewed interest in "the situated ways in which individuals use objects in the construction of identity, social formations, and culture itself" (Hardin and Arnoldi 1996:8). It is only very recently that objects and artifacts have come to attract once more the attention of Amazonianist specialists (Van Velthem 2001, 2003; Chaumeil 2001; Erikson 2001; Myers and Cipoletti 2002; Barcelos Neto 2004; Bilhaut 2006). The past indifference toward material life might be a reaction to the obsessive detail with which our modernist predecessors described the objects of Amerindian everyday life in order to determine cultural similarities and differences (e.g., Koch-Grünberg 1917; Métraux 1928; Nordenskiöld 1929; Tessmann 1930). It might also be, as Stephen Hugh-Jones suggests in this volume, that the Amerindian fascination with animals and the emphasis on people in recent theories of native Amazonian political economies have conspired to make the world of objects somewhat invisible. As the chapters in this volume indicate, however, objects figure as prominently, if not more prominently, than animals in native Amazonian cosmologies and imaginaries. This suggests that the paucity of studies on the material culture of Amazonian indigenous peoples should be credited to our own preconceptions rather than to any alleged Amerindian indifference with respect to objects.

The last important attempt to present an overview of Amerindian material culture was that of Julian H. Steward (1946) in volume 5 of his

Handbook of South American Indians. Since this work came to light, the topic has hardly been the subject of fresh anthropological reflection. The term "material culture" has itself become out of fashion, and rightly so, for it imposes a Western perspective on Amerindian phenomena. By focusing on the materiality of things and grouping objects on the side of cultural production, this notion obscures the fact that, in Amazonian ontologies, things—or at least some things—are considered to be subjectivities possessed of a social life. More importantly, as we shall see, it obscures the "natural"—in the sense of given—dimension of objects, and particularly artifacts, and the important role they play in the production of what we understand as Nature—including humans, animals, and plants.

This book does not intend, therefore, to revive the topic of "material culture." Rather, it strives to explore how native Amazonian peoples envision the lives of material objects. In other words, its purpose is to examine the "occult life of things"—occult because their lives are extraordinary, and occult because their personas are normally not visible to lay people. In the recent past, there has been a renewed interest in the notion of "animism" both within and without Amazonia (Descola 1992; Århem 1996; Howell 1996; Ingold 1998, 1999; Morris 1998, 1999; Bird-David 1999; Stringer 1999; Morrison 2000; Pedersen 2001; Harvey 2006). By placing emphasis on the "animic" character of Amerindian cosmologies, these authors have called for the need to expand the notion of Amazonian sociality beyond the sphere of human relations to include plants, animals, and even spirits. Similarly, a great deal has been said about the "perspectival" quality of relationships between all beings in the world, a quality whereby each category of being regards its own members as human while viewing other kinds of beings as nonhuman predators or prey (Århem 1990; Stolze Lima 1996, 1999, 2005; Viveiros de Castro 1996, 1998, 2004a and b; Vilaça 1992).

Objects, however, have been conspicuously absent from these analyses. In their pioneering works on Amerindian perspectivism, Kaj Århem (1990), Tânia Stolze Lima (1996), and Eduardo Viveiros de Castro (1996) concentrate on what they consider to be the three basic categories of living beings: humans, animals, and spirits. Viveiros de Castro (1998:470), who turned what was a fertile ethnographic intuition into a stimulating theory of Amerindian perception and thought, asserts that artifacts are only "occasionally" considered as subjectivities—adding, almost as an afterthought, that "the spiritualization of plants, meteorological phenomena or artefacts seems to [be] secondary or derivative in comparison with the spiritualization of animals" (Viveiros de Castro 1998:472). The studies gathered in this volume demonstrate otherwise. Animic and perspectival notions also encompass the world of "things," a term used here to refer not only to artifacts—objects made by gods and humans, including images, songs, names, and designs—but also to natural objects and phenomena that are believed to be central to human life and reproduction. As we shall see, objects are not derivative. Rather, they are often attributed the role of primordial building blocks in Amerindian constructional cosmologies and composite anatomies.

The widespread distribution in the Americas of the myth of the "revolt of objects"—objects rebelling against their masters—attests to the pervasiveness of the idea that in primordial times, things (or at least some of them) were human (Lévi-Strauss 1969). Even objects that are not thought to have an intrinsic living dimension are nevertheless believed to be capable of becoming endowed with properties generally attributed to living beings. Some objects are imbued with the power to attract those persons with whom they come into contact; other objects become, through intimate contact, of one essence with their makers/owners, and may be as much the subject of sorcery as the people to whom they belong; still others are believed to have important fertilizing powers that increase with the passage of time and with their transmission from generation to generation as family or collective heirlooms. In brief, there are multiple ways of being an object in Amerindian lived worlds.

The contributors to this volume focus on three domains regarding native Amazonian conceptions of things. First, there is the issue of the "subjective life of objects." Which things have a subjective dimension? And how is this subjectivity manifested? Second, there is the issue of the "social life of things," by which we understand not the way things move in and out of various "regimes of value" à la Arjun Appadurai (1986),[1] but rather the diverse ways in which human beings and things relate *qua* subjectivities. Lastly, there is the issue of the "historical life of things." Because of their high value as ritual objects, prestige goods, or family heirlooms, some things (e.g., flutes, masks, shamanic stones, feather headdresses) have both a social history—a history that recounts who made them and how they changed hands—and a biography—a personal history recounting their life cycle. Contributors to this book address these issues combining linguistic, ethnological, and historical perspectives. Their works draw on a wealth of information gathered from ten Amerindian peoples belonging to seven different linguistic families. Together, the authors have identified the basic tenets of what can be considered a native Amazonian theory of materiality and personhood. These tenets I discuss in the following pages.

Constructional Cosmologies

The notion that in mythical times, all beings were human—or appeared to each other as human—constitutes one of the most widespread native Amazonian mythemes. In times of indifferentiation, the predecessors of all living beings—humans, animals, plants, and spirits, but also a variety of objects—shared the primordial mythscape with powerful creator gods, cultural heroes, or mischievous tricksters. This idyllic existence, native Amazonians say, came to an end due to the fallibility of the ancient people, at which point emerged the different categories of beings that populate the world nowadays. This emergence was not, however, a straightforward process. It involved multiple metamorphoses, by which primordial people passed through different modalities of existence before acquiring their (more or less) definite form. It entailed processes of bodily deconstitution and reconstitution marked by extreme forms of interspecific permutation of body parts, including artifacts that were formerly body parts and body parts that were formerly artifacts. And it implied the intervention of powerful demiurges whose creative capacities often took the form of divine "technological acts" (Van Velthem 2003:90). More importantly, the coming into being of the present-day world was not the result of a creation *ex nihilo*, but rather the product of the transformation of pre-existing things (Viveiros de Castro 2004a:477). These characteristics endow Amerindian cosmologies with a "constructional" character that contrasts strongly with the "creationist" emphasis of other cosmologies such as the Judeo-Christian. This does not mean that Amerindians cannot conceptualize a creation ex nihilo, as Stephen Hugh-Jones (this volume) has very well demonstrated is the case of the Tukano. But even Amerindian cosmologies that evoke an initial creation ex nihilo can be described as being constructional, insofar as subsequent creative acts assumed the form of creations via transformation.

According to Viveiros de Castro (1998), in Amerindian cosmologies humans and animals appear as the primordial forms, whereas plants and objects seem to be derivative. Proof of this would be the extended notion that cultural artifacts originated when humans borrowed or stole the prototypes possessed by nonhuman beings (Viveiros de Castro 2004a:477). This, however, is far from being a universal notion, as is attested by the native Amazonian cosmologies discussed in this book and elsewhere. In these cosmologies, objects and artifacts appear as having existed prior to other forms of being. More interestingly, they are often attributed a crucial function in the creation and constitution of humans, animals, and plants.

Tukano people assert that in the beginning, there was only the creator god and his Instruments of Life and Transformation, artifacts of great ceremonial and shamanic significance (Hugh-Jones, this volume). These instruments, made of white crystal, were constituent parts of the creator god's body and later on became the bones of true humans. Similarly, the Wakuénai claim that the body of Kuwái, the primordial human being and creator god, is made up of a variety of sacred flutes and trumpets (Hill, this volume). In Mamaindê cosmology, the first beings to come into existence were humans and their artifacts, which were themselves human (Miller, this volume). When a child opened the gourd that contained the night, the primordial people and their artifacts turned into animals. Axe became a tayra, arrows were transformed into poisonous snakes, and Carrying Basket turned into a jaguar. A similar conception is found in the Cashinahua myth of the great flood that ended with the transformation of ancient people and artifacts into animals (Lagrou, this volume). For example, the boa came into being as the result of the transformation of a couple lying down in a patterned hammock—this explains the beautiful designs of its skin. Wayana people claim that the demiurges' first creations were the primordial people and their instruments, which were made out of the same raw materials and had a bodily existence (Van Velthem 2003:93, 120). At the end of the time of indifferentiation, the bodies or parts of bodies of these primordial beings turned into present-day animals, plants, and artifacts. Because they were created by the demiurges, objects have the capacity to transform into other beings, mostly animals.

A slight variant of this theme is found in Yanesha (Santos-Granero, this volume) and Piro (Peter Gow, personal communication) cosmologies, which recount how present-day animals are ancient human beings transformed into animals. The artifacts they possessed in mythical times became emblematic parts of their bodies. The blood-covered axe of the primordial Curassow became the red beak of the present-day curassow, the straw mat on which Armadillo slept became the plated shell of its animal counterpart, and the beautifully woven hammock of Spider became the spider's subtle web. In other Amerindian cosmologies, some artifacts are said to have appeared even before the creator gods themselves. The

Miraña claim, for instance, that before coming into existence, the Creator was pure, disembodied consciousness (Karadimas 2005:259–66). In such a condition, he created a stool on which he sat, thereby giving shape to his own body. With the help of Yurupari, who was flute and earthworm simultaneously—and was the only other living being—he created the animal and plant people.

What becomes clear from these ethnographies is that in native Amazonian thought, the creation of life is a constructional process in which primordial bodies and body parts—often conceived of as prototypical artifacts—play a crucial role. Based on his data on the Miraña, who assert that human beings were made up of different fish species, Dimitri Karadimas (2005:402) refers to primordial creations as acts of "corporeal organization of species," each species being fabricated from the bodies and body parts of other natural species. Given the widespread belief that most living beings contain within themselves the bodies and body parts of primordial artifact-people, I would suggest that it might be more accurate to understand demiurgic acts as a form of "artifactual organization of species." Because artifacts were believed to be people or parts of people that were later transformed into other beings, it can be said—as suggests Lúcia Van Velthem (2003:119)—that in native Amazonian ontologies, people and objects share the same "symbolic frame of fabrication." They are simultaneously things and embodied social relations.[2]

Artifactual Anatomies

It has long been accepted that in Amerindian societies, bodies are the main instruments to convey social and cosmological meanings (Seeger et al. 1979; Turner 1995). They are the privileged means for imprinting and preserving both self-identity and the memory of changes of status (Clastres [1973] 1998; Viveiros de Castro 1979). Viveiros de Castro (1998:480) has argued that the ultimate aim of the social construction of the body is to "particularize a body still too generic" in order to make it different from that of other human and nonhuman beings. He further contends that whereas the model of the spirit is the human spirit, that of the body is animal. From this point of view, the maximum social objectification of bodies, which generally takes place in ceremonial contexts, would coincide with its maximum "animalization"—when the bodies of participants are clad with impressive feathers, pelts, and other emblematic animal body parts (Viveiros de Castro 1998:480). However, since animal bodies are frequently conceived of as being constructed out of cultural objects—and this is confirmed by the fact that animals themselves see their body parts as cultural instruments (Viveiros de Castro 1998:470)—we are forced to conclude that the model of the human body is not the body of animals but rather the body of artifacts.

This has some important corollaries. If bodies are, as Viveiros de Castro (1998:478) has suggested, the main site of differentiation between different life forms, and if they are, as they seem to be, composite or even artifactual constructions, then interspecific bodily differences are never absolute but just a matter of degree. If bodies are indeed "bundles of affects and capacities" (Viveiros de Castro 1998:478)—and there is much evidence to support this conclusion—then they would be made up of a combination of affects and capacities derived from different living beings, among which artifacts figure prominently. From this perspective, there would be no pure species, but rather a variety of species manifesting the affects and capacities of a diversity of other living beings.

This should not be all that surprising given native Amazonian theories of personhood, which place emphasis on the incorporation of the Other as an indispensable feature in the making of Self. Persons are not born as such, but must be intentionally manufactured or shaped through the input of a variety of substances and affects provided by parents and kin (Londoño Sulkin 2005). The person is a complex amalgam of substances and influences. Since kin are originally Others, alterity becomes a crucial component in the making of human bodies (Vilaça 2002). Marilyn Strathern's (1990:13) dictum with regard to Melanesian notions of personhood, namely, that "persons are frequently constructed as the plural and composite site of the relationships that produce them," is thus also valid for lowland South America. Els Lagrou (this volume) has aptly labeled this particular way of conceiving personhood as the "Amerindian mode of relatedness," a social mode by which every being is a synthesis of the combined efforts of all the beings who have contributed—socially and bodily—to his or her existence. Such a constructional and relational perspective, which is basic in the fabrication of social bodies, could not be absent in the acts of the creator gods.

As we have seen, in mythical times, artifacts were the bodies or parts of bodies of primordial human beings. At the end of the times of indifferentiation, they became constitutive parts of human and other-than-human persons, such as animals, plants, and spirits. In some Amerindian cosmologies, it is said that the artifactual mode of reproduction preceded the genital mode (see Hugh-Jones, this volume). Often, however, native Amazonians view both modes of production/reproduction as being homologous. More importantly, as I suggest below, there is evidence supporting the idea that in Amerindian ontologies, it is craftsmanship rather than childbearing that provides the model for all creative acts. If this is true, it could then be asserted that the artifactual mode of production/reproduction is not only prior to the genital mode but also to the paradigmatic mode of creation.

Artifacts were important not only in the fabrication of primordial human and other-than-human persons in pre-subjective, pre-objective mythical times. Their contribution to the construction of persons continues to be salient even today. Among Urarina, baby hammocks, elaborated by mothers, and hammock rattles, made with animal parts and a variety of objects presented by fathers and other kinspeople, are believed to shape, protect, and fortify the bodies of their baby owners (Walker, this volume). Parents carefully select the components of hammock rattles, which are generally gender specific, to instill into their babies highly valued artifactual or animal qualities. Cashinahua boys and girls undergoing ritual seclusion are presented with stools made from the buttress roots of the lupuna, so that they acquire from this powerful tree the knowledge of how to live a tranquil life (Lagrou, this volume). Objects are important components of the bodies of all living beings, having been incorporated either through primordial processes of creation or through ceremonial body-making techniques. The same can be said of objectified animal and plant subjectivities, which, like Urarina hammock rattles or Cashinahua ritual stools, are considered to be vitally important in the production of well-formed and competent human beings. As a result, all living beings appear as composite beings possessing eminently artifactual anatomies. This is why, as Joana Miller suggests in this volume, a native Amazonian theory of objects must be a theory of the person.

Multiple Objectivities

One of the notions that transpire from this volume is that there are "multiple ways of being a thing" in the Amerindian lived world. Without attempting to exhaust all possibilities, in this volume I mention at least five categories of objects with this notion in mind: (1) objects originating through self-transformation, (2) objects originating through metamorphosis, (3) objects originating through mimesis, (4) objects originating through ensoulment, and (5) plain objects. Objects in the first four categories, which are amenable to some kind of subjectivation, encompass a large number of "things": ceremonial items, shamanic paraphernalia, personal ornaments, songs, names and images, tools and weapons, cooking utensils, sleeping accessories, baby accouterments, personal documents, and a broad range of industrial objects—only recently incorporated into Amerindian societies—including not only shotguns and flashlights but even airplanes (see Turner, this volume). These objects differ from others not only in the way they have become subjectivized but also in terms of the degrees of animacy and agentivity they are thought to possess (Santos-Granero, Erikson, Guzmán-Gallegos, and Hill, this volume).

Ellen Basso (1985) was the first to point out that in Amerindian ontologies, not all beings were attributed the same kind of powers. On the basis of Kalapalo data, she suggested that each class of beings—including objects—is characterized by possessing particular forms of communication skills and by being able to act only upon beings of the same class or of classes with lower degrees of animacy. Philippe Descola (1996:375–76) has also noticed that communicational skills were the basis for Achuar hierarchies of animate/inanimate beings. From an Achuar point of view, he contends, such skills depend on the possession of or lack of a *wakan* (soul), as well as on the strength of the wakan of each species. At the bottom of the Achuar hierarchy of life forms, there are some animate beings and inanimate objects that, having no wakan of their own, can be said to be the only beings that properly belong to the sphere of "nature" as understood in Western thought.

In a similar vein, María Guzmán-Gallegos (this volume) suggests that "subjectivity does not necessarily presuppose the presence of a soul, whereas not all agency presupposes will and intentionality." Some objects are "subjective" objects. They are conceived of as "persons" insofar as they possess an independent "soul" and are "agents of meaningful action" (Pollock 1996:320). Other objects are simply "subjectivized" objects. They possess some kind of soul substance, but not in the quantity or quality needed to be able to act on their own. They require the intervention of human beings to activate their agency and, in this sense, they can be described as "secondary agents" (Gell 1998).[3] Thus, the Kawoká flutes of the Wauja, possessed of a strong *apapaatai* animal spirit (Barcelos Neto, this volume), contrast greatly with Yanesha objects, which are mostly subjectivized rather than subjective objects and are thus incapable of autonomous agency (Santos-Granero, this volume).

Since the communicative aspect is crucial in native Amazonian classification of animate/inanimate beings, the only objects recognized as such
from an Amerindian point of view are those that lack any kind of soul
stuff and with which no communication is possible. All other "objects" are
actually subjectivities more or less endowed with soul substance, which
is tantamount to possessing communication skills. It is this capacity for
communication that turns "things" into social beings (Douglas and Ney
1998:46). From a native point of view, the more powerful among these
objects/subjects are those that can engage in actual dialogues with human
beings, whether in dreams, spirit trips, or supernatural encounters—and
particularly those that can impart important life-giving or life-taking
knowledge. Tukano flutes, Urarina shamanic stone bowls, and Wauja
drums are among these hyper-communicative objects. Thus, from a
native point of view, materiality is both a social and a communicative
process. However, since communication is always subjective and meaning
unstable, the degree of subjectivity attributed to objects, as well as their
meaning, is always open to negotiation and debate. Indeed, the subjectivity of objects reveals itself to, or is perceived by, different categories
of people in very different ways, shamans being recognized as the most
capable of engaging objects as subjects.

Native Amazonians also distinguish objects according to their use-
value, opposing artifacts of daily use to those used in ceremonial contexts.
Tukano people, for instance, consider all human artifacts as *gaheuni* or
things capable of subjectivation (Hugh-Jones, this volume). The paradigmatic gaheuni, however, are the Instruments of Life and Transformation,
the fertilizing ceremonial objects that are indispensable for ensuring the
continuity of all forms of life. Likewise, Kayapo designate all personal
possessions or valuables—including names and rights to ritual roles and
songs—by a single term, *nêkretch* (Turner, this volume). They make, however, a further distinction between "common" and "beautiful" nêkretch,
the latter being mostly names and valuables transmitted through complex
collective ceremonies, as opposed to common names and objects whose
transmission is confined to the sphere of the extended family.

Objects are also classified according to their origin, the main distinguishing factor being the opposition between native and industrial goods.
Foreign objects have been gradually incorporated into native societies
since the time of their contact with European peoples, to the point that
some of these objects are conceived of as constituting an intrinsic part of
"traditional" lifeways. Native Amazonians do not always agree, however,

as to the animacy of these alien objects and their place in local hierarchies of life forms. In some societies, such as the Matis and Yanesha, only native objects are believed to be animated or capable of becoming animated (Erikson and Santos-Granero, this volume). This is also true for the Yekuana, who consider that only locally made objects possess subjectivity and are thus capable of relating or being social (Guss 1990). In other societies, such as the Urarina (Walker, this volume), both native and foreign objects are thought to have a subjective dimension. Likewise, the Tukano term *gaheuni* and the Kayapo term *nêkretch* encompass both native and industrial objects (Hugh-Jones and Turner, this volume). In both cases, these objects are endowed with subjectivity, being the objectivation of the capacities, affects, and knowledges of the people who made them. Not all of the objects, however, are thought to possess the same kind of potency—some are more powerful than others and should thus be taken care of more conscientiously.

As Hugh-Jones has proposed in this volume, not only are there multiple ways of being an object in Amerindian ontologies, but there are also important differences in terms of what he calls "object regimes." The wealth and social prominence of objects in societies such as the Tukano, Kayapo, and Wauja contrast with the simpler "material culture" of the Urarina, Yanesha, and Matis, and even more with the paucity of the material life of the Mamaindê. This volume has only pointed toward such fascinating differences, which certainly deserve further analysis. The existence of inalienable objects, individually or collectively owned, that escape the common fate of native Amazonian artifacts once their owners die and that are transmitted from generation to generation (see below) must have, undoubtedly, important social and political implications of which we are still unaware. Differences between object regimes do not obviate, however, the existence of many shared notions about the world of things that point to a common, underlying native theory of materiality.

Linguistic Markers

Animic peoples do not consider that all forms of existence are endowed with animacy and agentivity. Some objects are just plain objects. In turn, some living beings are considered to lack souls or other attributes of personhood and for this reason are distinguished from other animate beings that possess them (Descola 1996:375–76; Camargo 2006). Distinctions between animate and inanimate beings or between more and less animated beings are often marked through a variety of linguistic devices (Harvey 2006:33). These may be positive or negative; that is, they can operate either by adding markers to distinguish a group of items from others groups or by not marking them, thus implicitly grouping all unmarked items into the same category. On the side of positive forms of marking, we find the Cashinahua, who, through the use of a series of possessor elements, distinguish between human and nonhuman beings according to whether the latter are assimilated or not to the category of "humanness." Eliane Camargo (2006) asserts that in the Cashinahua language, the opposition between humans and nonhumans (animals and nonanimals) is not pertinent. Rather, the main opposition is that between humans and nonhumans assimilated to humanness versus nonhumans. Artifacts are conceived of as belonging to the class of nonhumans and in genitival phrases are morphologically treated as they are. Subjectivity and agentivity are attributed, however, to certain manufactured objects, particularly in shamanic contexts. On the side of negative forms of marking, we find the Urarina, who do not distinguish objects from animals, plants, or humans either through the use of pronouns for animateness or nominal classifiers, thus indicating that all these forms of existence are capable of subjectivity (Walker, this volume).

In other societies, such as the Wayana, personal belongings and body parts cannot be named without a possessive pronoun, a marker underlining their subjective quality (Van Velthem 2003:141). This is also the case for the Yanesha people, who consider body parts (arms, legs, heart), immaterial aspects of self (vitalities, shadow souls), and objects of personal use (tunics, beads, chestbands) as being equally animated (Santos-Granero, this volume). In this case, however, the common subjectivity of these forms of existence is emphasized by marking the non-possessed forms of these terms with a privative suffix. This linguistic practice is connected to the widespread native Amazonian belief that, through intimate contact, objects of personal use become gradually "ensouled" or infused with the soul substance of their owners, thus acquiring a certain degree of subjectivity. This particularity is not always linguistically marked, however. Although the Matis share the notion that personal ornaments become subjectivized through long-term contact, they classify those ornaments as being *chu*—"belongings" or "inanimate possessions"—rather than *wiwa*—"pets," the term they use to classify nonhuman "subjected beings" (Erikson, this volume).

Among the Wakuénai, levels of animacy and power are marked through the use of numeral classifiers that arrange different beings and objects into noun sets according to common interactional properties, such as edibility, utility, gender, and place. According to Jonathan Hill (this volume), "Things most likely to become subjectivized are those that come into bodily contact through eating, using, and touching; things that come in pairs or that are otherwise involved in quantitative expressions; and things that are believed to have exceptional power to cause harm in ritual and myth." The cases discussed in this volume provide a glimpse of the rich semiotic resources that are available to describe materiality and materialization in native Amazonian languages. These resources include not only grammatical aspects but also sounds, music, and gestures, constituting as much a way of speaking as a way of feeling/being. A deeper knowledge of the kinds of things that are amenable to subjectivation in different Amerindian societies, together with more detailed linguistic studies focused on the issues of animacy and agentivity, such as Camargo's (2006), would certainly contribute to a better understanding of native Amazonian constructional cosmologies. It would also provide much necessary linguistic data to enhance our comprehension of native Amazonian forms of animism and perspectivism.

Subjectivations

Whereas some objects are thought to possess strong, autonomous souls, others are credited with weaker forms of subjectivity or none at all. In other words, not all objects are believed to be subjective in the same way. These "states of subjectivity" (Stolze Lima 2005:214) depend to a great extent on the amount and quality of the "soul substance" that they are thought to possess. Objects that lack autonomous souls are often dependent on some kind of human intervention to become subjectivized or personified. This is in consonance with Amerindian theories of personhood, which view persons as beings that possess a soul or vitality. It is the possession of a soul that allows for awareness of oneself and of others, as well as for the ability to think. From this point of view, "persons" are volitional and relational social beings with whom communication and reciprocity is possible (Harvey 2006:xvii; see also Taylor 1993). They know themselves through the relationships they maintain with others. More importantly, as Beth Conklin (2001:141) has suggested, the capacities of the self are thought to be activated only through interaction with others. Indeed, it is through relationships with persons different from oneself that creativity and vitality are possible. Amerindian personhood is, in this sense, a "fractal personhood" insofar as it involves relations of incorporation of the Other into the Self at different scales, which are always similar to each other (Luciani and Antonio 2001). As Viveiros de Castro (2004a:480) has so compellingly put it, from an Amerindian point of view, "the self is always the gift of the other."

The subjectivity or personhood of objects is also relational, particularly in the case of objects lacking autonomous souls, which depend on a subject to realize their subjectivity. The subjectivation or subjectification of such objects is achieved through intimate contact or through the activation of a pre-existing, latent subjectivity. In the first situation, which involves mostly but not exclusively artifacts, a series of objects—which may or may not have been produced by their owner—become subjectivized through the gradual diffusion of the soul stuff of their owners into their most personal belongings (Miller, Walker, Lagrou, Santos-Granero and Hill, this volume). Subjectivation through ensoulment entails a kind of embodiment by which the ensouled objects become a sort of "extension of their owners' bodies" (Santos-Granero, this volume). This notion seems to be very widespread in native Amazonia. The Urarina view baby hammocks as being simultaneously extensions and constitutive parts of their baby owners; indeed, each appears as an extension of the other (Walker, this volume). The same is true of Mamaindê personal ornaments or gender-specific objects (Miller, this volume). According to Philippe Erikson (this volume), among the Matis, those objects that are in closest contact with their owners become, as it were, "extra-somatic body parts." Since in many native Amazonian ontologies souls and bodies are seen as "doubles" (Vilaça 1992), any addition or subtraction to the one must be reflected in the other. This explains why human and other-than-human people seen in dreams or shamanic spirit trips always appear clad in their emblematic clothes, ornaments, and weapons. Viveiros de Castro (1998:482) is thus right when claiming that "it is not so much that the body is a clothing but rather that clothing is a body" (see also Santos-Granero 2006).

From an Amerindian point of view, the boundaries of a person are not coterminous with his or her body, not only in the sense that bodies are relational and subjectivity communal but also because a series of personal objects become part of the body (Harvey 2006:113). Certain personal, generally inalienable objects are even thought to stand for the qualities and/or subjectivity of their owners. Mamaindê bead necklaces (Miller, this volume), Kayapo "beautiful" nêkretch valuables (Turner, this volume), and Runa identity documents (Guzmán-Gallegos, this volume) are some of the many objects that are thought to possess this metonymical quality. Because of the close association, or even identity, between bodies and personal objects, actions that affect personal objects are thought to affect their owners in similar ways (Santos-Granero, this volume). Furthermore, because personal objects are constitutive parts of their owners, they may be used by enemies or evil agents to bewitch their owners under the principles of what James George Frazer (1982) dubbed "contagious magic."

The second form of subjectivation involves objects that are not the product of human efforts, but rather of supernatural agency. Being the result of their productive agency, these objects embody the powerful intentionalities and affects of their supernatural makers. They are generally not credited with possessing an independent soul and thus depend on human intervention to become active. This is the case with Yanesha panpipes, whose subjectivity and generative powers—derived from the creator gods associated with them—can be activated only by means of offerings of manioc beer, coca juice, and tobacco smoke (Santos-Granero, this volume). Other objects of supernatural origin, such as Runa curing stones or Urarina shamanic stone bowls, are thought to possess an autonomous soul and thus to have intentionality and agency of their own (Guzmán-Gallegos and Walker, this volume). Their subjectivity, however, finds full expression only when activated by the shaman who found them and took possession of them. Modes of activation vary significantly. In order to utilize *egaando*, or stone bowls, Urarina shamans must first capture and tame them through ritual dialogue, songs, and dieting. As Harry Walker (this volume) asserts, the egaando have to be "coerced into full personhood." In contrast, Runa shamanic stones can neither be tamed nor controlled (Guzmán-Gallegos, this volume). Their subjectivity and agency can be activated in positive ways only by establishing amicable relationships with them. Only when Runa shamans have managed to befriend a particular stone does the latter become an active helper in the context of curing sessions. Similar relationships of friendship between shamans and their stones are found among the Zapara (Bilhaut 2006; see also Santos-Granero 2007 on friendly relations between shamans and their familiars).

Whether subjectivized through intimate contact or appropriation, these objects are always conceived of as extensions of their owners' bodies. When their owners die, they appear—in the words of Terence Turner (this volume)—as an "unburied part of the dead person's corpse" and thus have to be destroyed. If they are not destroyed, the soul of the dead person might linger around the objects that were a constitutive part of that person in order to haunt the living and drag their souls away to live in the afterworld. To avoid this, all the possessions of a dead person, including ornaments, weapons, utensils, pets, houses, and gardens are destroyed, burned, killed, or abandoned. In the past, this practice included even captive slaves, who were often killed and buried with their masters to serve them in the afterworld (Santos-Granero 2009). Despite its widespread character, this belief is not, however, universal and does not apply to all objects. In certain native Amazonian societies, generally those exhibiting more "opulent" object regimes, some artifacts are spared from being destroyed when their owners die. These particularly esteemed objects, such as Tukano feather headdresses, Wauja Kawoká flutes, and Kayapo nêkretch names, are kept and transmitted from generation to generation (Hugh-Jones, Barcelos Neto and Turner, this volume). Some of these objects, like the peccary tusk necklaces of Guiana, are enhanced throughout time, representing the accumulated prowess not only of the wearer but also of his ancestors (Im Thurn 1893:196). They have the character of "inalienable possessions," objects imbued with the intrinsic and ineffable identities of their owners— often a social collectivity—that are never given away and are passed on from one generation to the next within the closed context of clans, descent groups, or moieties (Weiner 1992:6).

Objectivations

Amerindian ontologies contemplate both the possibility of objects turning into subjects and that of subjects turning into objects. Processes of objectivation or objectification are thus the counterpart of the processes of subjectivation/subjectification discussed above. There are at least three ways in which subjects can be turned into objects: through craftsmanship, through ritual action, and through de-subjectivation. The first situation entails the direct production of artifacts, which appear as the materialization of the subjective dimensions of their makers (Erikson, Hugh-Jones, Lagrou, and Santos-Granero, this volume). The situation assumes the form of a material embodiment of nonmaterial intentionalities (Viveiros de Castro 2004a:470). Artifacts constitute the objective expression of the knowledge, skills, and affects of their makers, and thus partake of their makers' subjectivity (Karsten 1923:12; McCallum 2001:93). This agrees with the Amerindian notion that views makers and their artifacts as being related in terms of filiation. As Els Lagrou, following Joanna Overing (1988), suggests in this volume, artifacts are often described as the "children" of their makers.

Less well acknowledged is the fact that Amerindian people conceive of their actual children as being as much artifactual creations as blowguns and pots. Cashinahua people describe the processes of fabrication of babies and artifacts in similar terms (McCallum 2001:16–17). And the Wayana use the same verb (*tihé*) to refer to the production of both children and objects (Van Velthem 2003:119). Since production is understood as the process through which something is created, made to appear, or made to happen, the Wayana designate all things "fabricated" by a person, including children, hunted animals, and captured enemies, by a single term that translates as "my made things" (Van Velthem 2003:141). This explains why children are often placed in the same category as other personal "belongings" and are said to be "owned" by their parents (Rivière 1969:243; Santos-Granero 1991:211; Belaúnde 2001:121). The artifactual character of Amerindian children is powerfully expressed by Mamaindê parents, who affectionately call daughters undergoing puberty initiation rituals "my thing" (Miller, this volume).

Like children, artifacts are the result of the input of substances and affects belonging to their makers/genitors and, thus, also constitute a sort of extension of their bodies. Urarina baby hammocks constitute the embodiment or materialization of the love and affection of the mother who made it, as well as that of her female kin, who contribute to its making through gifts of selected items that belonged to the hammocks of their own children (Walker, this volume). Cashinahua artifacts and designs constitute, in turn, the "crystallized memory" of the persons who made them, as well as that of the invisible network that links their makers to other human and nonhuman beings (Lagrou, this volume). This characteristic of artifacts was already pointed out by Marcel Mauss (1954) in his essay *The Gift*. In this work, he argues that gift-giving must be reciprocated—both because gifts retain attributes of the person by whom they were given and because they embody the relationship that exists between two persons by virtue of their mutual obligation to receive and reciprocate gifts. This is so because craftsmanship involves a double process of objectivation/subjectivation. By transforming raw matter by means of his or her affects, skills, and intentionality, the maker produces an object that is simultaneously a subject—a subjectivized object that acts as an objectified subject.

The second form of objectivation is related to the sphere of ritual, often shamanic, action. It involves a process of objectivation of supernatural subjectivities, which Jonathan Hill (this volume) has very aptly labeled the "materialization of the occult." Here, too, the process entails the production of an object that is simultaneously a subject. In shamanic contexts, subjective relations (fear of death, illness and misfortune, conflict and anger) are turned into tangible materialities under the guise of pathogenic objects (Guzmán-Gallegos and Hill, this volume). Native Amazonians often conceive of shamanic darts as thwarted desires transformed by shamans into harmful objects (Gow 2003). The fabrication of certain ritual objects is frequently viewed as a means of materializing supernatural subjectivities. The ritual operations aimed at giving material shape to such normally invisible entities are surrounded by great secrecy and involve ascetic practices, such as fasting, vigils, and sexual abstinence, as well as numerous supernatural precautions. They often involve singing and chanting, as is the case with Wakuénai shamans who "sing into being" the cord that connects the world of the ancestors to the world of the living (Hill, this volume).

In some instances, artifacts thus materialized are thought to possess strong, independent souls. They are often attributed great agency and extraordinary powers, including the power of self-transformation. Such is the case of Wauja flutes, masks, drums, and other objects embodying powerful apapaatai animal spirits, which are made by ritual specialists for the purpose of shamanic curing (Barcelos Neto, this volume). These objectified subjects are thought to possess different degrees of power and agentivity, determined according to the hardness and durability of the materials out of which they are made. Wayana and Miraña masks are also believed to be the embodiment of the powerful, monstrous beings or masters of different animal species that they represent (Van Velthem 2003:125, 198–99; Karadimas 2005:322). For this reason, the masks require very careful ritual handling. Their making, often entailing the efforts of the entire collectivity, involves not only great skills of craftsmanship but also the input of nonvisual elements such as movement, sound, and fragrances. All these elements are indispensable in order to bring to life the powerful supernatural beings that the masks represent and to engage them in ritual operations in favor of the collectivity.

The aim of processes of objectification through craftsmanship or ritual action is always the production of an object-as-subject. In contrast, the third form of objectification involves the de-subjectivation of a subjective, or subjectivized, object in order to turn it into an inanimate thing. Such operations are effectuated, for instance, before transferring personal objects or powerful ritual objects to a third party. In such situations, objects are deprived of their subjectivity to prevent them from harming the receiver or from being used by the receiver to harm the donor. Before passing tobacco tubes and other powerful shamanic artifacts on to someone else, Yanesha people thoroughly cleanse them (Santos-Granero, this volume). Likewise, Matis men conscientiously scrub curare pots destined to be sold (Erikson, this volume). Native Amazonians often refuse to sell used items unless they have undergone a process of de-subjectivization. Even new items may be manufactured in ways that will prevent their subjectivity from becoming manifest. Thus, Wauja masks made for sale lack eyes, mouths, and/or teeth so that their monstrous subjectivity will not be activated due to lack of proper ritual tending (Barcelos Neto, this volume). In other native Amazonian societies, highly subjectivized artifacts are taken out of public circulation in order to de-subjectivize them. Urarina baby hammocks, carefully kept out of the way by mothers until they rot, are a case in point (Walker, this volume). Sometimes, extremely powerful subjective objects may also be mutilated prior to taking them out of circulation. After ceremonial masks have fulfilled their function, Wayana people deprive them of their feathers before leaving them to rot under the ceiling of the ceremonial house (Van Velthem 2003:214). By doing so, they seek to weaken the masks' subjectivity and render them harmless.

These practices suggest that the life of Amerindian artifacts follows a cycle similar to that of other living beings. They are brought to life through craftsmanship or ritual operations; they actively participate in a variety of economic, social, or ceremonial contexts; and once they are worn out or unable to continue performing the tasks for which they were made, they are left to die or are "magically killed" (Turner, this volume). Often, however, Amerindian artifacts are unable to fully complete their life cycles. When a person dies, most of his or her possessions are burned, destroyed, or abandoned in an effort to de-subjectivize them so that they will not haunt the living. On such occasions, the lives of objects come to an abrupt end. Since artifacts, like people, have a life cycle, they also possess a biography (Kopytoff 1986)—that is, a personal history recounting how and when they came to life, who brought them into being, what life experiences they had, what relations they entertained with other living beings, and, sometimes, how their lives came to an end. This aspect of the occult life of things, which has been insufficiently explored in this volume, could be a very promising area of research, especially key to understanding the connection between artifacts and sociopolitical organization in opulent object regimes.

Objectual Relations

Animic ontologies consider the world to be full of persons, only some of whom are human. Sociality in such contexts encompasses not only humans but also other-than-human persons. Human life is always lived in relationship with these other persons (Harvey 2006:xi). Intersubjective relations between humans and objects, like those between humans and animals, are not exempt from conflicts and power struggles. Indeed, relations between humans and objects are often expressed in terms of power asymmetries. Such asymmetries generally derive from absolute differences in terms of the degree of animacy and agentivity attributed to different life forms. In such contexts, the place of each life form is more or less predetermined in hierarchical classifications such as those found among the Kalapalo (Basso 1985), Achuar (Descola 1992), or Yanesha (Santos-Granero, this volume). The signs of the relations between humans and objects in these hierarchies vary, however, considerably.

Among the Urarina, for instance, human-object relations always entail some kind of subjection of objects by their makers or owners (Walker, this volume). This is particularly the case with respect to powerful objects such as shamanic stone bowls, which need to be tamed and subjected before they can be safely used. For the Urarina, objects are always "subjected companions." The Matis hold a similar view (Erikson, this volume). Human-object relations are always seen as relations between subjects of unequal standing. They are described either as a relationship between "master/owner" and "wiwa/pet" or as one between "master/owner" and "chu/belongings." In either case, objects occupy the position of semi-autonomous subordinates. They are, in Erikson's words, "obedient things." A weaker version of this conception is found among Yanesha people, who conceive of objects and artifacts as being dependent on the whim of their owners, for they lack true souls, which are the source of full agency and subjectivity (Santos-Granero, this volume). The power of some objects may be greater than that of their owners, but since they lack an autonomous soul, they depend on human intervention for their agency to become activated.

In other native Amazonian societies, some objects are thought to be not only more powerful than humans but also potentially dangerous for human existence. These powerful subjective objects can neither be coerced nor tamed. At most they can be appeased, so that they stop being dangerous to their owners and to the collectivity at large. These objects occupy a dominant position, demanding much attention from their owners. This is the case with Wauja flutes and masks, which must be given periodic offerings of food lest they become angry and transform into the animals they represent in order to punish their uncaring owners (Barcelos Neto, this volume). The ornaments that Mamaindê shamans obtain from the spirits of the dead are also thought to occupy such a dominant position (Miller, this volume). Shamans must appease them with offerings of manioc beer in order to secure their help when curing patients. A similar process of pacification, this time occurring through singing, takes place in Cashinahua puberty rituals to persuade the predatory lupuna-tree spirit, contained in the stools on which those being initiated sit, to impart its knowledge to them instead of devouring them (Lagrou, this volume).

Human-object relationships are not always hierarchical and predatory. In order to be able to cure, Runa and Zapara shamans must establish friendly relationships with powerful shamanic stones (Guzmán-Gallegos, this volume; Bilhaut 2006). Egalitarian, amicable relationships between shamans and spirit helpers—whether animals, plants, or objects—are not uncommon in native Amazonia, as the examples of the Tapirapé, Matsigenka, Kaingáng, and Juruna attest (Santos-Granero 2007; Stolze Lima 2005:100, 112). In some cases, shamans even claim to interact on a sexual level with spirits as they would with human partners, marrying and having children and families in the other world (Saladin d'Anglure and Morin 1998; Miller, this volume). In brief, in Amerindian ontologies, people and objects may interact in both egalitarian and hierarchical ways. The sign of the relationship mostly depends on the degree of animacy and agentivity attributed to objects.

Native Amazonian ontologies are not only "animic" and "perspectival." They also have a strong "constructional" dimension. Amerindian constructivism is particularly salient in mythical accounts narrating the creation of the world and the different life forms that populate it. It conceives of all living beings as composite entities, made up of the bodies and parts of bodies of a diversity of life forms, among which artifacts occupy a prominent place. According to these cosmologies, at the beginning there were only people and their artifacts—and sometimes, only artifacts. These artifacts are conceived of as the primordial building blocks out of which the bodies of people, and even gods, were first created. In this Amerindian view, artifacts fall on the side of the "natural" or the given—they were the first divine creations—whereas humans, animals, and plants fall on the side of the "cultural" or the constructed. In Amerindian ontologies, Culture—as understood in Western thought—preceded Nature, whereas what we understand as Nature appears as a cultural construct.

It can thus be said that Amerindians are not only intellectual "brico-leurs," as Claude Lévi-Strauss (1967) proposed in *The Savage Mind*, but, above all, that they conceive of all creative acts as taking place in the key of "bricolage." All visible and invisible occurrences in the world have origi-nated through processes entailing the deconstitution and reconstitution of the bodies of ancient demiurges and primordial humans. Present-day living beings are the result of this original act of bricolage in which objects, and particularly artifacts, played a crucial role. In Amerindian construc-tional cosmologies, creation is always a process entailing the destruction and re-creation of bodies. In other words, it is always about composite, namely artifactual anatomies.

Much has been said about the transformational character of bodies in native Amazonian ontologies. Bodies, it is argued, are highly unstable and prone to transformation and metamorphoses. Corporeal existence is extremely fluid. Amerindian body-making ritual techniques are meant to fix human bodies in their humanity. Other ritual practices are meant to fix the bodies of nonhuman beings in order to prevent them from transforming into more dangerous beings. Offerings, songs, and proper rules of behavior are some among the many Amerindian practices aimed at hindering objects from turning into rabid animals, animals from trans-forming into predatory monsters, or plants from becoming blood-sucking creatures. This capacity for transformation, I argue, derives to a large extent from the composite character of all life forms. Humans are made out of artifacts or plant and fish species; animals are made out of fish and a variety of artifacts; plants are made out of animals and artifacts. Designs are made out of boas or the language of spirits; flutes are made out of forest fruits, birds, and animals; songs are made out of the divinities' breath or the smoke of their cigars. These composite, often artifactual life forms are thought to be held together by a dominant affect, capacity, or habitus that makes them what they are.

Often, however, these anatomical arrangements are extremely unsteady. It suffices for an animal spirit to steal the personal ornaments of a human being to induce a change of perspective and thus the trans-formation of the affected person into the animal that attacked him or her. By simply answering the call of an aquatic spirit, a person opens the door to becoming a spirit of the same category and thus being abducted (Santos-Granero 2006). Thus a hunter who kills too many individuals of the same species runs the risk of inducing the transformation of that animal into human form and becoming the subject of the animal's attacks. The possibility, inherent in all beings, of imposing their point of view onto other beings also derives from their composite character. I suggest, however, that the "struggle between points of view," which Stolze Lima (1999:48) posits as the crux of Amerindian perspectivism, is not as much a struggle to impose one's point of view onto that of other life forms as it is a perpetual effort to prevent one's point of view from becoming tainted with that of others. This is particularly true with regard to human beings, the only beings that are fully aware of the perspectival nature of reality (Stolze Lima 1999:50; Santos-Granero 2006:74–75). Since in Amerindian ontologies it is the body that shapes consciousness, most efforts aimed at preserving the integrity of the human point of view center around the body. The Amerindian obsession with body-making and body-shaping techniques, including the ingestion of sublime substances—such as coca, tobacco, and hallucinogens—and the use of particular body ornaments, is aimed at internalizing the "moral" and "civil" values that make humans human (Londoño Sulkin 2005; Seeger 1975). Through these means, native Amazonians seek to firmly anchor in their composite, artifactual bodies a properly human point of view.

Acknowledgments

I wish to thank Philippe Erikson for his contribution to the organization of the symposium "The Occult Life of Things: Native Amazonian Theories of Materiality and Sociality" (52nd International Congress of Americanists; July 17–21, 2006; Seville, Spain), on which this volume is based. His comments and suggestions on an earlier draft of this introduction were very helpful. I would also like to thank Olga F. Linares for her invaluable help with improving my English style.

Notes

1. In Arjun Appadurai's seminal work on the circulation of commodities, things are said to have a "social life" insofar as they acquire value through exchange, that is, through circulation in networks of relations that are both socially and politically defined. It is this argument that, according to Appadurai (1986:3), "justifies the conceit that commodities, like persons, have social lives." When we refer to the social life of things in this work, we do not use the phrase as a metaphor, but rather as a notion that reflects native Amazonian perceptions.

2. This conception of the world, which at first glance appears to be similar to the notion of "commodity fetishism" developed by Karl Marx and elaborated by Michael Taussig (1980), is, nonetheless, its opposite. Whereas native Amazonians conceive of people and things as being always the product of social relations, members of capitalist societies perceive the products of social relations (time, space, land, labor) as things disconnected from social life.

3. Objects lacking subjectivity, will, and intentionality may also have agency in Alfred Gell's (1998) or Marilyn Strathern's (1999) sense, insofar as they can cause events to happen and can have an effect on a variety of entities ("patients"), including people. Here, however, we use agency in the more classical sense of a subject's conscious capacity to act upon or exert power over other beings and the surrounding world. Such capacity varies depending on the subject's degree of subjectivity, which from a native Amazonian point of view is always associated with the amount of soul substance he or she is believed to possess.

References

Appadurai, Arjun. 1986. *The Social Life of Things: Commodities in Cultural Perspective*. Cambridge: Cambridge University Press.

Århem, Kaj. 1990. Ecosofía makuna. In François Correa (ed.), *La selva humanizada: Ecología alternativa en el trópico húmedo colombiano*, pp. 105–22. Bogotá: ICAN-Fondo Editorial CEREC.

———. 1996. The Cosmic Food Web: Human-Nature Relatedness in the Northwest Amazon. In Philippe Descola and Gísli Pálsson (eds.), *Nature and Society: Anthropological Perspectives*, pp. 185–204. London: Routledge.

Barcelos Neto, Aristóteles. 2004. *Visiting the Wauja Indians: Masks and Other Living Objects from an Amazonian Collection*. Lisboa: Museu Nacional de Etnologia.

Basso, Ellen B. 1985. *A Musical View of the Universe*. Philadelphia: University of Pennsylvania Press.

Belaúnde, Luisa Elvira. 2001. *Viviendo bien: Género y fertilidad entre los Airo-Pai de la amazonía peruana*. Lima: Centro Amazónico de Antropología y Aplicación Práctica / Banco Central de Reserva del Perú.

Bilhaut, Anne Gaëlle. 2006. Biographie d'un esprit au corps brisé. Les pierres magiques des ancêtres zapara d'Amazonie: des sujets du passé. *Journal de la Société des Américanistes* 92(1–2):237–54.

Bird-David, Nurit. 1999. "Animism" Revisited: Personhood, Environment, and Relational Epistemology. *Current Anthropology* 40:167–91.

Camargo, Eliane. 2006. Animate/Inanimate in Cashinahua (Huni Kuin) Grammar and Sociability. (unpublished ms.)

Chaumeil, Jean-Pierre. 2001. The Blowpipe Indians: Variations on the Theme of Blowpipe and Tube among the Yagua Indians of the Peruvian Amazon. In Laura Rival and Neil Whitehead (eds.), *Beyond the Visible and the Material: The Amerindianization of Society in the Work of Peter Rivière*, pp. 81–99. Oxford: Oxford University Press.

Clastres, Pierre. 1998. Of Torture in Primitive Societies. In Pierre Clastres, *Society Against the State*, pp. 177–88. New York: Zone Books.

Conklin, Beth A. 2001. Women's Blood, Warriors' Blood, and the Conquest of Vitality in Amazonia. In Thomas A. Gregor and Donald Tuzin (eds.), *Gender in Amazonia and Melanesia: An Exploration of the Comparative Method*, pp. 141–74. Berkeley: University of California Press.

Descola, Philippe. 1992. Societies of Nature and the Nature of Society. In Adam Kuper (ed.), *Conceptualizing Society*, pp. 107–26. London and New York: Routledge.

———. 1996. *The Spears of Twilight: Life and Death in the Amazon Jungle*. Glasgow: HarperCollins Publishers.

Douglas, Mary, and Steven Ney. 1998. *Missing Persons: A Critique of Personhood in the Social Sciences*. Berkeley: University of California Press / New York: Russell Sage Foundation.

Erikson, Philippe. 2001. Myth and Material Culture: Matis Blowguns, Palm Trees, and Ancestor Spirits. In Laura Rival and Neil Whitehead (eds.), *Beyond the Visible and the Material: The Amerindianization of Society in the Work of Peter Rivière*, pp. 101–21. Oxford: Oxford University Press.

Frazer, James George. 1982. *The Golden Bough: A Study in Magic and Religion*. Franklin Center, PA: Franklin Library.

Gell, Alfred. 1998. *Art and Agency: An Anthropological Theory*. Oxford: Clarendon Press.

Gow, Peter. 2003. *An Amazonian Myth and Its History*. Oxford: Oxford University Press.

Guss, David M. 1990. *To Weave and Sing: Art, Symbol, and Narrative in the South American Rain Forest*. Berkeley: University of California Press.

Hardin, Kris L., and Mary Jo Arnoldi. 1996. Introduction: Efficacy and Objects. In Mary Jo Arnoldi, Christraud M. Geary, and Kris L. Hardin (eds.), *African Material Culture*, pp. 1–28. Bloomington: Indiana University Press.

Harvey, Graham. 2006. *Animism: Respecting the Living World*. New York: Columbia University Press.

Howell, Signe. 1996. Nature in Culture or Culture in Nature? Chewong Ideas of "Humans" and Other Species. In Philippe Descola and Gísli Pálsson (eds.), *Nature and Society: Anthropological Perspectives*, pp. 127–44. London: Routledge.

Im Thurn, Everard. 1893. Anthropological Uses of the Camera. *Journal of the Anthropological Institute of Great Britain and Ireland* 22:184–203.

Ingold, Tim. 1998. Totemism, Animism, and the Depiction of Animals. In Marketta Seppälä, Jari-Pekka Vanhala, and Linda Weintraub (eds.), *Animals, Anima, Animus*, pp. 181–207. Pori: Pori Art Museum.

———. 1999. Comment on Nurit Bird-David's "Animism Revisited." *Current Anthropology* 40:181–82.

Karadimas, Dimitri. 2005. *La raison du corps: Idéologie du corps et représentations de l'environnement chez les Miraña d'Amazonie colombienne*. Paris and Dudley, MA: Peeters.

Karsten, Rafael. 1923. *Blood Revenge, War, and Victory Feasts among the Jibaro Indians of Eastern Ecuador*. Washington, D.C.: Government Printing Office.

Koch-Grünberg, Theodor. 1917. *Vom Roraima Zum Orinoco*, vol. 3: Ethnographie. Stuttgart, Germany: Strecker and Schroder.

Kopytoff, Igor. 1986. The Cultural Biography of Things. In Arjun Appadurai (ed.), *The Social Life of Things: Commodities and Cultural Perspectives*, pp. 64–91. Cambridge: Cambridge University Press.

Lévi-Strauss, Claude. 1967. *The Savage Mind*. Chicago: University of Chicago Press.

———. 1969. *The Raw and the Cooked*. New York: Harper and Row.

Londoño Sulkin, Carlos. 2005. Inhuman Beings: Morality and Perspectivism among Muinane People (Colombian Amazon). *Ethnos* 70(1):7–30.

Luciani, Kelly, and José Antonio. 2001. Fractalidade e troca de perspectivas. *Mana* 7(2):95–132.

Mauss, Marcel. 1954. *The Gift*. London: Cohen and West.

McCallum, Cecilia. 2001. *Gender and Sociality in Amazonia: How Real People Are Made*. Oxford: Berg.

Métraux, Alfred. 1928. *La civilisation matérielle des tribus Tupi-Guarani*. Paris: Paul Geuthner.

Morris, Brian. 1998. *The Power of Animals: An Ethnography*. Oxford: Berg.

———. 1999. Comment on Nurit Bird-David's "Animism Revisited." *Current Anthropology* 40:182–83.

Morrison, Kenneth M. 2000. The Cosmos as Intersubjective: Native American Other-than-Human Persons. In Graham Harvey (ed.), *Indigenous Religions: A Companion*, pp. 23–36. London: Cassell Academic.

Myers, Thomas, and Maria S. Cipoletti (eds.). 2002. *Artifacts and Society in Amazonia*. Bonn: Bonner Amerikanische Studien 36.

Nordenskiöld, Erland. 1929. *Analyse ethno-géographique de la culture matérielle de deux tribus indiennes du Gran Chaco.* Paris: Les Éditions Genet.

Overing, Joanna. 1988. Personal Autonomy and the Domestication of Self in Piaroa Society. In Gustav Jahoda and Ioan M. Lewis (eds.), *Acquiring Cultures: Cross-Cultural Studies in Child Development,* pp. 169–92. London: Croom Helm.

Pedersen, Morten A. 2001. Totemism, Animism and North Asian Indigenous Ontologies. *Journal of the Royal Anthropological Institute* 7:411–27.

Pollock, Donald. 1995. Masks and the Semiotics of Identity. *Journal of the Royal Anthropological Institute* 1(1):581–97.

———. 1996. Personhood and Illness among the Kulina. *Medical Anthropology Quarterly,* n.s. 10(3):319–41.

Reichel-Dolmatoff, Gerardo. 1988. *Goldwork and Shamanism.* Medellín, Colombia: Editorial Colina.

Ribeiro, Bertha. 1980. A civilização da palha: A arte do trançado dos índios do Brasil. Doctoral thesis, Universidade de São Paulo.

———. 1988. *Dicionário do artesanato indígena.* São Paulo: Editora da Universidade de São Paulo.

——— (coord.). 1987. *Suma etnológica brasileira,* vol. 2: Tecnologia indígena. Petrópolis: Editora Vozes.

Rival, Laura. 1996. Blowpipes and Spears: The Social Significance of Huaorani Technological Choices. In Philippe Descola and Gísli Pálsson (eds.), *Nature and Society: Anthropological Perspectives,* pp. 145–64. London: Routledge.

Riviére, Peter. 1969. *Marriage among the Trio: A Principle of Social Organisation.* Oxford: Clarendon Press.

Saladin d'Anglure, Bernard, and Françoise Morin. 1998. Mariage mystique et pouvoir chamanique chez les Shipibo d'Amazonie péruvienne et les Inuit du Nunavut canadien. *Anthropologie et Sociétés* 22(2):49–74.

Santos-Granero, Fernando. 1991. *The Power of Love: The Moral Use of Knowledge Amongst the Amuesha of Central Peru.* London: Athlone Press.

———. 2006. Sensual Vitalities: Noncorporeal Modes of Sensing and Knowing in Native Amazonia. In Fernando Santos-Granero and George Mentore (eds.), In the World and about the World: Amerindian Modes of Knowledge. Special issue in honor of Prof. Joanna Overing. *Tipiti: Journal of the Society for the Anthropology of Lowland South America* 4(1–2):57–80.

———. 2007. Of Fear and Friendship: Amazonian Sociality Beyond Kinship and Affinity. *Journal of the Royal Anthropological Institute* 13(1):1–18.

———. 2009. *Vital Enemies: Slavery, Predation, and the Amerindian Political Economy of Life.* Austin: University of Texas Press.

Seeger, Anthony. 1975. The Meaning of Body Ornaments: A Suya Example. *Ethnology* 14(3):211–24.

Seeger, Anthony, Roberto Da Matta, and Eduardo Viveiros de Castro. 1979. A construção da pessoa nas sociedades indígenas brasileiras. *Boletim do Museo Nacional* 32:2–19.

Steward, Julian H. (ed.). 1946. *Handbook of South American Indians*, vol. 5: The Comparative Ethnology of South American Indians. Washington, D.C.: Government Printing Office.

Stolze Lima, Tânia. 1996. O dois e seu múltiplo: reflexões sobre o perspectivismo em uma cosmología tupi. *Mana* 2(2):21–47.

———. 1999. Towards an Ethnographic Theory of the Nature/Culture Distinction in Juruna Cosmology. *Brazilian Review of Social Sciences*, special issue, 1:43–52.

———. 2005. *Um peixe olhou para mim: O povo Yudjá e a perspectiva*. São Paulo: Editora UNESP: ISA / Rio de Janeiro: NuTI.

Strathern, Marilyn. 1990. *The Gender of the Gift*. Berkeley: University of California Press.

———. 1999. *Property, Substance and Effect: Anthropological Essays on Persons and Things*. London and New Brunswick, NJ: Athlone Press.

Stringer, Martin D. 1999. Rethinking Animism: Thoughts from the Infancy of Our Discipline. *Journal of the Royal Anthropological Institute* 5(4):541–56.

Taussig, Michael T. 1980. *The Devil and Commodity Fetishism in South America*. Chapel Hill: University of North Carolina Press.

Taylor, Anne-Christine. 1993. Des fantômes stupéfiants: Langage et croyance dans la pensée achuar. *L'Homme* 33(126–28):429–47.

Tessmann, Günter. 1930. *Die Indianer Nordost-Peru*. Hamburg: Friederichsen, De Gruyter and Cy.

Turner, Terence S. 1995. Social Body and Embodied Subject: Bodiliness, Subjectivity, and Sociality among the Kayapo. *Cultural Anthropology* 10(2):143–70.

Van Velthem, Lucia Hussak. 2001. The Woven Universe: Carib Basketry. In Colin McEwan, Cristiana Barreto, and Eduardo Neves (eds.), *Unknown Amazon: Culture in Nature in Ancient Brazil*, pp. 198–213. London: British Museum Press.

———. 2003. *O belo é a fera: A estética da produção e da predação entre os Wayana*. Lisboa: Assírio and Alvim.

Vilaça, Aparecida. 1992. *Comendo como gente: Formas do canibalismo wari (Pakaa Nova)*. Rio de Janeiro: Editora UFRJ.

———. 2002. Making Kin Out of Others. *Journal of the Royal Anthropological Institute* 8(2):347–65.

Viveiros de Castro, Eduardo. 1979. A fabricação do corpo na sociedade xinguana. *Boletim do Museu Nacional* 32:40–49.

———. 1996. Os pronomes cosmológicos e o perspectivismo ameríndio. *Mana* 2(2):115–44.

———. 1998. Cosmological Deixis and Amerindian Perspectivism. *Journal of the Royal Anthropological Society* 4(3):469–88.

———. 2004a. Exchanging Perspectives: The Transformation of Objects into Subjects in Amerindian Ontologies. *Common Knowledge* 10(3):463–84.

———. 2004b. Perspectival Anthropology and the Method of Controlled Equivocation. *Tipiti: Journal of the Society for the Anthropology of Lowland South America* 2(1):3–22.

Weiner, Annette B. 1992. *Inalienable Possessions: The Paradox of Keeping-While-Giving*. Berkeley: University of California Press.

Whitten, Dorothea S., and Norman E. Whitten Jr. 1988. *From Myth to Creation: Art from Amazonian Ecuador*. Urbana: University of Illinois Press.

———. 1993. Creativity and Continuity: Communication and Clay. In Dorothea S. Whitten and Norman E Whitten Jr. (eds.), *Imagery and Creativity: Ethnoaesthetics and Art Worlds in the Americas*, pp. 309–56. Tucson: University of Arizona Press.

Wilbert, Johannes. 1975. *Warao Basketry: Form and Function*. University of California, Museum of Cultural History, Occasional Papers, No. 3. Los Angeles.

I
Artifactual Anatomies

1
The Fabricated Body

Objects and Ancestors in Northwest Amazonia

Stephen Hugh-Jones

Contemporary Amazonian ethnography has given relatively little attention to the world of objects. One reason for this might be that "material
culture" was the focus of an earlier, no longer fashionable approach to
studying the region. There is also the salience of animals and plants in
Amerindians' everyday experience and cosmological thinking, one that
has its analogue in the prominence of "nature" in European constructions
of Amazonia and Amazonians. Against this animated backdrop—the twin
product of Amerindian and Western imaginations—inanimate objects
would seem to pale into insignificance. The three main theoretical styles
that continue to influence the ethnography of the region (see Viveiros de
Castro 1996) also have an inbuilt tendency to downplay the significance
of objects. This is evident in Peter Rivière's (1984) characterization of the
Amazonian political economy as one more of people than of goods, in
Cecilia McCallum's (1988) denial of the relevance of notions of wealth or
political economy in this context, and in claims (see Overing and Passes
2000) that native Amazonian societies are inherently egalitarian. The
diminished sociological weight of objects is also implicit in the view,
shared by all three styles, that Amazonians fall under the rubric of Jane
Collier and Michelle Rosaldo's (1981) bride-service societies where, in
contrast to bridewealth societies, substitutions between people and things
do not occur. Finally, as Fernando Santos-Granero notes in his introduction to this volume, objects play a decidedly secondary role to animals in
Eduardo Viveiros de Castro's influential theory of perspectivism, a theory
that has its roots in Amerindian ethnography.

In this ethnography, Amazonians are sometimes described as "object-
poor," an epithet that suggests they are being compared, implicitly or
explicitly, to the peoples of other regions—the Andes, Melanesia, or "the

West." Such comparisons often take present conditions as representative of all times and neglect both the archaeological and historical reality of the region and the extensive material and intellectual exchanges between highlands and lowlands. The analogue of this temporal flattening is the spatial homogenization that occurs when particular manifestations of Amerindian society and culture are taken as typical of the whole.

In "Exchanging Perspectives" (2004), a paper that brings his arguments concerning affinity, predation, and perspectivism to bear on the world of artifacts, Viveiros de Castro writes:

> The idea of creation *ex nihilo* is virtually absent from indigenous cosmologies. Things and beings normally originate as a transformation of something else. . . . Where we find notions of creation at all, what is stressed is the imperfection of the end product. Amerindian demiurges always fail to deliver the goods. . . . And just as nature is the result not of creation but of transformation, so culture is a product not of invention but of transference. . . . In Amerindian mythology, the origin of cultural implements or institutions is canonically explained as a borrowing—a transfer (violent or friendly, by stealing or by learning, as a trophy or as a gift) of prototypes already possessed by animals, spirits or enemies. (Viveiros de Castro 2004:477–78)

Viveiros de Castro goes on to contrast this characteristic Amerindian emphasis on transformation and exchange with a more typically Western emphasis on creation and production and speculates that this may be connected with an Amerindian emphasis on affinity over consanguinity. He suggests that this difference is reflected in myth, for if old-world mythology is haunted by parenthood and especially fatherhood, the protagonists of the major Amerindian myths are related agonistically as in-laws (ibid).

In this chapter, I discuss a set of Tukanoan myths from the Uaupés region of northwest Amazonia that are indeed about creation ex nihilo and squarely in the idioms of parenthood. These are myths about divinities who, in the end, do indeed deliver the goods—and they do so by means of goods. My aim is not to prove Viveiros de Castro wrong—he is already well aware that the Tukanoans fit uneasily into the general Amazonian pattern.[1] Instead I want to suggest that, in effect, he is right, for the Tukanoans' patriliny and exogamy produce a transformation in mythic structure that can be predicted from his suggestions above. This transformation, which plays lineal inheritance and transmission off against themes of affinity, violence, and theft, is also reflected in a shift away from the violent appropriation of body parts and trophies and toward the elaboration of sets of highly crafted artifacts that become personified heirlooms transmitted across generations. These heirlooms are both the spirit manifestations of ancestral powers and objectifications of body parts that point to human capacities, intentions, and responsibilities. All this suggests that we should avoid overly hasty generalizations about Amazonia and Amazonians. As Amazonian peoples have varied patterns of kinship, shamanism, architecture, etc., so they may have different theories and ideologies of materiality and live in different object worlds.

Despite the universal theme of "ensoulment" (Santos-Granero, this volume) of objects by those in their proximity and the frequent associations of body ornaments with "spirit" or "soul" (Hill, Miller, and Turner, this volume), one thing that emerges clearly in this collection is diversity and variation. There are not only "multiple ways of being a thing" in particular Amerindian societies (Santos-Granero, this volume) but also significant differences between the overall object regimes of different groups. The collectively owned valuables and heirlooms of northwest Amazonia and central Brazil (Turner, this volume) are a far cry from the shamanic stones of the Yanesha and Urarina (Santos-Granero and Walker, this volume). Likewise, the intense circulation of ritual objects and ordinary possessions in northwest Amazonia and the upper Xingú (Barcelos Neto, this volume) contrasts with the Matis' insistence on the moral imperatives of self-sufficiency (Erickson, this volume). One aim of this chapter is to suggest that there is a certain fit between different object regimes, different social structures, and different cosmologies.

Tukanoan Creation Myths

As suggested above, Tukanoan creation myths are unusual both because they do indeed tell of a creation from nothing, of gods who bring the world and its contents into being through their thoughts, and because their main focus is on objects and artifacts rather than on animals. The myths I have in mind can be found in a remarkable series of publications, the *Coleção narradores indigenas do Rio Negro*, each authored by an elderly Tukano or Desana *kumu* ("priest-shaman") paired with a younger, literate amanuensis.[2] As Geraldo Andrello (2006:282–83) points out, these books, with their myths about ancestral creation from potent artifacts, have themselves become recent additions to the sets of heirlooms owned by each Tukanoan group. The myths are close variants of those discussed by Jonathan Hill (this volume); his chapter should be read as a performative, musical accompaniment and complement to this one.

Starting with an initial, dark, formless, and invisible state, these Tukanoan creation myths run through several attempts at creation that culminate in the emergence of the fully human ancestors of the peoples of today. The process of this emergence involves a progressive materialization and embodiment from an initially immaterial, disembodied state and a transition from a pre-human, artifactual mode of reproduction to a fully human, genital mode.

Briefly summarized and keeping objects to the fore, a Desana version of the primary creation myth, complemented where appropriate by other variants,[3] runs as follows:

> [19–26] Grandfather of the Universe, both Thunder and the Primal Sun, appears spontaneously in a state of total darkness. He lives alone {lives with his daughter and the Master of Food (Tõramü Bayar and Guahari Ye Ñi 2004:27)} in a house in the sky. He has with him the following items, the Instruments of Life and Transformation: rattle lance,[4] shield,[5] stool, cigar, forked cigar holder,[6] gourds of coca and other substances, hour glass-shaped gourd stands,[7] adze,[8] split-palm screen,[9] and maraca, each made of white crystal {and each a part of his body (Ñahuri and Kümarõ 2003:21, 27)}(see fig. 1.1).
>
> On a support made from two crossed rattle lances—one made of female bone, the other of male bone—he places five sieves, spinning them round to make a layered world comparable to a gourd on a stand. He spreads split-palm screens on the earth to bring Ũmüari Niko, Grandmother of the Universe, into being.[10]
>
> Blowing spells, Grandfather of the Universe conjures up a stool on which he then sits, eating coca. To create people, he smokes a cigar, blowing smoke and blessings over a gourd of sweet *kana* berries[11] covered with another gourd and placed on a stand. These gourds are Grandmother of the Universe, the earth itself. Seeing that Grandfather of the Universe has failed to create life, Grandmother of the Universe takes over, blowing smoke and spells on the gourd (see fig. 1.2). Five male and two female beings, the Universe People, Ũmüari Masa {Yepá Masa, the Earth People (Ñahuri and Kümarõ 2003:22); the Thunders (Umúsin Panlõn Kumu and Tolamãn Kenhíri 1980:52)} come to life and emerge from the gourds: Sun (Abe[12]); Deyubari Gõamü,[13] Master of Hunting and Fishing; Baaribo, Master of Cultivated Food[14]; Buhsari[15]

Figure 1.1. Instruments of Life and Transformation: cigar, cigar holder, gourd on stand, stool, and ceremonial staff. *Source*: Redrawn from cover illustration of M. Maia and T. Maia 2004.

Figure 1.2. Grandmother of the Universe creating the Ūmüari Masa or Universe People. *Note*: Seated on a ceremonial stool and smoking a cigar in her cigar holder, Grandmother of the Universe makes appear a new being, the Grandson of the Universe, creator of light, of the layers of the universe, and of humanity. *Source*: Drawing by Feliciano Lana (in U.P. Kumu and T. Kenhíri 1980). Reproduced with permission from the author.

Gõamü, Master of Time, Seasons, Nature, and Living Beings; Wanani[16] Gõamü, Master of Poison; Wisu; and Yugupó.

[35–41] Wanani creates a woman for Deyubari Gõamü, vomiting her up after drinking water mixed with forest vines. Like all women at that time, she has no vagina; the beings make her one using the cigar holder's pointed end. {Getting up near dawn, Abe's son Kisibi vomits up two women, Pui/Diakapiro and Wisu/Yuhusio. Had he obeyed his father and gotten up earlier, he would have vomited up men, self-sufficient beings capable of autonomous reproduction by vomiting (Tõramü Bayar and Guahari Ye Ñi 2004:49–51)}.

[143–155] The Universe People need the beverage yagé to enable the future humanity to have visions. Realizing yagé is in their own bones, they decide to kill and eat their younger brother Wanani Gõamü. They turn him into a caimo fruit, which they offer to their sisters Wisu and Yugupó to eat. Yugupó refuses the fruit, but Wisu eats it and becomes pregnant. Lacking a vagina, she is delirious with pain, her delirium being also the effects of yagé. Abe cuts a vulva for her with his gold earring, using the cigar holder as a template. The house fills with blood, the visions of yagé, as her child is born as Yagé, his body made up of all its varieties. The Universe People eat Yagé's head, arms, and legs, leaving his denuded trunk as a penis/flute. He now assumes the name Yuruparí, Master of Forest Fruits; his body parts are flutes, forest fruits, birds, animals, and fishes.

{Sun and Moon have coca in a Gourd of Life guarded by poisonous insects that change their skins and spiders that carry their abundant young in bags on their stomachs. Using the gourd, a cigar, and a cigar holder, the brothers try in vain to emulate these creatures' special reproductive powers. Their two sisters, created when the men vomit water and vine sap, smoke the cigar and eat from the gourd. This gives women the power to reproduce through pregnancy but diminishes the powers of the cigar and gourd. The women become pregnant but lack vaginas. The men give them caimo juice to drink; a drop indicates where their vaginas should be. The men use the cigar holder to make vaginas. The elder sister gives birth to Yuruparí; the younger sister gives birth to birds with colored feathers, to snakes, and to Yagé (Maia and Maia 2004:57–61)}.

Yuruparí later avenges his brothers' shameful act by eating their sons. They, in turn, burn him on a fire. From his ashes springs a paxi-uba palm, which is cut up and distributed to all Tukanoans as their flutes, Yuruparí's bones.

Wisu and Yugupó steal the Yurupari flutes from the men. The men recapture the flutes from their enemies, the women {urged on by Opossum, who tells the men that they do not need women and can emulate his own extra-uterine, marsupial mode of reproduction (Ñahuri and Kümarõ 2003:141)}. As the men seize the flutes, the women also retain them in another form and hide them in their vaginas. Wisu flees to the west and Yugupó to the east. {Wisu becomes Amo, Mistress of Feather Ornaments, who lives in a house made from the molted plumage of migrating birds. The younger sisters go to the east, where they become Clothes Women who transform ceremonial ornaments into manufactured objects that they send to their brothers upstream (Maia and Maia 2004:33–39; Tõramü Bayar and Guahari Ye Ñi 2004:70–71)}.

[163–177] Grandfather of the Universe and Buhsari Gõãmü decide to transform the Universe People into true human beings. Grandfather of the Universe has two transformation gourds, one in the sky and one on earth. The Universe People fly to the upper gourd and then travel via a kana vine down to the lower gourd, the Milk Lake in the east, where they become fishes. They make the Anaconda Canoe of Transformation (*pamüri pino, pamüri gasiro*).[17] {Sky/Sun and Earth/Moon seek help from Grandmother of the Universe and Grandfather of the Universe in the sky. Grandfather of the Universe vomits up paired ceremonial ornaments onto a split-palm screen, each pair corresponding to a future Tukanoan group. Sky sends two avatars down to the Milk Lake in the east. In the underworld, Earth acquires a maraca and a stool with three different designs, gaining strength and becoming Yepa Oakü. One of Sky's avatars becomes Transformation Anaconda, a female snake who swallows her children, the future humanity, in the form of fish (Maia and Maia 2004:40–43)}.

Inside the anaconda canoe, the Universe People travel toward the center of the world. As they travel, they undergo a gestation period, leaving animals and fish behind them and becoming diversified Transformation People, each speaking a different language and now related as cousins. After nine months, they arrive at Ipanoré, the center of the world, emerging through a hole in the rocks of the rapids as fully human ancestors.

As they emerge, Grandfather of the Universe offers them four gourds (for future generations: blood, milk, pure air, and health), a hat and a gun (the sources of technical intelligence and manufacturing industry), and two more gourds, one for white skin and one for skin changing and eternal life. The ancestors eat from the five gourds. The whites' ancestor also bathes in the gourd for white skin but does not dare confront the snakes and spiders that are present around the rim of the gourd for skin changing. Instead, he puts the hat on his head and fires the gun. Angered by his behavior, Grandfather of the Universe sends the whites' ancestor to live in the east. The Indian ancestors bathe in the remaining water from the gourd for white skin—but only enough to whiten the palms of their hands and soles of their feet. {The Transformation People acquire the Instruments of Life and Transformation, now as their own bones, wa'í-ōari or "fish bones" (Maia and Maia 2004:46–51)}.

[177–188] The myth ends with the dispersal of the different Tukanoan groups, an account of the internal composition and hierarchical ranking of the Desana, the distribution of ritual goods amongst the Desana and other Tukanoans, the Desana's post-mythical history, and the genealogy of the narrator's own group.

The Sexual Life of Things

In their myths, the Tukanoans envisage the human body as made up of cultural artifacts and present creation as human reproduction carried out in the modes of fabrication and assemblage. The following correspondences between objects and body parts are all evident in complete versions of the creation myths summarized above:

    stool: placenta, pelvis, buttocks
    rattle lance: bone, vertebral column, penis
    shield: placenta, skin
    cigar holder: penis, legs, labia
    cigar/tobacco: penis, part of vertebra; bone marrow, semen
    tobacco smoke: semen
    gourd: vagina, womb, stomach, heart/soul, head
    gourd stand: human body (especially thighs), waist and thorax
    caimo and kana fruits/ juice: semen, milk
    coca: bone from vertebral column, semen, milk
    gourd and kana vines: umbilical cord, women with children
    flute: bone, penis, vagina
    feather ornaments: skin
    fish bones: all Instruments of Life and Transformation

Beyond such term-by-term correspondences, some "cross-references" should also be noted. In Tukanoan myths, the world is supported on crossed rattle lances that form a *saniro*, or "stand" (also "holder, enclosure"), a Barasana word that also appears in the term for cigar holder—*muno* ("tobacco") *saniro*. The cigar holder has stool-shaped "hips" (the Barasana word *isi-kumuro*, "buttock stool") that are often carved in symbol form as paired stools separated by a gourd stand (see fig. 1.3). Functionally, stools are also stands or supports. The cigar holder and rattle lance are both made of dense, red wood and both have sharp points that are stuck in the ground—and used as a penis in the context of the myths. The two bone prongs on the top of the rattle lance also reproduce in miniature the cigar holder's two forked arms (see fig. 1.4). Below these prongs are two roundels, the Sun and Moon; seen from the side, these can also be read as either stools or gourd stands. Inverted, the cigar holder symbol resembles a man, with the cigar appearing as an erect penis. Finally, the spiral-wound cigar may appear as a miniature Yuruparí trumpet, an object that is also bone and penis.

The Instruments of Life and Transformation fall into three classes: (1) tubes: flute, cigar, and rattle lance; (2) containers: cigar holder, gourd, shield, canoe, beer trough, screen enclosure, feather box, feather ornaments,[18] and house; and (3) supports: stool and gourd stand. These also correspond to the major skeletal features and organs of the body; in Tukanoan myth, the total human form is imagined as a cigar in a holder stuck inside a gourd supported by a gourd stand and standing on a stool (see fig. 1.5 and Diakuru and Kisibi 1996:261).

In Tukanoan myths, the Instruments of Life and Transformation appear in male-female pairs and some of the objects themselves form "natural" pairs, specifically the cigar and holder, the rattle lance and shield, and the flute and gourd (see Hugh-Jones 1979). If these pairings have to do with sexual reproduction, they also displace and substitute for it, for the myths present normal bodily sex as a sterile diversion from the urgent task of creation, a sign of laziness and a cause of disharmony. Instead of sex, we have insemination and gestation in artifactual modes. Divine bodies made up of tubes, cigars, flutes, and rattle lances spew forth seminal breath and vitality in the equivalent registers of color and sound: tobacco smoke, fruit juice, flute music, and feather ornaments, a fertile, dangerous synaesthesia encapsulated in the figure of Yagé—at once blood of parturition; colored vision; throbbing ears; Yuruparí; colored, biting snakes; and colored, singing birds. Like manioc mash mixed with saliva, the stuff that fertilizes beer, these seminal substances then fill gourds and beer troughs, where fermentation culminates in new life: the Tukanoans or Fermentation/Transformation People (*Pamüri Masa*).

Figure 1.3. Desana cigar holder. *Source*: Drawing based on a photograph in Hartmann 1975:147.

Figure 1.4. Upper end of a ceremonial rattle lance. *Source*: Redrawn from Vincent 1987.

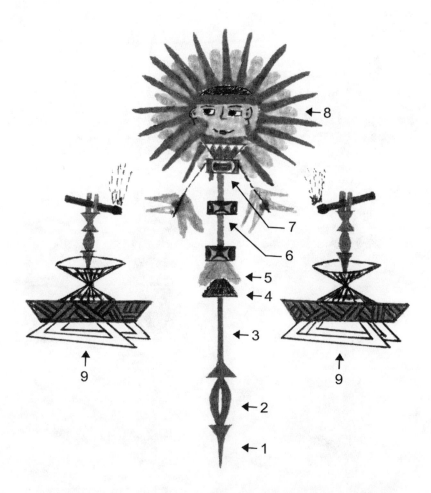

Figure 1.5. Symbolism of the rattle lance. *Key*: The rattle lance is the support or bone of the world: it symbolizes the layers of the world as envisaged by the Desana of the Guahari Diputiro Porã clan. (1) part of the lance stuck in the earth to make safe/support the world; (2) part that represents the world where we (Indians, whites, blacks) live; (3) support of the sky; (4) House of Clouds or of Rain; (5) House of Moon (Abe); (6) House of Star-People; (7) House of Thunder; (8) House of Sun (Abe), who is ornamented with macaw and oropendola feathers; (9) the stool, gourd support, gourd, coca, cigar holder, and cigar are the artifacts used to bring about the transformation of humanity. *Source*: Drawing based on cover illustration of T. Bayar and G. Ye Ñi 2004.

Showing consistency with other myths concerning creation and parenthood, Tukanoan myths clearly use tubes and containers to stand (in) for the normal reproductive organs that the divinities lack. This substitution of artifact for reproductive organ is underscored in the spells that accompany the divinities' acts of creation. Recapitulating these acts as they sit on stools and blow smoke over gourds of coca and kana fruits, human kumus now use these same spells to manage pregnancy, birth, and naming. It is only when the ancestors become fully human that they fully internalize and embody their reproductive and other organs, only then that cultural artifacts are externalized and disembodied as objects and possessions, and only then that men and women become fully distinct. This brings us to the issue of gender.

From Sex to Gender

If, in the myths, there is no separation between persons and things, there is also no separation between genders. Rather, a set of androgynous demiurges with overlapping identities and ambiguous kinship statuses inseminate—and are inseminated by—each other. This androgyny, latent in the fuzzy boundary between tube and container (or anaconda and canoe), is encapsulated in the cigar holder, an object that inseminates gourds and women and, by implication, the smoker as well. At once a man with an erect penis and a penis thrust between female legs or labia, the holder encompasses gourd stand, stool, and rattle lance within its own form.

This androgyny also applies to normal human beings. In most respects, the bodies and body parts of men and women are quite similar, and the penis and vulva/vagina that we treat as diacritics are here imagined as transformations of one another, androgynous object-organs that are simultaneously given up—as flute/penis—and retained—as flute/vagina following the women's theft of Yuruparí flutes.[19] This same androgyny appears in the Makuna idea that women have a right/male and left/female side and that menstruation is the *yuruparí*—that is, "reproductive power"—of the left side (Århem et al 2004:184, 207). All this suggests that, rather than reducing gender to sex, we should recognize that gender, as one kind of relation, serves a device to imagine many others. Rather than seeing these myths as a discourse about human sexuality in the code of material culture, which Gerardo Reichel-Dolmatoff's work erroneously does, it would be more appropriate to see artifacts as expressions of more abstract capacities and dispositions shared in common by men and women, albeit in different gendered modes.

While women's ability to create life may be primarily bodily and only secondarily artifactual, in the analogous culinary processes of cooking and fermentation, the story of the theft and recuperation of Yuruparí suggests that for men, the case is the opposite. In getting back as artifacts what women retain in their bodies, men's role in sexual reproduction plays second fiddle to their rituals of reproduction and dominance of ceremonial goods. This is the message of Opossum, who links flutes to an extra-uterine, marsupial mode of reproduction; of men who sleep too long and thus forgo the ability to reproduce solely by vomiting; and of women who, in stealing the ability to become pregnant, diminish the potency of the men's Gourd of Life.

As androgyny is transmuted to the ambiguities of ethnicity, the play between male and female, body and artifact reappears in the pairing of bows with guns and of feather ornaments with merchandise. Today, men dominate all such objects but, in Tukanoan myths, if bows/guns are "male"—chosen by the male ancestors of Indians and whites—ornaments/ merchandise are unequivocally "female"—controlled by two sisters who stand for Indians and whites. All these objects are ultimately forms of "clothing," things made from transformed body ornaments by Clothes Women. They are signs for gendered capacities and dispositions, "destruction" in the case of weapons and "creation" in the case of ornaments and manufactured goods. Clothes are also changeable skins, things that can be taken on and off to produce transformations in being and appearance equivalent to insect pupation or the sloughing of skins by snakes. Clothing, the Clothes Women, and Amo—a name meaning molting, sloughing the skin, ecdysis, pupation, and menstruation (itself an internal change of skin; see Hugh-Jones 1979), and whose house is made from molted feathers—all encapsulate reproduction, transformation, and periodicity. Like the feathered wings of birds, the paws and claws of jaguars, or the spiked shoes of an athlete, clothes are affects (see Viveiros de Castro 2004:474), at once sign and substance of capacities and dispositions.

From Objects to Affects

In myth, divinities—prototypical kumus or priest-shamans existing as pure spirit—act through a set of artifacts that stand for absent bodies. As their blessings make clear, these artifacts are the outcomes and indices of their thoughts and intentions and signs of the capacities of the human bodies they will eventually create, a creation that moves from thought through artifact to body. Likewise, in ritual contexts, invisible ancestors are made present by assembling the ceremonial items that correspond to their body parts (see Hugh-Jones 1979:153–54). At birth, naming, puberty, and initiation, the kumu controls bodily transitions and transformations by manipulating artifacts identified with body parts. This identity is affirmed in blessings first uttered by divinities, but here the process moves in the opposite direction—away from concrete bodies and toward more abstract artifacts that serve as signs for the "spiritual" components of those bodies. This allows the socialization of thoughts and behavior (compare to Mamaindê ornaments as souls [Miller, this volume]).

This move from body to thoughts, intentions, and responsibilities through artifacts is illustrated in the following account from a Makuna text (Århem et al. 2004, my translation):

> During the first stage of the life cycle, the kumu's blessings relate to the maintenance of the baby's stools of birth. These stools, which contain the life and thoughts of the newborn child, relate to its mother's arms and legs because it is these that give it comfort and support in its first months. The baby is not given other stools, as it does not yet think about its own future, so the kumu gives it a stool of infancy, the legs of its mother. At this stage, the baby will also have the stool of crying and tears. At the second stage of the life cycle, at puberty, the kumu changes the stools of birth into stools of thoughts; for boys, these relate to Yuruparí and for girls, to menstruation. At this time, the stool of the mother becomes prohibited; the child is isolated from the mother and takes on another life, the "stool of forgetting the mother" (200). Through the blessings a young girl receives when she begins to menstruate, she changes her skin and exchanges her childhood stools for those of thoughts, of cultivated plants—coca, tobacco, manioc—of menstruation, and of red paint. From this time on, much of the life of the young girl will depend on looking after these stools (205). Because women are the only ones who can give life, they are considered to be the "birth stools of the universe" (184). When boys see Yuruparí for the first time, the stools of thought that are blessed are those of coca, tobacco, red paint, yagé, and Yuruparí (215).

If containers and tubes relate to more immediate capacities and processes of reproduction, the above account suggests that stools relate not just to different capacities, but also to different behaviors, competencies, and responsibilities more generally. For the Tukanoans, a "stool" is not just an object or part of the anatomy but also an abstract notion of a support, base, foundation, location, and comportment. When a newborn child is named, the kumu gives it a stool to fix its name-soul in its body; at puberty, this stool is exchanged for a new set of stools: the gendered thoughts, concerns, and responsibilities of adult life. Similarly, sitting—an activity described as cooling, relaxing, and peaceful—is synonymous with learning, contemplation, and meditation and has connotations of stability, rootedness, and fixity. A wise person has a "cool seat," an irritable person a "hot seat," and a thoughtless or flighty person "does not know how to sit." A person's "stool" is thus an aspect of his or her character.

Stools are also an index of rank and authority, objects reserved for men of higher status—namely, dancers and kumus. The kumu sitting on a stool (in the Barasana language, *kumu-ro*, or "kumu's thing") is conceived of as a gourd filled with knowledge and wisdom, which travels between the layers of the cosmos with smoke as mediating breath, stool as clouds, and sky resting on mountain-legs (see Beksta 1988). Sitting in a canoe (*kumu-a* in Barasana), the kumu also travels in horizontal space in a vessel whose counterparts appear as the beer trough (*kumu-a hulia*, "canoe section") or Anaconda/Fermentation Canoe.

In short, and as the myths suggest, stools and gourds are not only objective forms of shamanic knowledge but also objectifications of human life and capacities—not just buttocks and wombs, but also hearts, souls, heads, and minds. The myths also suggest a theory of mind and agency in which thoughts, designs, and intentions are given material form in the objects that the intentions produce. It is a theory in which a diversity of artifacts connotes not only different body parts but also different bodily capacities and dispositions controlled, regulated, and inspired by different areas of self-discipline and responsibility.

Making and Self-Making

In Tukanoan society, technical and symbolic competence go hand in hand. The ability to make objects is a mark of adult status, leaders and ritual experts are typically expert craftsmen, and the objects they make are the hallmarks of a particular civilization. If people are progressively built up and socialized as assemblages of objects, so may objects socialize people. Girls undergoing puberty seclusion spend their days making pottery, while initiate boys are trained to make basketry. This training is as much moral, intellectual, and spiritual as it is technical, for sitting still and making things are forms of meditation. Post-initiation is also the favored time for more knowledgeable, newly adult males to make feather ornaments and other ritual objects, a dangerous pursuit whose counterpart, performed by females, is the production of red paint: both activities involve the seclusion and dietary restrictions that mark a bodily state akin to that of menstruation.

The seclusion, fasting, and other bodily regimes that follow first menstruation and initiation are processes of transformation in which the body is trained to make objects of beauty and is itself made into an object of beauty. Beauty is a social, not natural, quality: natural materials such as feathers are thought to become beautiful only when they have been transformed, a socialization of nature that parallels the way in which the making of things and the wearing of ornaments socialize the body. The recursive relation between bodies and objects is manifest in the fact that ritual objects are decorated in the exact manner in which bodies are decorated: the same designs are applied to baskets, to the skin of dancers, and to the stools they sit upon. The same recursive relation is also underlined in spells and other shamanic discourse concerning training, discipline, and socialization, in which the subject is portrayed as an artifact—a solid, contemplative stool or a basket progressively filled with knowledge, wisdom, and responsibility. Making things is thus self-making and the mastery of technique is a mastery of the self.

Possessions

All human artifacts are referred to using the Barasana word *gaheuni*,[20] but above all, gaheuni are the Instruments of Life and Transformation. In mythological terms, the Instruments of Life and Transformation are not human productions at all, but divine bodies existing as bone and crystal, substances whose qualities of hardness, durability, scarcity, whiteness, purity, brilliance, and luminescence all emphasize their otherworldly nature. In human terms, gaheuni are quintessentially highly crafted objects made from fine hardwoods and decorated with intricate painting, engraved designs, and delicate featherwork. The few who know how to make such things are deemed to possess special gifts. Gaheuni are thus items of wealth and objectified forms of knowledge whose value condenses labor, know-how, and controlled power.

Many of these valuables are heirlooms that connect their owners to the known past of previous generations; all of them connect to the otherworld of ancestors and divinities. These gaheuni, their names, and the names of their owners are collective property that signal group identity and embody its vitality, spiritual powers, and potency; they are items quite similar to the Kayapo *nêkrêtch* (Turner, this volume). They are accumulated and displayed as inalienable possessions but were once the prime object of inter-group raiding and occasionally enter into prestigious exchanges. They thus have connotations of alterity, primarily that of divinities and dead ancestors and secondarily that of other peoples and affines.

As animals have degrees of animality, with jaguars occupying pride of place, so objects have relative degrees of materiality. These hierarchies of subjectivity and value also correspond to the social hierarchies of rank and prestige that are a characteristic feature of Tukanoan society. Members of the higher-ranking clans typically control sacred ritual paraphernalia; like their possessions, such people are "big," "beautiful" and "heavy," more material than the less substantial commoners (compare Turner, this volume).

As immaterial possessions that define Tukanoan clans-houses (Hugh-Jones 1995), language and names may also be gaheuni. Likewise, material valuables come attached to mythological pedigrees that are recited when the objects are displayed and that serve to differentiate apparently similar objects as the body parts of different group ancestors. We have already met this verbalization of things and materialization of language in the synaesthesia of color and sound, the identity between tobacco smoke, flute music, and feather ornaments mentioned above. As I have shown elsewhere (Hugh-Jones 2006), names and ornaments are like two versions of the same thing, both of them manifestations of soul. Thus feather ornaments and the name-soul are both described as a "second body," and naming at birth also confers a protective covering (*küni oka* in the Barasana language) made up of invisible artifacts, split-palm screens, and shields. Artifacts are the material traces of thoughts and intentions, just as name and spirit point to artifacts. In Andrello's words, in the Tukanoan case, "objectification is the same as personification" (2006:262–63).

Clothing and Merchandise

Manufactured goods may also be *gaheuni*, but here again some are more so than others. In historical times, at the top of the hierarchy were guns, swords, machetes, and axes, potent tools and weapons also used as items of dress and adornment alongside glass beads, clothes, silver coins, and mirrors. There were also bibles, images of saints, calendars, and letters patent, paper items treasured more as potent objects in their own right than as materials to be read. Coming from faraway peoples and places and possessed with extraordinary qualities and efficacy, white peoples' objects were also considered as things not made but simply existing—and to some extent, they are still thought of that way. Today, the historical hierarchy is giving way to one favoring electrical and electronic goods and the land titles and other bureaucratic documents involved in dealings with the state. In addition to high-ranking individuals' control of ritual goods, it was typically they who controlled trade with white people, who were appointed as chiefs by the colonial authorities, and who received the hats, swords, epaulettes, medals, and letters patent that went with such appointments (see also Andrello 2006, ch. 4). Today, too, there is still a strong correlation between traditional rank and status and occupancy of positions of leadership in indigenous organizations and local government.

As gaheuni, ancestral heirlooms and manufactured goods are alternative versions of the same thing, objectifications of capacities and knowledge that come in two different but complementary forms. Thus the world of dead ancestors is imagined as a white peoples' city, a place with streetlights and abundant material wealth. The equivalence between indigenous heirlooms and Western goods and between the capacities that these objects connote is also made clear in a series of mythic permutations and choices.

In Tukanoan creation myths, women have to give up flutes to men but they still manage to retain these flutes in another form as their vaginas; "flutes," as artifacts or body parts—as musical instruments, penises, or vaginas—are thus objective material correlates of the reproductive capacities of men and women. This differentiation between men and women through an apparent loss of flutes then results in a differentiation between Amo, the Mistress of Dance Ornaments, who lives at the headwaters where Indians live, and her sister, the Mistress of Clothing, who lives downstream with white people. Instead of the "flutes" of men and women, it is now indigenous dance ornaments and Western merchandise that are rendered equivalent as two versions of "clothing." Like "flutes," this "clothing" is at once stuff and capacity: as dance ornaments connote ritual and the capacity to reproduce in indigenous society, so Western clothing connotes the capacity to produce all manufactured goods and to reproduce Western society. Changes of ornaments or clothes connote processes of reproduction and transformation that are on a par with the molting of birds, the shedding of skins by snakes and insects, and also with menstruation—a process that is understood as an internal change of skin. So "flutes," dance ornaments, "clothing," and merchandise are all permutations or transformations of the same thing—capacities that allow people to reproduce themselves sexually, materially, and socially. Clothing, a metonym for all merchandise, is an exotic version of molted feathers and the shed skins of insects and snakes, the objective, material correlates of menstruation and reproduction—capacities encapsulated in the name Amo, which means "Chrysalis/Menstruating Woman." Finally, like the "choice" between flute and vagina or that between Amo and her sister, a further choice determines the difference between white people and Indians. This choice is presented in three different registers: a bath that determines skin color, a choice between weapons, and a choice between items of clothing. These registers suggest that the difference should be understood as simultaneously physical, technological, behavioral, and moral. One reading of all this would thus be that women and white people stand together as thieves who stole goods, powers, and capacities that rightfully belong to men. The other would be that, in their use of ancestral heirlooms and white peoples' merchandise, men are appropriating, in object form, the powers and capacities of those in the position of potent Others: women, enemies, and potential affines.

Conclusion: Separations and Continuities

In Amazonian mythology, there is typically no separation between humans and animals. After the appearance of sex, death, and time, humans and animals become separated in this world but remain united at the level of the spirit or soul in a parallel world, where human culture provides the common frame of reference for beings that operate in different bodies with different perspectives. If this is also true of the rest of Tukanoan mythology, what is striking in the culture's creation myths of the different groups is that objects appear to take up the space normally occupied by animals. People and things are not separated, we see a profusion of different artifact-body parts, and instead of an elaborate external differentiation of animal species, animals are reduced to "fish," a generic category of which ordinary fish are the prototype, the anaconda is the hyper form, and land animals (*wai büküra* or "mature fish" in the Barasana language) are a subspecies. In this scheme of things, objects also play a key role in the differentiation of men and women (flutes), Indians and white people (weapons, clothes), and humans and fish (ornaments). Since we have already discussed the differentiation of men and women and Indians and whites, let us turn to the myth describing that of humans and fish, following Geraldo Andrello (2006:381 ff.).

After a journey (gestation, childhood, and socialization), the ancestors emerge from a hole (birth and initiation). As they emerge, they abandon their fish skins and put on ornaments. These ornaments are the final additions that allow the ancestors to achieve a new, definitively human status; combined with external skins added to internal organs that figure as stools, gourds, and so on, these ornaments demarcate the ancestors from fish. They underline the transformation from fish to human because, from the perspective of the divinities, ornaments are themselves people. Humans are thus doubly human: they clothe their bodies with goods that are not just aspects of persons—their skins—but also persons in their own right—their ornaments. This means that Tukanoans are Real People—different from both animals and other peoples not only in their own eyes but also in the eyes of the divinities that have tried so hard to create them.

This foregrounding of objects has knock-on effects on the relations between humans and fish. If people see themselves as human and fish as fish, fish, too, see people as humans and not only as predatory animals. Because fish are resentful at having failed to make the grade, they seek to drag humans back down to their own level by making them ill. Thus Tukanoans hold Fish-People (*wai masa*) responsible for most of their illnesses and afflictions (see also Lasmar 2005, Cabalzar 2006). From the human point of view, to see fish as human would be to go along with these plans, an invitation to sickness or death. So rather than a transitive or affinal relation between people and fish, in which each sees the other through human eyes, we have a linear, nonreciprocal relation between fish, humans, and divinities that appears to correspond both to an emphasis on hierarchy and to creation in the idioms of fabrication and parenthood.

But the classical Amazonian themes of affinity, enmity, and theft are not entirely absent from the picture. Tukanoan creation myths move from the universal to the particular, from alterity to identity, and from potential affinity through real affinity to consanguinity. More concretely, they move from generic divisions between (1) men and women, (2) humans and fish, and (3) whites and Indians to deal with the differentiation of the Tukanoans into affinally related groups, which are then further divided according to genealogy and internal rank.

In the earlier stages of Tukanoan myths, women, fish, and white people all figure as hostile enemies. From these virtual affines, humans appropriate spiritual powers and capacities objectified in flutes, feather ornaments, exotic names, and white peoples' "clothing." In the middle stages of the myths, these generic powers and their material correlates are divided between different Tukanoan groups, appearing as their ancestral inheritance and inalienable heirlooms. Here, differences between objects signal differences between people. The Real People, related as real affines of the same general kind, order their lives by exchanges of sisters and ritualized exchanges of goods. Some of the items we have met above—yagé and beer, coca and tobacco, stools and gourds—figure prominently in these exchanges. Flutes and feather ornaments, inalienable objectifications of group spirit and potency, are more typically displayed than exchanged. Their display is an affirmation of both power and rank, but when they are exchanged, the groups involved enter into a special kind of ritual or spirit alliance (*hee tenyü* or "ancestral affine" in Barasana), as if the groups had exchanged sisters—or as if goods and people were equivalent and substitutable. If this is not quite the same as the bridewealth system, there can be little doubt that, for the Tukanoans, objects can also be subjects and persons.

At the end of the creation myths, these same goods underwrite internal differences in rank and status. At the level of groups, such goods are the prerogatives of high-ranking clans and part of a politico-ritual system that allows those clans to dominate lower-ranking groups. At the level of individuals, power and influence go hand in hand with control of sacred property—and of white people's merchandise, technology, and learning.

Tukanoan culture and society thus display two complementary tendencies, one that appears to be restricted to northwest Amazonia, and the other appearing to be more widespread. At the level of shamanism, these two tendencies are those of the kumu ("priest") and *yai* ("jaguar-shaman"—see Hugh-Jones 1994). The kumu is concerned with "vertical," hierarchical relations of divine creation, lineal transmission, and ancestry, and he controls relations between the living and their ancestors by processes of personification and objectification. His prototypes are the Grandparents of the Universe sitting on their stools blowing out tobacco smoke, the creator divinities that figure throughout this discussion. The yai tendency is more concerned with "horizontal" relations between humans and various kinds of others—spirits, enemies, and animals. The province of the yai or jaguar-shaman, a more typically Amazonian domain, is the focus of a different, complementary body of mythology, common to Amazonia as a whole, in which humans and animals intermarry and exchange perspectives on equal terms. And here, as for the Mamaindê (Miller, this volume), objects figure not as divinities whose human creations were once fish, but rather as the body parts of birds and animals who were once people. In these other myths, and as Viveiros de Castro would predict (2004:477–78), the origins of cultural institutions are indeed explained as borrowings of prototypes possessed by animals, spirits, and enemies—i.e., taking. Thus, while virtual affinity and transfers from enemies do also figure in Tukanoan creation myths, in this case, they are set alongside themes of creation in the bodily and artifactual idioms of parenthood and fabrication—i.e., making.

The Tukanoans' ritual and symbolic elaboration of a range of highly crafted ceremonial goods and the coexistence, amongst them, of two kinds of shamanism, two rather different bodies of mythology, and two modalities for the origin of cultural institutions, have some wider comparative and theoretical implications.

Characterizing Amazonia as "object poor" compared with other parts of the world, ethnographers of the region have tended to accord relatively little sociological weight to material items. However, this apparent poverty may be as much or more a product of the ethnographers' theories as it is a reflection of things on the ground, for, as suggested above, current theoretical trends share in common an inbuilt tendency to downplay the significance of objects, albeit in different ways and for different reasons.

In addition, generalizations about objects in Amazonia, like generalizations about Amazonians' political, moral, or symbolic economies, always reflect particular ethnographic and historical perspectives. One thing that emerges clearly from this volume is that different Amazonian peoples may have quite different object regimes, a point that is yet more evident if one examines the historical and archaeological record (see McEwan, Barreto, and Neves 2001).

In the case of the Tukanoans, the importance accorded to the Instruments of Life and Transformation and the parental idioms of creation that these artifacts imply—in mythology, in ceremonial exchange, and in daily life—are part and parcel of the Tukanoans' emphasis on hierarchy, patriliny, exogamy, and exchange—social structural features that are also reflected in the physical and symbolic elaboration of their architecture (see Hugh-Jones 1995). The "fit" between the domain of objects and materiality and other social structural and cosmological features suggests that attention to different object regimes might itself provide new insights into some wider similarities among and differences between Amazonian peoples.

A final point concerns the relative attention given to objects and animals by Indians and by ethnographers. In the past, objects played a dominant role in several comparative works on Amazonia—consider, for example, William Edmund Roth's (1924) *An Introductory Study of the Arts, Crafts, and Customs of the Guiana Indians*. Today, with the current interest in animism and perspectivism, it is animals that have moved to center stage. The focus on animals certainly reflects one dominant concern of Amazonian peoples, the Tukanoans included. But, like the Waura and other Xinguanos (Barcelos Neto, this volume), the Tukanoans are also preoccupied with the circulation of goods, and, like the Kayapo (Turner, this volume), they discriminate between ordinary goods and a category of valuables to which manufactured goods are assimilated. Further, when it comes to manufactured items, their interest can sometimes border on an obsession (see Hugh-Jones 1992; also Gordon 2006). However, rather than assigning relative priority to one or the other category in the minds of Amerindians, the chapters of this book suggest that animals and objects can, and should be, considered together. It is not just humans and animals that are undifferentiated in Amerindian mythology; this lack of differentiation can apply equally between humans, animals, and objects.

Notes

1. See Viveiros de Castro 1993.

2. See Umúsin Panlõn Kumu and Tolamãn Kenhíri 1980, Diakuru and Kisibi 1996, Ñahuri and Kümarõ 2003, Maia and Maia 2004, and Tõramü Bayar and Guahari Ye Ñi 2004.

3. This version is based on the text in Diakuru and Kisibi 1996. Relevant page numbers appear in square brackets. Variants, in curly brackets, are from the sources in note 2 above; orthography has been standardized and simplified.

4. The rattle lance is an approximately two-meter-long staff decorated with feather mosaic, engraved designs of the sun and moon, and two bone or teeth prongs. Above the staff's pointed end is a bulbous, maraca-like swelling that contains small crystal pebbles. The staff is used to mark divisions of time in major rituals (see Koch-Grünberg 1909–10, I: abb. 219–21).

5. This accompanies the rattle lance (see Koch-Grünberg 1909–10, I: abb. 218; abb. 221).

6. See Koch-Grünberg 1909–10, I: abb. 159–60.

7. See Koch-Grünberg 1909–10, I: abb. 145.

8. See Koch-Grünberg 1909–10, I: abb. 225.

9. See Koch-Grünberg 1909–10, II: abb. 18; abb. 19. The split-palm screen is used to construct fish traps, as a compartment to seclude officiating shaman-priests during rituals and young persons during puberty rites, and as a mat to protect objects from dirt. It is called *parí* in Lingua Geral; Yuruparí, the name of the mythological hero, decomposes into *yuru-*, "mouth" and *-parí*, "enclosure."

10. Also variously called Yepa Büküo ("Old Earth Woman"), Yepa Maso ("Earth Woman"), the "Grandmother of Transformation" (Maia and Maia 2004:21), and Romi Kumu ("Woman Shaman") (Hugh-Jones 1979).

11. *Sabicea amazonensis*, a vine found in abandoned clearings, is a key ritual item (see Hugh-Jones 1979:126).

12. The Tukano word *muhihu* refers to a composite "sun/moon." In Tukanoan mythology, Sun and Moon, ancestors of the Desana Sky/Day People and Tukano Earth/Night People, sometimes change roles (see Hugh-Jones 1979:272–73). This role change, and the affiliation of the narrator (whether Tukano or Desana), will affect who is specified and who is senior/junior.

13. The Desana Gõamü, equivalent to the Tukano Õakü—often glossed as "God"—could also be "man of bone" (compare the Wakuénai Iñápirríkuli, "he inside of bone"; see Hill, this volume). The Tukano Yepa Oakü is the Barasana Yeba Hakü; *hakü*, or "father," is phonetically and semantically close to *oakü*.

14. His body is made of manioc and cultivated plants (Ñahuri and Kümarõ 2003:19), as Yuruparí's body is made of forest fruits (Ñahuri and Kümarõ 2003:42) and as ancestors of white people are described as having bodies made of manufactured items.

15. The Desana/Tukano word *buhsari* means "ornaments."

16. The Barasana word *wanari* refers to a bird of the species *Anhinga anhinga*.

17. The Tukano *pamü-* means "to emerge, surface, ferment"; *pino* means "anaconda"; and *gasiro* means "skin" and "canoe"—thus, "pamüri pino" literally means "fermentation anaconda" and "pamüri gasiro" means "fermentation canoe," with fermentation being a process of transformation. The canoe is also the trough (in the Barasana language, *kumua-hulia* or "canoe section") in which beer is brewed. Essentially, therefore, "pamüri pino" and "pamüri gasiro" can be understood as "fermentation anaconda," "fermentation canoe," "transformation canoe," or "beer trough."

18. Amo's house (container) is made from feathers; the Barasana word *hoa*, meaning "feather" or "hair," is also "bag, container."

19. See also Hugh-Jones 2001.

20. *Gahe-*, "other"; *-uni*, "thing(s)."

References

Andrello, Geraldo. 2006. *Cidade do índio*. São Paulo: Editora UNESP: ISA / Rio de Janeiro: NUTI.

Århem, Kaj, et al. 2004. *Etnografía Makuna*. Gothenburg and Bogotá: Acta Universitatis Gotoburgensis / Instituto Nacional de Antropología y Historia.

Bayar, Tõramü, and Guahari Ye Ñi. 2004. *Livro dos antigos Desana-Guahari Diputiro Porã*. São Gabriel da Cachoeira: ONIMRP / FOIRN.

Beksta, Kasys. 1988. *A maloca Tukano-Dessana e seu simbolismo*. Manaus: SEDUC / AM.

Cabalzar, Aloisio (org.). 2006. *Peixe e gente no alto rio Tiquié*. São Paulo: Instituto Socioambiental.

Collier, Jane, and Michelle Z. Rosaldo. 1981. Politics and Gender in Simple Societies. In Sherry B. Ortner and Harriet Whitehead (eds.), *Sexual Meanings*, pp. 275–329. New York: Cambridge University Press.

Diakuru and Kisibi. 1996. *A mitologia sagrada dos Desana-Wari Dihputiro Põrã*. São Gabriel da Cachoeira: UNIRT / FOIRN.

Fulop, Marcos. 1954. Aspectos de la cultura Tukana: Cosmogonía. *Revista Colombiana de Antropología* 4:123–64.

Gordon, Cesar. 2006. *Economia selvagem: Ritual e mercadoria entre os índios Xikrin-Mebêngôkre*. São Paulo: Editora UNESP.

Hartmann, Günther. 1975. Sitzbank und zigarrenhalter. *Tribus* 24:137–56.

Hugh-Jones, Stephen. 1979. *The Palm and the Pleiades: Initiation and Cosmology in Northwest Amazonia*. Cambridge: Cambridge University Press.

———. 1988. The Gun and the Bow: Myths of White Men and Indians. *L'Homme* 106–7:138–56.

———. 1992. Yesterday's Luxuries, Tomorrow's Necessities: Business and Barter in Northwest Amazonia. In Caroline Humphrey and Stephen Hugh-Jones (eds.), *Barter, Exchange, and Value: An Anthropological Approach*, pp. 42–74. Cambridge: Cambridge University Press.

———. 1994. Shamans, Prophets, Priests and Pastors. In Nicholas Thomas and Caroline Humphrey (eds.), *Shamanism, History and the State*, pp. 32–75. Ann Arbor: University of Michigan Press.

———. 1995. Inside Out and Back to Front. In Janet Carsten and Stephen Hugh-Jones (eds.), *About the House: Lévi-Strauss and Beyond*, pp. 226–52. Cambridge: Cambridge University Press.

———. 2001. The Gender of Some Amazonian Gifts. In Thomas Gregor and Donald Tuzin (eds.), *Gender in Melanesia and Amazonia: An Exploration of the Comparative Method*, pp. 245–78. Berkeley: University of California Press.

———. 2006. The Substance of Northwest Amazonian Names. In Gabriele vom Bruch and Barbara Bodenhorn (eds.), *The Anthropology of Names and Naming*, pp. 74–96. Cambridge: Cambridge University Press.

Koch-Grünberg, Theodor. 1909–10. *Zwei Jahre unter den Indianern: Reisen in Nordwest-Brasilien 1903–1905*. Stuttgart: Strecker and Schröder. (2 vols.)

Kumu, Umúsin Panlõn, and Tolamãn Kenhíri. 1980. *Antes o mundo não existia*. São Paulo: Livraria Cultura Editora.

Lasmar, Cristiane. 2005. *De volta ao lago de leite*. São Paulo: Editora UNESP: ISA / Rio de Janeiro: NUTI.

Maia, Moisés, and Tiago Maia. 2004. *Üsâ yêküsümia masîke*. São Gabriel da Cachoeira: COIDI / FOIRN.

McCallum, Cecilia. 1988. The Ventriloquist's Dummy? *Journal of the Royal Anthropological Institute* 23(3):560–61.

McEwan, Colin, Christiana Barreto, and Eduardo Neves. 2001. *Unknown Amazon: Culture in Nature in Ancient Brazil*. London: British Museum Press.

Ñahuri (Miguel Azevedo) and Kümarõ (Antenor Nascimento Azevedo). 2003. *Dahsea Hausirõ Pora ukũsehe wiophesase merãbueri turi*. São Gabriel da Cachoeira: UNIRT / FOIRN.

Overing, Joanna, and Alan Passes (eds.). 2000. *The Anthropology of Love and Anger: The Aesthetics of Conviviality in Native Amazonia*. London: Routledge.

Rivière, Peter. 1984. *Individual and Society in Guiana*. Cambridge: Cambridge University Press.

Roth, William Edmund. 1924. *An Introductory Study of the Arts, Crafts, and Customs of the Guiana Indians*. Thirty-eighth Annual Report of the Bureau of American Ethnology: 25–745. Washington: Government Printing Office.

Vincent, Murray. 1987. Mascaras. In Berta Ribeiro (coord.), *Suma etnológica brasileira*, pp. 151–71. Petropolis: FINEP / VOZES.

Viveiros de Castro, Eduardo. 1993. La puissance et l'acte. *L'Homme* 33(2–4):141–70.

———. 1996. Images of Nature in Amazonian Ethnology. *Annual Review of Anthropology* 25:179–200.

———. 2004. Exchanging Perspectives. *Common Knowledge* 10(3):463–85.

2
Things as Persons

Body Ornaments and Alterity among the
Mamaindê (Nambikwara)

Joana Miller

In 1938, Claude Lévi-Strauss visited a Nambikwara band camped near one of the numerous telegraph stations built by the Rondon Commission across the Brazilian states of Mato Grosso and Rondônia.[1] During his stay, the local shaman suddenly vanished, an event recalled by Lévi-Strauss in his study on the social life of the Nambikwara (1948—later partly republished in *Tristes tropiques* [1955]).[2] I refer to this episode because it constitutes, to my knowledge, the first evidence of the importance of body ornamentation in this ethnographic region—the theme I intend to explore in this chapter.

Lévi-Strauss reports that the shaman in question was late in returning to the camp and that his kinsfolk were very worried. Sometime later, he was found, completely naked, at a location near the encampment. The shaman told the people who found him that he had been carried far away by the thunder, who had stolen his ornaments. The following morning, he was once again wearing his ornaments without anyone questioning his version of the events that had taken place the previous day.

The conclusion that Lévi-Strauss draws from this episode is mainly political: the shaman had left to meet with a hostile band but subsequently explained his absence as the result of capture by supernatural beings. While not necessarily disagreeing with the episode's political connotations, I wish to draw attention to the fact that the shaman described his abduction by the thunder as resulting in the theft of his body ornaments. In spite of the differences that exist between Nambikwara groups, my observations among the Mamaindê, Nambikwara-speakers living in the northwest of Mato Grosso state, may help explain this particular detail of the episode.

The Mamaindê establish a close link between their body ornaments and the components of the person, a link that receives particular emphasis in the contexts of shamanism and female puberty rites. An understanding of the Mamaindê notion of personhood cannot, therefore, dispense with an inquiry into the status of objects and, more specifically, of body ornaments. I argue that among the Mamaindê, the ownership of body ornaments defines the subject, conferring upon her consciousness, direction, intentionality, and memory. For this reason, illness—conceived of as a process of transformation—is frequently described as the loss of body ornaments, or as the exchange of one's body ornaments with those of other beings. In these cases, the adornments are associated with the concept of spirit (*yauptidu*). An analysis of the status of objects in general, and of body ornaments in particular, reveals the means through which the person is constituted out of the wide spectrum of humanity characteristic of Amerindian ontologies. The analysis of these items is, thus, crucial to understanding how the Mamaindê conceive of themselves and others.

Nambikwara

The groups generically denominated "Nambikwara" have traditionally occupied the region extending from the northwest of the state of Mato Grosso and the neighboring areas of the state of Rondônia, between the affluents of the Juruena and Guaporé rivers, as far as the headwaters of the Ji-paraná and Roosevelt rivers. This large territory encompasses three geographically, linguistically, and culturally distinct areas: the region known as the Serra do Norte, the Chapada dos Parecis, and the Guaporé Valley.

All the groups inhabiting these areas speak dialects of the Nambikwara language family. These can be divided into three groups of languages spoken in different parts of the Nambikwara territory and are classified as southern Nambikwara, northern Nambikwara, and Sabanê (Price 1969). This latter language is spoken by a group designated by the same name, and it is more distantly related to the other two Nambikwaran languages. The Mamaindê are situated at the northern end of the Guaporé Valley and speak a northern Nambikwara language. They currently number some 190 people, most of whom live in a single village situated between the Pardo and Cabixi rivers. All my fieldwork data was obtained in this village, although it is possible to extend my observations to other Nambikwara groups.[3]

The episode reported by Lévi-Strauss occurred among the Sabanê and Tarundê (the latter probably speakers of a northern Nambikwara language), who were, at the time, assembled in a single camp next to the Vilhena telegraph station at the northern limits of the Nambikwara territory.

Things

The Mamaindê assert that they have both external and internal body ornaments. The latter can be seen only by shamans, who make them visible to others during curing sessions. Both inner and outer ornaments are each generically called *wasain' du*, "thing," a term also used to refer collectively to all the belongings of a person. Visibility or invisibility is not an intrinsic property of the object, but rather the result of a visual capacity of the observer. From the viewpoint of the shaman, a being capable of adopting multiple perspectives, a body always reveals itself as a decorated body.

During curing sessions, the shaman often removes the internal ornaments of his patient, rendering them visible. Rubbing his hands on the head of the patient, he pulls out a "cotton thread" (*kunlehdu*) that, to his eyes, is a band of black beads (*yalikdu*[4]) (see fig. 2.1). According to the shaman, however, not only our heads are adorned with this thread/band: our whole body is, in fact, draped with black-beaded bands.

On one occasion, I observed a shaman healing an elderly woman whose body was wracked with pains. He removed beads from her knee and stomach and explained that she was in pain because the bands contained inside her body had broken. He added that this had happened because the woman had stored her bands at home in the wrong manner: she should have stored them carefully stretched out rather than bundled in coils. This indicates that what happens to a person's ornaments affects her in the same way regardless of whether they are external or internal, provoking ailments that can lead to death. In the case of an ailment, it is up to the shaman to fix the broken bands and then put them back inside the patient's body.

The shaman may also recommend that those who are ill begin to use more bands around their bodies. During a curing session, I observed a shaman remove beads from within a man's body and hand them over to the latter's wife. The woman then proceeded to make a new band, which she subsequently tied around her frail husband's wrist. Thus, although the inner threads/bands are invisible to the eyes of common people, they can become visible during curing sessions. In this sense, they are not

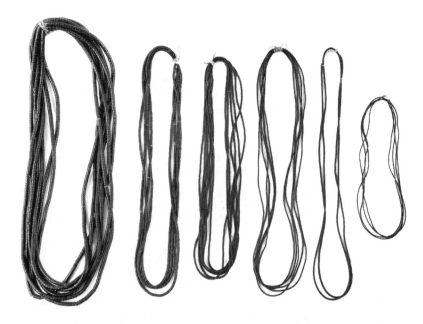

Figure 2.1. Bands of black beads that all Mamaindê can possess as external and internal ornaments. *Photo*: Carlos Miller, 2007.

conceived to be fundamentally distinct from the bands that the Mamaindê use externally.

The Mamaindê affirm that these threads/bands are our path, our memory, and also that which causes us to dream.[5] Without these bands, we do not know where we are; we fail to recognize our kin and we become lost and sick. When this happens, a person is said to have lost her "spirit" (yauptidu) or her "things" (wasain' du). Indeed, in this context, the Mamaindê frequently translate the term "wasain' du" into the Portuguese word for "spirit" (*espírito*), indicating that the loss of the thread/band is equivalent to the loss of one's spirit. If the shaman does not retrieve the lost thread/band, the person may die.

The same occurs when someone loses other body ornaments. While making a toucan feather headdress to be used by her daughter in the festival that closes the female puberty rite, a woman told me that were someone to steal the headdress, her daughter would die instantly, since she would lose her spirit (yauptidu). Marcelo Fiorini (1997) reports a similar idea among the Nambikwara groups living to the south of the Guaporé

Valley. He observes that the Wanairisu consider certain objects, particularly body ornaments, to be an extension of their own spirit (*yãukit'isu,* in the southern Nambikwaran language) and adds that children often wore many necklaces, since their spirits were considered more vulnerable to the attacks of malevolent spirits. David Price also briefly mentions the importance that the Nambikwara groups of the Chapada dos Parecis attach to bodily adornments:

> Necklaces of all sorts belong to a category of things that the Nambiquara call *yegnk'isu.* This is a generic term for "things made by people"—as opposed to natural objects like plants or animals. . . . Some kinds of handiwork, notably those that do not have a utilitarian function, are "spirit handiwork," charged with a certain element of mystery, and worn close to the body, especially on ritual occasions. (Price 1989:681)

The above examples indicate that, in this ethnographic context, body ornaments may often be associated with the notion of spirit and are therefore considered to be a constitutive part of the person (see Santos-Granero and Walker, this volume, for similar notions among the Yanesha and Urarina). For the Mamaindê, at least, illness is frequently described as a loss of body ornaments. Thus, the shamanic practices that seek to attach the spirit to the body very often involve adorning the latter with numerous bands of black beads.

Although, for the Mamaindê, the ownership of bands of black beads confers people with consciousness, memory, and intentionality—qualities that are equated with the spirit—it should be noted that, under certain circumstances, the ornaments themselves can act as subjects. I became aware of this during a curing session when the acting shaman removed a thread/band from inside the head of a patient and, rubbing it between his hands, placed it close to his ears. People explained that the thread/band was speaking to the shaman, telling him what had happened to the patient's spirit. Some even claimed that the thread/band was the person's own spirit speaking. After listening to it, the shaman told everyone what had happened to the sick man, who only then regained his memory and began to recover his health.

It is not only in the context of shamanism, however, that body ornaments may act as subjects. During the period of seclusion central to female puberty rites, the secluded girl cannot wear body ornaments lest these transform into dangerous animals. People say that in the darkness of the hut, where the girl is confined, bands, cotton anklets, and cotton bracelets can turn into snakes or giant centipedes.

The end of the seclusion is celebrated with a large feast, during which the girl is removed from the small hut where she was confined by guests coming from other Nambikwara villages. When the girl leaves the hut, her body needs to be hyper-adorned with a variety of ornaments and numerous bands of black beads (see fig. 2.2). This contrasts with her nudity during the seclusion period. One of the ritual songs sung on these occasions refers to the girl indirectly through reference to the bands that she wears.[6] When the girl finally emerges from the seclusion hut, her parents, who must make numerous bands of black beads to give to those who remove her from seclusion, often call her affectionately "my thing" (*da wasain' du*). Thus although during the seclusion period, body ornaments are dangerous because they can transform into animals, during the feast that marks the end of seclusion, they become indispensable. They are identified with the girl to such an extent that both become a single "thing" (wasain' du).

David Price (1977:125) observes that among the Nambikwara groups of the Chapada dos Parecis, pubescent girls—who are actively "made" through human agency—can be considered the "handicraft" of their parents, just like their bodily adornments. According to this author, what enables the comparison between pubescent girls and the bands they wear is the fact that the Nambikwara see both as the products of human agency. It should be added, however, that by tracing such a comparison, Mamaindê people are not conceiving pubescent girls as objects, but rather conceiving objects as subjects.

The human quality of the ornaments and objects made by people is even more evident in myths. An important Mamaindê myth narrates how people were transformed into animals when a child opened the gourd that contained the night (darkness). Until then, those animals that had existed were kept in a hole controlled by a shaman "owner" of animals. The sun never set and everything was clearly visible. Then, one day, the children disobeyed the shaman's orders and opened the hole where the animals were kept, allowing them to escape. In punishment, the shaman gave one of the children a gourd that contained the night. The gourd was filled with wasps, which stung the child when he opened it. Unable to endure the stings, the child dropped the gourd, shouting that it was going to become dark, as night spread throughout the world. The child was transformed into an *urutau*, a bird of the Nyctibiidae family that cries during the night. The older people became white-furred monkeys (*kõndadu*). The stone axe

Figure 2.2. Pubescent girl profusely adorned for the ceremony celebrating the end of her ritual seclusion. *Photo*: Joana Miller, 2004.

said that it liked to chop down trees in order to eat honey and so transformed itself into a tayra (a sharp-toothed, weasel-like animal that eats honey). The poisoned arrows used for hunting became poisonous snakes. The shaman's cotton anklets became giant centipedes. A type of container made from a gourd announced that it would become a tortoise because it did not want to get wet from the rain. The carrying basket became a jaguar, which is why the jaguar is spotted like the weave of the basket. At the end of the myth, we are told that "all animals are made of people," which suggests that human-made objects had the status of subjects.[7]

The myth indicates that the objects possessing subjectivity are precisely those produced by people, which makes them, in this sense, into bearers of human agency. When defining the term "wasain' du" ("thing"), the Mamaindê emphasize precisely this characteristic: "*wasain' du* is everything that we make or use." The set of things people make can thus be called *nusa wasainãã* ("our things"), or *nusa wekkinãã* ("that which we make," literally "our makings").[8]

As Eduardo Viveiros de Castro (2004:471) has observed, "Artifacts have this interestingly ambiguous ontology. They are objects that necessarily point to a subject; as congealed actions, they are material embodiments of nonmaterial intentionality." Likewise, we could assert that, for the Mamaindê, body ornaments and other human-made things (wasain' du) are an epitome of the concept of spirit insofar as they are conceived of as bearers of human agency and are always linked to a subject.

Whenever an object ceases to be linked to whoever made it, it can revert to the state described in myth and transform once again into an animal. The Mamaindê affirm that, even today, a carrying basket abandoned in the forest can become a jaguar and return to attack its owner. It is as though objects must be constantly "domesticated" lest they transform into animals. From a Mamaindê perspective, it could be asserted that objects are "potential animals" that constantly need to be made into objects.

Things of the "Owners"

As we have seen, body ornaments, particularly black-bead bands, can be conceived of both as subjects and as what defines a subject capable of having consciousness, memory, and intentionality. However, according to the Mamaindê, humans are not the only beings possessing ornaments. The spirit of the *da'yukdu* cannibal monster—identified as the "owner" (*wagin'du*) of the spider monkey and described as a hyper-version of this species—is said to steal the inner threads/bands of the Mamaindê while they dream and replace them with his own. A person whose thread/band has been stolen by the spirit of this monster grows very ill, forgets her kin, and loses her way. Her spirit goes away to live in the forest, accompanying the spirit that took her body ornaments. The Mamaindê also assert that the person whose thread/band has been stolen or swapped by the da'yukdu marries him and starts to see her own kin as beasts (*nadadu*, "large and dangerous animals" or "predators"). Thus, the exchange of body ornaments also entails an exchange of perspectives.

The ornaments of those beings deemed to be the "owners" of specific animal or vegetable species and natural phenomena are often described as being made from materials different from those used by the Mamaindê. The thread of the owner of the spider monkey is described as a black, greenish, or grey thread that, to the shaman's eyes, appears like a spider web. The beads used to make the bands of the owner of the peccary are made from annatto seeds instead of the fragments of tucum palm used by the Mamaindê.

Many illnesses are caused by the exchange of threads/bands with beings that are described as hyper or monstrous versions of the species that they "own," particularly the da'yukdu (the owner of the spider monkey).[9] When this type of illness happens, the shaman has to remove the thread left by the da'yukdu in the head of the patient and replace it with a new one, putting an end to the process of transformation begun with the theft of the thread/band. The patient once again recognizes her own kin, and her spirit ceases to wander through the forest in the company of the da'yukdu. Hence, the Mamaindê describe the experience of transformation as the result of an exchange of body ornaments. It can thus be said that the possession of body ornaments not only defines a subject endowed with consciousness and perspective but, above all, it confers the possibility of transforming into another type of person.

Things and Spirits

In a recent article, Aparecida Vilaça (2005) reconsiders some of the questions found in studies of Amerindian corporality, drawing attention to the body's instability. Focusing on the relationship between the concepts of "body" and "soul," she observes that, for the Wari', a Txapakuran-speaking people from the Brazil-Bolivia border, all beings that possess *jam-* ("soul" or "spirit") can be defined as human or potentially human.

"Jam-" implies the ability to transform, to change affects, to adopt other habits. In sum, it allows the subject to be perceived as similar by other beings. Hence, people say that an animal *jamu*-ed, particularly in the context of an extraordinary action, to indicate that it acted like a human being, for example by killing a Wari' (an event that, to the eyes of the Wari', appears as the victim's disease). Likewise, a shaman is said to *jamu* when he interacts with his animal partners, perceiving them and being perceived by them as a member of their species. According to Vilaça:

> It seems evident that we cannot speak of the body without speaking of the soul. . . . However, the reason, at least for the Wari' . . . *seems to be not that the soul gives this body feelings, thoughts and consciousness, but that it gives it instability.* This is conceived as a capacity typical to humanity which must be controlled, since transformation may always be the result of the agency of other subjects rather than ego's desire. (Vilaça 2005:452–53, my emphasis)

Vilaça thus draws attention to the common native Amazonian practice of affixing the soul to the body as a means of controlling the possibility of corporeal transformation. As we have seen, among the Mamaindê, the act of affixing the spirit to the body often involves covering the body with ornaments, particularly bands of black beads wrapped around the neck, waist, and wrists. The Mamaindê do this especially to protect their young children, since the spirits of infants are thought to be more vulnerable to the attacks of malevolent spirits. The process of shamanic curing also involves adorning the body with many bands. In such cases, the shaman reintroduces the lost thread/band into the victim's body and suggests that she should adorn herself with as many bands as possible.[10]

Nonetheless, at the same time as they affix the spirit to the body, ornaments make the body visible to other types of beings, conferring upon them the kind of "instability" mentioned by Vilaça. As we have seen, it is the ownership of ornaments that makes a person visible to the da'yukdu cannibal monster. The theft of these ornaments by the da'yukdu is therefore equivalent to an exchange of perspectives. Similarly, it is no accident that shamans, who are capable of adopting multiple perspectives, always see the bodies of different beings as ornamented. The same happens in dreams—the preferred locus for the actions of spirits—when the dreamer meets the spirit (yauptidu) of a dead kinsman or the spirit owner of an animal species: they always see their bodies covered in ornaments. The anaconda, for instance, may appear in dreams as a man decorated with harpy eagle feathers. The spirit owner of the tortoise may appear as a man draped in necklaces made from tortoise shell. Whenever the Mamaindê recount their dreams of dead kin, they stress the beauty of the ornaments their kin were wearing. In dreams, as in myth, everything has the potential to reveal itself as human—even natural objects. A woman once told me that she dreamed she was fishing when, suddenly, a large stone began to walk. She was very frightened and for a while refrained from fishing, fearing that stones could become people.

The definition of the word "yauptidu"—"spirit"—provided to me by a young Mamaindê man, is perfect to summarize the notion of spirit that I have been trying to delineate here. According to this young man, "the spirit is the part of the body that we do not see." It is precisely this "part of the body" that makes the body visible for other beings.

It has been frequently claimed that the concepts of "body" and "soul" found in native Amazonian cosmologies are primarily perspectival relations, or positions. In an article on the concept of the body among the Juruna, a Tupi-speaking people of the Xingu basin, Tânia Stolze Lima (2002:12) explores this theme, noting that the body "does not represent a visible part in contradistinction to an invisible one." Although the young Maimandê man's translation may suggest such an opposition, the way the Mamaindê conceive of visible and invisible ornaments—relating these to the concept of "spirit/soul" (yauptidu)—suggests precisely the contrary. We have noted that what is visible or invisible is a matter of perspective. For this reason, the outer and inner ornaments are not understood as being two fundamentally distinct things. Stolze Lima explicates this point:

> The visibility or invisibility of a body does not depend on a character-istic intrinsic to it, but rather on a visual capacity of the observer. If I do not see a spirit, it is because my eyes lack the capacity to see it. If a spirit sees me, it only sees an aspect of myself that I am unable to see: my soul, which represents my whole body for it, my whole person. (Lima 2002:12)

Stolze Lima's claim, based on her ethnography of the Juruna, applies equally well to the Mamaindê, particularly if we substitute "soul" for "ornament" (wasain' du). Hence, we can say that from the perspective of other beings, the spirit (yauptidu) is an ornamented body, or indeed the body ornament itself (wasain' du).

It should also be noted that, according to the Mamaindê myth cited earlier, the time in which people and the objects they made were transformed into animals was a time in which the sun never set and everything was clearly visible—a time, therefore, in which there was no time, no distinction between day and night, light and dark, visible and invisible. As Viveiros de Castro (2002:419) has observed, Amerindian mythology records precisely "the process through which the present state of things is actualized from a pre-cosmos that is absolutely transparent, in which the spiritual and corporeal dimension of beings had not yet reciprocally concealed each other." What myths describe, he goes on to suggest, is how this state of transparency bifurcates into an invisibility (a soul), and an opacity (a body), that remain relative, given that such a state is always reversible. As we have seen, among the Mamaindê, only the trained eyes of the shaman can nowadays see the body preserved in the original transparency described in myths without eclipsing the ornaments that have become invisible to normal people.

It is, however, important to emphasize that although ornaments can be associated with the concept of the spirit/soul, the possession of body ornaments should not be taken as a fixed ontological attribute of each and every kind of subject. Whenever I asked the Mamaindê whether they were born with ornaments inside their bodies, the answers I obtained varied considerably. Some people said yes, while others vehemently denied this claim. Nonetheless, everyone agreed that shamans must always introduce new ornaments into the bodies of their sick patients. It seems, then, that what matters to the Mamaindê is not whether they are born already decorated, but rather the possibility of losing their ornaments—the risk of having them stolen or replaced with those of other beings. Hence, it only makes sense to conceive of body ornaments as components of the person when that person is inserted within a relationship.

The Shaman's Things

The Mamaindê describe shamanic power as the possession of many ornaments acquired from the spirits of the dead, as well as from the shaman who oversees the shamanic training. Shamans are the ones who possess the greatest number of body ornaments. The two who are currently active in the Mamaindê village can be quickly distinguished from other people since they always wear numerous bands of black beads. One of them also always wears cotton bands around his arms and head.

The process of shamanic initiation can be described as a type of death. The future shaman is beaten with the club of the spirits of the dead and faints (/*do*-/ = "dies"). When this happens, the spirits of the dead give him a variety of ornaments and objects, such as bands of black beads, cotton bracelets and anklets, toucan feather headdresses, gourds, arrows, and the *waluka'du*, a wooden spear that some Mamaindê refer to as "the shaman's sword."[11] These items are called "the shaman's things" (*wa'ninso'gã na wasaina'ã*) or "magical things" (*wa'nin wasaina'ã*), and are the basis of a shaman's power.[12]

Future shamans also receive a spirit-woman from the spirits of the dead, who will become "his wife" (*na de'du*). This spirit-woman is said to be a jaguar (*yanãndu*), who from then onwards accompanies the shaman, always sitting next to him during curing sessions "as if she were his dog." A shaman refers to his spirit-wife as "my pet" (*da mãindu*),[13] "my jaguar" (*da yanãndu*), or, more generically, "my thing" (da wasain' du). This suggests that spirit-wives are conceived of as being in the same category as the shaman's other magical objects and ornaments.

After obtaining these ornaments and objects from the spirits of the dead, shamans come to see the world as these spirits do. This enables them to acquire shamanic knowledge. It also allows them to see the ornaments that remain invisible to lay people and to make these ornaments visible to the latter. The shaman's ornaments (wasain' du) can thus be considered "objectifications" of the relationships established with the spirits of the dead. I suggest that this explains why a shaman's spirit-wife is called "his thing" (*na wasain' du*).

According to the Mamaindê, it is the relationship between shamanic knowledge and the acquisition of body ornaments that explains why forest spirits constantly strive to steal their ornaments. A shaman once explained to me that the da'yukdu spirit, the owner of the spider monkey, steals ornaments from the Mamaindê in order to have shamans of its own. Just as the Mamaindê depend on the perspective of the dead to obtain shamanic knowledge "objectified" in the form of body ornaments, forest spirits acquire shamanic knowledge by stealing the ornaments of the Mamaindê.

In order not to lose their shamanic power or "magic" (*na wa'nindu*), as the Mamaindê put it, shamans must observe a series of alimentary and sexual prohibitions. By doing so, they ensure that their spirit-wives will not abandon them, taking away their ornaments. When this happens, the shaman's wasain' du, or "things"—including both his ornaments and his spirit-wife—are said to have "gone away" (*na wasain' du 'ailatwa*).

Shamans must observe a series of alimentary restrictions in order to consummate their marriage with their spirit-wives. Among the Mamaindê, marriage is defined as a relationship based on the sharing of food. For many Amerindian peoples, commensality is an important vector for the creation of kinship, being conceived of as a sign of perspectival identity. Sharing food and attitudes toward food creates links between people and makes them similar. As Carlos Fausto states, "eating *like* someone and *with* someone is a primary vector of identity, much like abstaining for or with someone else" (2002:15; see also Vilaça 2002, 2006). In light of this, it can be said that the alimentary restrictions observed by shamans enable them to share the perspective of the spirits of the dead. The Mamaindê often say, for example, that shamans cannot eat the flesh of the spider monkey because, from the viewpoint of the dead, this species of monkey is the pet (*mãindu*) of the da'yukdu spirit.

Married to spirit-women, and in possession of body ornaments acquired from the spirits of the dead, shamans become these spirits' companions and call them "my kin" (*da waintãdu*, literally "my many"). People say that shamans are never alone: whatever they do, the spirits of the dead will do with them. Hence, whenever a shaman makes an object, he must remember to leave a pot of manioc beer beside him so that the spirits of the dead can drink while he works.[14] There is no contradiction, therefore, in asserting that a given object was made by the spirits of the dead, even if everyone saw the shaman making it. This is possible because the relationship that shamans establish with the spirits of the dead is in no sense metaphorical. The shaman is not like the dead; rather, he is effectively a dead person among the living. The shaman and the spirits of the dead thus constitute a single "collective body" sharing the same body ornaments and the same food.

Made by the spirits of the dead, shamanic ornaments possess their makers' agency. This explains their power. During curing sessions, the spirits of the dead act as the shaman's auxiliaries, helping him to recover the ornaments stolen from his patients so that he can place them back into their bodies. On such occasions, the spirits of the dead can bring new threads/bands for the shaman to pass on to the person being cured. The act of wrapping the patient's body with new bands is a means of re-establishing the kinship relations that were interrupted when her ornaments were stolen. We have already seen that this theft is often explained as a marriage with other beings. Curing sessions can therefore be seen as a means for the (re)production of human people out of the possibility—always latent—that they can become kin to other kinds of beings (see Vilaça 2002). To achieve this, the Mamaindê must resort to the perspective of the dead, which is thereby revealed to be essential to defining the identity of the living.[15]

In order to continue acting as the shaman's auxiliaries, the spirits of the dead must also be offered large quantities of manioc beer during the curing sessions. If they are not well fed, the spirits of the dead might become enemies, sending snakes to bite the living and provoking accidents and storms. Most of the curing songs I have recorded mention the ornaments acquired from the spirits of the dead. Some also proclaim that the spirits of the dead are coming to eat, referring to the food as a form of "payment" (*na yohdu*) for the ornaments they bring to the shaman.

In an article on the vocal music of the Mamaindê, Thomas Avery (1977) mentions a song that was classified by them as a "curing song" (*wa'ninso'gã hainsidu*), despite the fact that its lyrics mostly referred to exchanges. The Mamaindê commented that the song indicated that the spirits of the dead were satisfied with the exchanges between themselves and the shaman. Curing sessions can thus be described as a type of exchange in which the spirits of the dead give threads/bands to the living in exchange for food and drink.

The confection of other ornaments, such as the buriti palm-leaf loincloth used in rituals, as well as mother-of-pearl earrings, also depends upon the establishment of exchange relationships with spirits considered to be the "owners" of the buriti palm and of the shells from which the earrings are made. When they gather the raw materials needed to make either the loincloth or the earrings, the Mamaindê must offer food and manioc beer to their spirit "owner" in exchange for the raw material. Through these exchanges, the spirits are placated and made to refrain from sending diseases to harm the living—particularly young children, whose spirits are more vulnerable to their attacks.

The acquisition of objects from the spirits does not always require a counter-prestation in food. In some instances, shamans have only to look at the ornaments of the spirits in order to obtain them. This was how the Mamaindê learned to make the toucan feather headdress used in female puberty rites. A shaman "saw/seized" (*eududenlatwa*) the headdress used by the "people of the water."

The body ornaments used by the Mamaindê are thus the result of a process of appropriation of something that was made by others (spirits of the dead or the spirits deemed to be the "owners" of plants and animals). This allows us to conceive of personal ornaments as indices of relationships. These relationships, objectified as body ornaments, are constitutive parts of persons precisely because they enable their transformation.

Conclusion

I would like to conclude this chapter by returning to the episode of the disappeared Nambikwara shaman reported by Lévi-Strauss in *Tristes tropiques*. As I have suggested, this incident indicates the importance of body ornaments in the cosmology of Nambikwara groups, since the shaman described his encounter with supernatural beings in terms of the theft of his ornaments. Following this lead, I sought to show—based on my own data from the Mamaindê—that, in this ethnographic context, body ornaments are intimately linked to the processes that constitute the person out of the wider backdrop of humanity that is characteristic of Amerindian ontologies.

Although Lévi-Strauss's account of the disappeared shaman is the first recorded indication of the central place occupied by body ornaments in the symbolic economy of the Nambikwara, his description of their material culture places emphasis on its extreme paucity, a feature that distinguished them from other neighboring peoples, and particularly from the Bororo, whom he had just visited. Lévi-Strauss observed that the material goods made and possessed by the Nambikwara could be easily stored in a woman's carrying basket. These rustic artifacts, he added, "hardly deserve to be called 'manufactured goods.' The Nambikwara basket contains mostly raw material from which they make objects as need arises: a variety of woods . . . , lumps of wax or resin, yarns of vegetable fiber, bones, animal teeth and claws, strips of animal hide, feathers, porcupine thorns, coconut shells and river shells, rocks, cotton and seeds" (Lévi-Strauss 1996:261).

The idea of a material culture reduced to fragments of things gathered in the forest that could be stored in a single basket seemed to match the simplicity and fluidity of Nambikwara social organization, which again, according to Lévi-Strauss, evaded any attempts at sociological systemization. This state of affairs led the author to conclude his monograph by claiming: "I had sought a society reduced to its most simple expression. That of the Nambikwara was such a society, so much so that in it I found only people" (Lévi-Strauss 1996:299). Indeed, I believe that the analysis of Mamaindê body ornaments reveals much about their notion of humanity.

In this sense, the animal and plant fragments contained in their baskets form the raw materials for a rich cosmology.

Since at least the mid-1970s, Amazonian ethnographies have focused on the constitution of persons, highlighting the importance of corporality in the region's socio-cosmological systems (Overing 1977; Seeger et al. 1979). On the whole, however, descriptions of native conceptions of the person have not taken into account the status of objects. As Stephen Hugh-Jones (this volume) observes, this neglect stems in part from the characterization of the Amazonian political economy as one based more on people than on goods (e.g., Rivière 1984). Hugh-Jones further suggests that the diminished sociological weight given to objects in lowland South America is also implicit in the widely shared view that, in Amazonia, objects cannot substitute for people. As Fausto observes, "Amazonian societies are primarily oriented toward the production of persons through ritual and symbolic work," and "in so far as things rarely have any trans-contextual value as substitutes for persons or relations, the mediation between 'us' and 'others' is done by persons, parts of persons, and non-material subjective qualities such as names, souls, and songs" (1999:934; see also Descola 2001). It should be noted, however, that objects have been the focus of greater attention precisely in those regions where they are involved in wider trade and exchange networks, such as in the upper Xingu (Agostinho 1974), the upper Rio Negro (Chernela 1993:110–22), central Brazil (Turner 1979), and the Andean piedmont (Santos-Granero 2002:30–31). In studies of these areas, even though objects still do not substitute for people as they can in gift and commodity economies, it has been amply observed that objects act to produce and stress distinctions within the group or between different social groups.

I have shown that for the Mamaindê, objects—and more specifically, body ornaments—are related to a system of exchange that points toward ontological rather than sociological distinctions. For these people, objects are immersed in an economy of subjectivities, being conceived of as subjects or as constituents of persons, insofar as they relate those persons to other species of subjects. In this sense, it is possible to say that, for the Mamaindê, a theory of objects must necessarily be a theory of the person. It is no accident that among the Mamaindê, the prototypical object, the one that can be generically called "thing" (wasain' du), is the body ornament. An understanding of the constitution of persons thus requires us to take into consideration both forms of production and conceptualization of objects.

Acknowledgments

I would like to thank Fernando Santos-Granero and Philippe Erikson for their invitation to participate in the symposium "The Occult Life of Things: Native Amazonian Theories of Materiality and Sociality," as well as the participants in the symposium for their comments. I also wish to thank Aparecida Vilaça, Carlos Fausto, Eduardo Viveiros de Castro, Luiz Costa, and David Rodgers for their comments.

Notes

1. In 1907, the Brazilian government nominated the army officer Cândido Mariano da Silva Rondon as the head of the Comissão de Linhas Telegráficas e Estratégicas de Mato Grosso ao Amazonas. This commission—the Rondon Commission—made numerous expeditions into Brazil's hinterlands in order to establish cable lines and telegraph stations that would connect the region with Rio de Janeiro, the country's federal capital at the time. The project also hoped to encourage the occupation of Brazil's hinterlands and to establish "peaceful" contacts with its indigenous population.

2. Lévi-Strauss also mentions this event in "The Sorcerer and His Magic" (1949b).

3. I carried out a total of thirteen months of fieldwork between 2002 and 2005. My research was funded by the Programa de Pós Graduação em Antropologia Social (PPGAS) of the Museu Nacional and the Núcleo de Transformações Indígenas (Nuti).

4. The term "yalikdu" refers to both the band and to the black beads that compose it.

5. The Mamaindê use the Portuguese word *rumo*. The term is commonly used in regional Portuguese and refers to one's direction, bearings, and path and also to the capacity to recognize places and people. To say that someone has "lost their path," the Mamaindê might say that she has lost her "thread" (*tehdu*) or her "things" (wasain' du).

6. One of the ritual songs translated by Price also stresses the relationship between the girl and her bands:

> Maiden becomes nubile; in seclusion for this reason.
> Maiden becomes black beads; in seclusion for this reason.
> Move, my maiden; black beads move.
> A black bead owner am I.
> I have many things . . . (Price 1989:687)

7. The ample diffusion of the myth of the "revolt of objects" throughout the Americas attests to the prevalence of the Amerindian idea that, during primordial times, objects were subjects (Lévi-Strauss 1969).

8. The term *wekkinãã* is derived from the verb root /*wek-*/ = "to make." This is also the term used to refer to "children" (*da wekdu* or "my child"). The morpheme /-*wek-*/ is also a classifier of humanness. To ask "whom," "which," or "what," the stem /*natog'-*/ is followed by a classifier indicating the form of what one seeks to know. For example: *natog' galdu* means "which flat thing" and *natog' wekdu* means "which person" or "whom" (Kingston 1991).

9. The Mamaindê also mention other causes for the loss or breaking of the thread/band: a heavy blow to one's head, falling suddenly, getting beaten, being startled, feeling very embarrassed/ashamed, eating hot foods, becoming very sad, working excessively, and carrying too much weight. All of these events are thought to cause illness.

10. Both children and shamans are considered particularly prone to transformations and, for this reason, they both need to use many bands around their bodies.

11. Shamans use this sword to kill forest spirits that cause disease. The walukaʾdu was also described to me as a lightning ray that, when manipulated by shamans, can make holes in rocks and tree trunks in order to retrieve the spirits of people that are being held captive.

12. The term *waʾnindu* is often translated by the Mamaindê as "magic" because it refers to the shaman's capacity to make things visible. Yet the same term can also be translated as "spirit/soul." I should note that, for the Mamaindê, the concept of "spirit" denotes, first and foremost, a quality or capacity of the subject more than a substantive attribute. In light of this, the two translations are neither contradictory nor mutually exclusive, but rather complement each other. Consequently, the term *waʾninsoʾgã*, used to refer to the shaman, can be glossed as "he who has magic/spirit." Marcelo Fiorini (1997) glosses the term *wanin*, as used by the Wanairisu—who speak a southern Nambikwaran language—as "soul" or "vital principle."

13. Mamaindê women also used to affectionately call their husbands "my pet" (*da mãindu*), because they feed them and take care of them in the same way that they feed and take care of pets.

14. The ability to consume great amounts of manioc drink is another sign of shamanic ability. A Mamaindê man told me that a powerful shaman should always drink at least two cups of manioc drink: one for himself and one for his spirit-woman.

15. This observation is equally valid for the definition of group identities. As is common in Amazonia, Nambikwara groups do not have self-designations; their names were conferred by neighboring groups. Ethnonyms are therefore the names given by others, markers of the differences between groups rather than emblems of group identity.

References

Agostinho, Pedro. 1974. *Mitos e outras narrativas Kamayurá*. Salvador: Universidade Federal da Bahia.

Avery, Thomas. 1977. Mamaindé Vocal Music. *Ethnomusicology* 21(3):359–77.

Chernela, Janet. 1993. *The Wanano Indians of the Brazilian Amazon: A Sense of Space*. Austin: University of Texas Press.

Descola, Philippe. 2001. The Genres of Gender: Local Models and Global Paradigms in the Comparision of Amazonia and Melanesia. In T. Gregor and D. Tuzin (eds.), *Gender in Amazonia and Melanesia: An Exploration of the Comparative Method*, pp. 91–114. Berkeley: University of California Press.

Fausto, Carlos. 1999. Of Enemies and Pets: Warfare and Shamanism in Amazonia. *American Ethnologist* 26:933–56.

———. 2002. Banquete de gente: Comensalidade e canibalismo na Amazônia. *Mana* 8(2):7–44.

Fiorini, Marcelo. 1997. Embodied Names: Construing Nambiquara Personhood Through Naming Practices. PhD dissertation, New York University.

Kingston, Peter. 1991. Gramática pedagógica mamaindé. Summer Institute of Linguistics. (ms.)

Lévi-Strauss, Claude. 1948. La vie familiale et sociale des Indiens Nambikwara. *Journal de la Société des Américanistes* 37:1–131.

———. 1949a. *Anthropologie structurale*. Paris: Plon.

———. 1949b. Le sorcier et sa magie. *Le Temps Modernes* 41:3–24.

———. 1955. *Tristes tropiques*. Paris: Plon.

———. 1969. *The Raw and the Cooked*. New York: Harper and Row.

———. 1996. *Tristes trópicos*. São Paulo: Companhia das Letras.

Overing (Kaplan), Joanna. 1977. Comments (Symposium "Social Time and Social Space in Lowland South American Societies"). *Actes du XLII Congrès International des Américanistes* 2:387–94.

Price, David. 1969. The Present Situation of the Nambiquara. *American Anthropologist* 71(4):688–93.

———. 1977. Comercio y aculturación entre los Nambicuara. *América Indígena* 37(1):123–35.

———. 1989. Mirian Is Awakening: A Nambiquara Puberty Festival. *The World and I* (May):678–89.

Rivière, Peter. 1984. *Individual and Society in Guiana*. Cambridge: Cambridge University Press.

Santos-Granero, Fernando. 2002. The Arawakan Matrix: Ethos, Language, and History in Native South America. In Jonathan Hill and Fernando Santos-Granero (eds.), *Comparative Arawakan Histories: Rethinking Language Family and Culture Area in Amazonia*, pp. 25–50. Urbana and Chicago: University of Illinois Press.

Seeger, Anthony, Roberto da Matta, and Eduardo Viveiros de Castro. 1979. A construção da pessoa nas sociedades indígenas brasileiras. *Boletim do Museu Nacional* 32:2–19.

Stolze Lima, Tânia. 2002. O que é um corpo? *Religião e Sociedade* 22(1):9–20.

Turner, Terence. 1979. Kinship, Household, and Community Structure among the Kayapo. In David Maybury-Lewis (ed.), *Dialectical Societies: The Gê and Bororo of Central Brazil*. Cambridge, MA: Harvard University Press.

Vilaça, Aparecida. 2002. Making Kin Out of Others. *Journal of the Royal Anthropological Institute* 8(2):347–65.

———. 2005. Chronically Unstable Bodies: Reflections on Amazonian Corporality. *Journal of Royal Anthropological Institute* 11(3):445–64.

———. 2006. *Quem somos nós: Os Wari' encontram os brancos*. Rio de Janeiro: Editora UFRJ.

Viveiros de Castro, Eduardo. 2002. Perspectivismo e multinaturalismo na América Indígena. In Eduardo Viveiros de Castro, *A inconstância da alma selvagem e outros ensaios em antropologia*, pp. 101–56. São Paulo: Cosac and Naify.

———. 2004. Exchanging Perspectives. The Transformation of Objects into Subjects in Amerindian Ontologies. *Common Knowledge* 10(3):463–84.

3
Baby Hammocks and Stone Bowls
Urarina Technologies of Companionship and Subjection

Harry Walker

In the face of a relatively modest inventory of material possessions, the relational and communicative potentials of things are widely exploited by the Urarina of Peruvian Amazonia. For the Urarina, things—like nature—can be "good to socialize" (Descola 1992), engaged in relationships that work together to shape personal identities and underscore the things' own person-like qualities. This chapter explores Urarina theories of materiality and personhood through a close analysis of these relationships formed between humans and things. Regarded in certain contexts as more than inert matter but less than fully autonomous subjects, things have "lives" that raise ambiguities, which challenge and thereby help to clarify the contours and outlines of local senses of personhood. These ambiguities further highlight aspects often neglected in earlier studies. While a focus on practices of conviviality and the particular concerns of medical anthropology have coincided to advance models of the person that are, as I read them, grounded squarely in the body and in corporeal processes of substance exchange (e.g., Conklin and Morgan 1996; Pollock 1996; Conklin 1996; McCallum 1996), personhood for proponents of animism and perspectivism is more structural than processual, the outcome of internalized relations with alterity (e.g., Taylor 2001; Viveiros de Castro 2001; Vilaça 2002) and evidenced less through shared bodily substance than through the capacity for language (e.g., Descola 1994:99). For proponents of perspectivism especially, the subject is treated as a "given" with the presence of a (universal) soul, rather than as the product of experience (e.g., Viveiros de Castro 1998:471; Descola 1992:114). This conflation permits the recourse to dualist models of soul versus body, or subject versus object, and overarching theoretical inversions such that the "soul" or "subject" is the "given" in Amazonia, while the "body" or "object" is the "constructed." In all these approaches, bodies alone are social sites. The perspectivist subject is relational only insofar as it occupies the position of "predator" or "prey," and there is little room for questions of gender difference or other types or degrees of subjectivity.

Drawing on the Urarina case, this chapter points to a notion of subjectivity that is potentially available to both persons and things, is inherently gendered and relational, and does not presuppose the presence of a soul. By emphasizing the importance of intimate but asymmetrical relations of dependency and control in the constitution of agency, I seek to complement and counterbalance prevailing understandings of the "soul" as essentially a "non-social condition" associated with individual uniqueness (e.g., Gow 2000:53), the cultural valorization of individual autonomy, and egalitarianism.

The Economy of Companionship

Amidst the ties of kinship that connect the Urarina within and beyond the local community, relations of companionship (*corijera* or *coriara*) are constructed and dissolved. Unlike kinship, companionship is not elaborated primarily through bodily idioms; "corijera" means literally "shadow-soul-fellow." Unlike the body soul (*suujue*)—bound up in notions of hardness, interiority, and the "heart" (*suujua*), as the seat of thought and emotion—the shadow soul (*corii*) is associated with reflections, doubles, and companions. Founded in complementarity and physical proximity, the informal but typically asymmetric ties of companionship last anywhere from the duration of a specific task to a lifetime, and they embody a local philosophy of mutuality. "Everyone has a companion," I was told by one Urarina man. "Otherwise, they could not live in peace . . . No one can live alone." A companion may be "of the same race/group" or simply "of the same activity." For example, birds may act as companions to people as they accompany those who walk in the forest, giving advice through song on a range of topics from rising water levels to the imminent death of a loved one. Trees may act as companions to each other, grouped into sets of companions based on whether species are found together or are held in similar esteem—for example, aguaje palms are the companions of shebon palms; mahogany is the companion of moena; lupuna is the companion of caupuri. Communicative facility and cooperation underpin the relationship: "Lupuna is always conversing with caupuri," my informant explained. "They coordinate their work together . . . they are neighbors." Large game animals are said to each have a special type of companion, known as its *cojoaaorain*, which takes the form of a small bird who advises that animal on a daily basis. The bird is "like its soul" and "for its protection," warning of approaching predators and other dangers. Cultigens have companions "in order to produce." Sweet potato, the companion of manioc, is the latter's "support" and "resistance," and each helps the other to grow. "Without help, one cannot work."

A thing, too, can be the companion of another thing, provided the relation between them is one of likeness and proximity but not identity. A sock's pair is its "other" (*laucha*) but never its companion. A canoe's companion may be another canoe, but necessarily one belonging to a different owner. Artifacts can be and often are considered the companions of humans, though the relation must be established slowly through continual use and ever-increasing familiarity, until the identity of each entwines with that of the other. In the Urarina language, things are not formally distinguished grammatically from animals, plants, or humans: there are no markers or pronouns for animateness or gender and no nominal classifiers. All things may, on occasion, be attributed life (*icha-oha*), a Mother or Owner (*neba* or *ijiaene*), and an animal or vegetal soul (*suujue* or *eeura*, respectively).[1] Ultimately, however, it seems that things are defined as particular kinds of subjects less by the explicit attribution of such qualities than by the attitudes held toward them, as well as by the ways of speaking about or to them in particular contexts. A shaman's ceremonial breast band is credited with a vegetal soul (eeura) when first fabricated, but it is considered to acquire a semi-autonomous subjectivity only after repeated use, when it displays affection for its owner by, for example, transforming into a boa and licking his face during a healing session. Many such possessions that partake of their owner's personhood in some way, such as the ceremonial paraphernalia of a shaman or the woven fan or cooking implements of a woman, remain inalienably connected to their owners even at death and must accompany them to their graves. The ontological status of a thing is by no means self-evident, nor is it immune to change, and it is perhaps the temporal dimension that is of the greatest importance in understanding the ambiguous position of things in Urarina social life.

A Gift of Love: The Baby Hammock

Among the most intimate of all companionships established by Urarina is that formed at the very outset of life between a newborn baby and its hammock (*canaanai amaa*). A baby enters the world in a highly vulnerable and ambiguous state of existence, and the fabrication and use of the baby hammock form part of an extensive series of parental interventions intended to form and fortify its body, protect it from disease, and ensure its successful entry into full social personhood. The mother weaves the hammock from palm fibers (*Astrocaryum chambira*) just prior to leaving the purpose-built annex (*jata*) of palm leaves in which she gave birth, and in which she must reside with her child in isolation until its umbilical cord falls. Like the hammock into which the child is then immediately transferred, the jata provides a protective environment designed to minimize contact with alterity, as well as a liminal space for the passage from one social status to another. When I once asked why a mother weaves the hammock, I was told simply, "Because she loves her baby." It is an act that materializes her maternal love, alongside relations with female kin who, during the term of pregnancy, present gifts of selected items from hammocks their own children have outgrown. Such gift giving is also a concrete expression of their love—and in fact, the terms for "gift giving" and "loving" are linguistically identical (*belaiha*). Through the mother's investment of labor and love, the hammock is identified with its maker as a partial extension of her person (see Erikson, this volume), explicitly intended to substitute for the mother as the child is progressively distanced from her.

The hammock is prepared for use, and the child for emergence from the birth annex, through the performance by the father or another male relative of a chant cycle known as the *canaanai mitu baau*. This blesses a preparation of achiote and the roots of a piri-piri plant, with which the child and hammock are each subsequently painted in order to "maintain the body" and protect it from harm. Performed throughout the night directly prior to the child's emergence from the jata and lasting for as long as several hours, the chant invokes an extensive repertoire of beings— from mythical ancestors to species of birds and fish to the sun, moon, and celestial jaguar—with the aim of appropriating desirable qualities or relations. Prominent among these is *acarera*, which means "vitality," "vital breath/strength," or "longevity." The chant gradually builds up a compound identity for the child/hammock until it is, finally, the entire

ensemble of vitalities that is painted, as the following extract from a
canaanai mitu baau indicates:

Chabana baitenachara	Never capable of dying
Leleno acarera	The vitality of the iguana
Rai corii acarera	And the vitality of the child's spirit
Necoulucuna que	Are being formed as in the womb
Aine calabi acarera	The boy's vitality
Coiainaritiin ne	Shall be painted with achiote
Caa ataebuinae	This jaguar
Cana ichoae que terequi	Who dwells in the sky
Catojoaain cotabaji	Tremendous beast
Chabana necoerateein	Never passes to this earthly side
Necoaauna caje	Since the creation
Chabana netabatacajeein	Is never diminished
Nii baitenacai	And there not forgotten
Nejoerate rai corii	As the child's spirit grows
Coiane que	Painting with achiote
Acarera caa calauri	This collectivity of vitalities
Elunai que	Shielded from dangers
Coiane ne najanoacoa	Painting the newborn
Cobiri que	With piri-piri
Rai acarera	His vitality
Coiane que coiainaritiin ne	Shall be painted with achiote

When not in the arms of its mother or sleeping in her bed at night, a
newborn baby spends most of its time in the hammock, under constant
supervision, for there are no baby slings or other carrying devices (see fig.
3.1). With time, it is said, the child's acarera permeates the hammock and
would remain there even when it is no longer in use; painting both the
baby and the hammock with achiote pre-empts this fusion. The hammock
gradually forms an integral connection to the baby, a kind of "ensoulment" (see Santos-Granero and Miller, this volume) through which
each becomes an extension of the other, and the hammock will not be
reused by another baby once outgrown, but guarded by the mother until
it deteriorates. In exchange for the investment of vitality bestowed by the
baby, the hammock actively forms the child's own nascent personhood,

Figure 3.1. Baby in hammock adorned with large rattle. *Photo*: Harry Walker, 2006.

a role prefigured by the performative force of the *canaanai mitu* chant. Of central importance is the hammock's rattle (*torara*), a heterogeneous collection of items affixed beneath the position of the baby's head. Its bulk is made up of dry, hollow seeds and gourds whose primary purpose is to produce sleep-inducing "lullabies" (*jororoa*) as they swing to and fro. By means of a long, taut string wound through her toes, a simple rocking of the caretaker's foot keeps the hammock in constant motion. Sleeping is considered the ideal state for a newborn baby, and the rattle's lullabies are often augmented with vocalized versions, personalized by the caretaker, which implore the baby to sleep, often promising union with its mother (or father)—recently departed for the garden or forest—by means of its hammock "canoe":

Chajaocha tijiquin	Come, lie in your hammock
Sinira canaanai	Sleep now, child
Chajaocha mama sacuniu	Go and follow Mummy,
canaanai	child

Nedai ne te chanatoriqui canaanai	If you stay behind, you will cry, child
Inae mama jourichaje elo canaanai	The rain already closes in on her, child
Cotihaniu canaanai	Go and call her, child
Mama que tacaain cotihaniu	Go and be together with Mummy
Chajaera laulautoracha canaanai	Come on, go by canoe, child
Chajaocha tijitijico canaanai	Go lying and swinging, child

The rattle's lullaby promotes more than sleep, for attached to the seeds and gourds is a diverse and often extensive collection of animal parts: bones, teeth, claws, beaks, and tails, woven together with remnants of foreign goods such as empty bottles, disposable razors, plastic spools, mirror frames, and sewing kits (see fig. 3.2). Each item is more or less explicitly associated with some useful quality to be instilled in the baby, evoking pan-Amazonian notions of the transmission of animal qualities: the shoulder-bone of the sloth, for example—an animal said to rarely defecate—is attached to build a child's resistance to diarrhea; the tongue of the paucar bird is attached to develop its vocal abilities; coati teeth are attached to transmit this animal's ability to find honey and avoid snake-bites. Snail shells might be tied to the rattle "so the baby's ear doesn't grow too big," while tiny glass vaccination bottles collected from the visits of local health workers, wrapped in colorful cotton jackets, help the child build resistance to diseases. Many items are gender specific: spent shotgun shells, collected from kills rather than misses, promote hunting ability; packets of needles might be affixed to a girl's rattle "so she will know how to sew—so she doesn't grow up useless," and plastic combs might be included so that her well-brushed hair will remain free from lice. A single rattle may boast dozens of such components, the meaning or value of which can be idiosyncratic or evident only to one familiar with its origins, and final interpretative authority always rests with the mother. The rattle is her unique and personalized contribution to the continuing formation of her child outside the womb. It embodies a technology for the production of persons founded in the controlled appropriation of alterity in the context of companionship.

Knowledge of the hammock's protective function, epitomized in the sonic transmission of resistance to diseases brought by the rattle attached to it, helps to interpret comments by Urarina that the hammock is not

Figure 3.2. Hammock rattle made of seeds, gourds, animal parts, and manufactured objects. *Photo*: Harry Walker, 2006.

only the baby's companion (coriara) but also "like its cojoaaorain," the avian caretaker or spiritual guardian of game animals. One informant defined the cojoaaorain as "one who communicates with you in order to care for your life . . . for your defense." The baby is emotionally as well as physically dependent on the hammock, and separation is considered highly distressing, as was first made clear to me when I once callously— and ultimately unsuccessfully—attempted to purchase a hammock still in use. The baby's emotional involvement (i.e., with the hammock) is further encouraged by the attachment of a series of "toys," typically pieces of wood carved by the mother for the baby's shadow soul (corii) to "play" with. Their location behind the head and out of reach reinforces this playing's immaterial nature. The most important such "toy" is the baby's own umbilical cord (*misi*), which is carefully wrapped in cloth inside a tiny string bag and attached to the rattle. Treated with great respect by adults, it cannot be touched or removed from the hammock by anyone but the child itself, who will ideally dispose of it or "lose" it in the course of playing. The umbilical cord is linguistically indistinct from the placenta (also "misi"), which the midwife has carefully buried in the same pit into which the baby is born. Because of the umbilical cord's enduring connection to the child, its accidental contact with an animal or harmful spirit is feared to result in illness. The baby's spirit or shadow soul is said to return to the placenta and umbilical cord after death, and their careful burial enables it to find and identify its family and birthplace, establishing a localized continuity between the womb and the afterlife. A spirit unable to find its umbilical cord and placenta is condemned to eternal wandering and discontent.

The canaanai mitu baau quoted above referred to the child's spirit growing in the hammock "as in the womb," and a series of additional gestures and ideas point to an implicit analogy between the hammock (with rattle) and placenta. The Urarina recognize that each becomes an integral part of both the mother and child, an extension of their collective person, and cannot be unambiguously interpreted as belonging to either. Much like the placenta, the hammock binds a baby to its mother and mediates between them; hence the encouraging references (in lullabies and elsewhere) to the hammock as a means for prolonging their union. It must similarly be carefully protected against accidental contact with alterity due to a quasi-material connection with the baby. An empty hammock is always untied and laid on the floor, lest the spirits of deceased children enter it and swing in it, inducing vomiting, diarrhea, and fever. The hammock fully contains the baby in a protective and nurturing space that facilitates growth, much like the womb, and the extensive collection of hollow seeds, gourds, and empty bottles on the rattle would further suggest this function of containment. Use of the hammock in daily life effectively serves to prolong the experience of intra-uterine life. Safely inside, the baby dwells in a sonic universe circumscribed by the sounds of the rattle and is insulated physically and symbolically from the outside world. Perhaps most importantly, the rapid swinging motion, in which the hammock ideally swings almost 180 degrees, subdues the child by resisting and ultimately overriding its tentative exercise of agency. A baby in a hammock is rarely spoken to outside the lullaby, and in this subordinate, preferably sleeping, dependent state, it is best protected and most receptive to the formative messages which inaugurate it as person and subject.

A Tamed Enemy: The Stone Bowl

At the other end of the life trajectory, experienced shamans wishing to increase their control over the dart-like media (*batohi*) of mystical attack engage in intimate companionships with small, naturally occurring stone bowls known as *egaando*. Like the baby and its hammock, the shaman and the egaando come to share a similar if asymmetrical mode of social existence in which each productively transforms the other through communication and substantive exchange. But in this case, it is the shaman who must wield greater authority in order to utilize the egaando and coerce it into full personhood. Such a task is considered both difficult and dangerous, given the egaando's renowned hostility and formidable abilities to ensorcel, even when lying undiscovered in rocky stretches of riverbed. Babies and small children are particularly susceptible to the egaando's attacks, often through the conduit of their parents' activities, and the resulting illnesses can be cured only by means of *baau* chants which, like the canaanai mitu baau used for preparing the child and hammock (and like the operation of the rattle itself), aim to instill desired qualities from diverse sources. A series of beings noted for their immunity to attack by egaando are invoked in turn:

Lauri conucue cocaratiri	In our river basin that has rocky rapids
Begaando que nenotajina rai jojiara	As his father looks at the egaando

Ne jana rai beluna que	With its terrifying power
Nenotajina rai jojiara ne jana	The egaando looks at his father
Rai coichana lomoritiin	His blood will be dyed
Nia rai cojoachucane jana	By the blessed contents of this bowl
Unaterinachara	Harm never ever befalls
Asae aroba necoerejete	The offspring of the giant otter

[Entire verse repeats, replacing "giant otter"/ "*asae aroba*" successively with:]

asisi jelai tijiain	otter chief
caoacha ate cosemane	tapir
asae baain	water jaguar
asae araracuru	water thunder people
jojona	ponpon duck

Prior to its appropriation by a shaman, the egaando is little more than a hostile concentration of will and "fearfulness" or predatory energy (*comaaori*). Although occupying a "point of view," capable of causing harm by "looking," its status as a person is ambiguous, diffuse, and devoid of individual identity. It is not readily distinguished as an entity separate from the rocky riverbed in which it rests, nor from their shared Mother or Owner, who has both a spiritual and locational aspect (respectively *caratiri neba*, "mother of rocky rapids," and *nacanocari*, a kind of alligator). The egaando, the rocky riverbed, and their Owners are all thought to collaborate in joint acts of predatory aggression. Even more significantly, the egaando dwells hitherto outside the moral sphere, which over and above all else instantiates the divide between humanity and animality, or between "real people" and others.

To utilize an egaando, one must first capture and "tame" it (*irilaa*). A suitable specimen, sought out in times of low water level, is around five to ten centimeters in diameter, with two depressions in its base, said to resemble the testicles of the white-lipped peccary. One woman described her late husband's egaando as being "very pretty" with natural designs on it similar to those painted by women on the ceremonial ceramic jars (*baichaje*) used for storing ayahuasca (*Banisteriopsis caapi*). Once an egaando is found, a shaman immediately blows tobacco smoke on the bowl and places it at the foot of a *Brugmansia* tree (*Brugmansia suaveolens*), where its cooperation is gradually enlisted through forms of ritual dialogue (*cojiotaa* and *chairetaa*). The Mother of *Brugmansia* and the egaando are directly addressed in turn in their potential capacity as subjects, with the aim of soliciting assistance, subduing the egaando, and instigating asymmetrical relationships of companionship between the three participants, though without any recourse to external relations of transference:

Ca egaando carai irilaara coaairi Brugmansia	Tame this egaando for me,
Aiyute coaairi neeine ecaoacha Brugmansia	Let your greatness be with him,
Jereronia neeine	Be at his side, accompanying
Ca egaando naainte	Speak to this egaando
Cojiotaaure cana inoaesiuru	Our ancestors prayed to you
Charijieenteeinte iachuruine	Do as before, that we shall replace them
Aiyute necocaae nianone	Yes indeed, as I drink
Canu necoca jeeune neeine	Let's accompany each other
Cairijitocora egaando	Just like this, egaando
Cairijitocote	You are just like this
Ca coaairi necaoacha aina	With this greatness of *Brugmansia*
Cairijitocotee coaairi necaoacha	Be like this greatness of *Brugmansia*
Jereronia neeincha egaando	You will accompany me, egaando

After several days at the foot of the *Brugmansia* tree, the bowl is transferred to a baichaje jar and brought inside the house. Some claim that the jar should be filled with water, to be changed every few days, for if the bowl dries out, it is liable to "run away" or ensorcel those in its immediate proximity. In further chants addressed to the egaando, the shaman uses his new role as "owner" to ask it to serve him obediently, to respect his family and not cause them harm, and to share its knowledge with him. Though silent at first, the egaando eventually capitulates to the requests in *Brugmansia* visions. It is used as a vessel for drinking concentrated tobacco juice, ingested continuously in conjunction with tobacco smoke. The shaman must learn to listen to the egaando's "darts" (batohi)— the tiny weapons used in mystical attack and the source of its power—which sing their songs "through" him as he drinks the tobacco juice:

Egaando egaando egaando	Egaando, egaando, egaando
Mariri mariri mariri	Lying out flat

Asara ne coberotee	Emptying out *asara* darts
Netajetia neeine egaando	You are laying your eggs, egaando
Necalabihaca	Reproducing, increasing in number
Nenatia cute	Let us play and sing here
Tabaquero aina	With the tobacco drinker
Cojoatojoi uureen nedareen	Your forces will come to stay
Nenatia caa ne te	Sing of this

The theme of playing, which is also a feature of the baby's relationship with its rattle, is emphasized here, as in much shamanic discourse. Play is pivotal in the consolidation of social relationships and references a productive, if incorporeal, interaction that generates affective closeness. My informant explained as follows: "The shaman is getting drunk with the tobacco juice, and also with the darts; he is playing with the darts, going around and around for fun . . . both sides are playing, together with egaando, they are all playing. The darts are making him sing. The darts are always singing. Wherever they are, they always have to demonstrate their manner." Said to resemble tiny worms, the darts are full of life (*ichaoha*), playful as well as lethal. The egaando "lays eggs" in the song in order "to have grandchildren," "to increase its numbers," and through these songs, through play, the darts are said to "empty out" into the shaman and multiply.

In exchange for the bowl's continued cooperation, the shaman submits to stringent dietary and other prohibitions. He avoids salt and animals with strong colors or designs, among other items, which cause the egaando's darts to "flee in fear." He leads a solitary existence, eating and sleeping alone, approached only by others on the same diet. With the material basis of his connection to the group effectively severed, he is free to "become like the egaando" and communicate with it more effectively. One dieting with egaando is said to resemble a convalescent, physically weak and incapable of hard work. The bowl is placed by his head when he sleeps and will approach him in his dreams, interrogating his motives for seeking it out and dieting with it. He will be asked about his wife, children, and relatives, and the bowl may make clear its desire to inflict harm, to "eat the liver" of one of them, for example. The shaman must have mastered the art of dreaming in order to dissuade it and contain its aggressive instincts. One who lacks mastery of the relevant chants, or the discipline to diet properly, will similarly be unsuccessful in restraining it. One woman recalled how her father possessed an egaando when she was small but was unable to tame it, and her brother became gravely ill and nearly died as a result.

Rigorous adherence to the diet becomes a form of leverage in such oneiric transactions for ensuring the bowl's continued cooperation. As long as the shaman's family stays in good health, the egaando is considered to be upholding its end of the bargain, its ability to keep to its word, indicating that the taming is proceeding well. After the shaman undergoes months of dieting, the bowl finally enters the moral universe, respectful and obedient, sharing a close affinity with its owner. "A good egaando loves its owner," I was told, and "is like a teacher in the school," instructing the shaman until he becomes a true *benane*—one with the facility to extract darts from an ensorcelled patient and redeploy them in retributive action. Such figures are the cornerstone of shamanic ideology and continue to command a sense of awe and a prominent place in everyday discourse that seems disproportionate with their now dwindling numbers. Possession of an egaando, the hallmark of the benane, is enshrouded in a kind of pseudo-secrecy, the topic of covert discussions that promote a suitable aura of fear better than any open advertisement. One of my informants recalled that his grandfather, after many months of dieting with an egaando, had successfully tamed it to the point where he could communicate with it in an everyday, waking, nonritual context. He taught his egaando to watch over and protect his house while he traveled upriver on hunting trips, instructing it to "insult," in their dreams, any passing travelers tempted to sleep in the house. Persons so insulted have been known to leap up from their beds, shouting, and run out of the house into the night. If they know how to dream, they will have realized that an egaando was responsible.

Gender and the Production of Subjects

Procedures for the fabrication and use of the hammock and egaando reference contrastive and complementary techniques for bringing into being determinate kinds of persons. Common to both is an intimate and mutually constitutive, but ultimately asymmetrical, relationship that is valued particularly for its ability to form or enhance personal identity through the inculcation of essential skills and other qualities. Use of things to this end circumvents an egalitarian ethos, according to which direct instruction by one's fellows is considered an undesirable imposition of authority. Just as the hammock's own agency necessarily exceeds that of the baby in order to effectively imbue it with the requisite qualities of a gendered, social person, the egaando is fully subjectivized only when and as the shaman successfully establishes his complete authority over it. As Philippe Erikson (this volume) has observed, the fact that something has a master in Amazonia does not impede its endowal with personality and intentionality. In fact, the cases developed here would point to having a master as a prerequisite of developing personality and intentionality, an apparent paradox that recalls recent inquiry into how "the subject is not only that which is oppressed by power but emerges himself as the product of this power" (Žižek 2000:251). The techniques for preparing and using an egaando, which encapsulate an Urarina theory of subjection, will be used to explore this further.

The egaando's progression from an unpredictable predatory force to a pet-like subordinate imbued with personality and a moral conscience is glossed by the Urarina as the outcome of *irilaa*, a term used to mean "taming" or "raising," for example, taming pets or raising orphans. Several authors have related taming to the conversion of affinity into consanguinity, encompassing it within the structural logic of predation (e.g., Fausto 2000, 2007; Taylor 2001; Descola 1997). Yet there is little to suggest the egaando's initial status as an affine, while its eventual relation to its owner was articulated in terms of the two being not like kin, but "like neighbors," and sharing not bodily substance, but mutual respect. Ideologies of predation and warfare are moreover far from salient in Urarina thought and practice, which emphasize peacefulness and passive forms of resistance over bellicose action. They figure as themes primarily in oral historical accounts in which the Urarina portray themselves as the innocent victims of Candoshi raiding parties. Whilst concurring with Carlos Fausto (2000:938) that "adoptive filiation" references prototypical relations of symbolic control in Amazonia, I suggest that taming can here be largely dissociated from warfare and predation and instead incorporated within a broader matrix of subjection, implying the simultaneous subordination and forming of subjects.

Taming comprises firstly the deployment of ritual discourse that demands the egaando's cooperation. Working in alliance with the Mother of *Brugmansia*, whose unrivaled power is revered, the shaman occupies a clear position of authority. The egaando's eventual response to his demands is said to be a kind of capitulation, a recognition of the power of those who call the egaando. We might say that it is hailed or *interpellated* into existence as a subject.[2] In aligning itself with authority and responding to the shaman's demands, the egaando is endowed with a moral conscience. It agrees to teach the shaman and promises not to harm his family, despite its desire to do so, and the shaman in return undertakes to diet. Demonstrating an ability to keep to its word is highly significant in the construal of the egaando as a moral person rather than a mere concentration of dangerous predatory energy. As Friedrich Nietzsche (1956:190) pointed out, one who promises something must be able to forge a continuity between an original determination and the actual performance of the thing willed, or between a statement and an act, across a time gap in which various other, competing circumstances or temptations might threaten to intervene. This protracted will enables the promising being to stand for itself through time. The deal struck with the egaando demands the suppression of its instinct to inflict harm and the adherence to social norms, such as respect for others and personal responsibility. It is the good moral sense thus adopted by the egaando that makes it most like a "true person" (*cacha*). From an Urarina point of view, it would seem that its newfound "consciousness," as represented by its ability to enter into increasingly coherent dialogues, is not somehow transferred or "captured" from its owner (cf. Gell 1998) but is rather the form taken by its own will—its innate hostility or predatory force—when prevented from simple expression as a deed. It is an aggression turned inward and back on itself, an internalization that creates an autonomous, internal space, producing conscience and the conditions for reflexivity.

Urarina claim that a tamed egaando is not only possessed of moral sensibilities and able to cooperate with others but is also highly dependent on, and fiercely loyal to—even "loving" toward—its owner and master. What might be the significance of this newfound emotional bond? If the egaando's identity as a person or subject was, from the very beginning, founded in a kind of "recognition" by and submission to an authority figure on whom it depended in every sense, then to embrace that submission, to form a "passionate attachment" to subjection (Butler 1997), is equivalent to embracing the very conditions of its continued existence. The situation of the baby in its hammock, though admittedly a more complex case, does not necessarily differ in general outline from this scenario. The baby experiences its physical dependency on the hammock as an intense emotional bond. Only specialized chants (cojiotaa) can placate a crying baby estranged from its hammock. The rattle's gentle messages, which shape and condition its new, human identity, similarly come from a protective authority who offers personalized recognition, but to whom submission is mandatory. The skills for achieving personal autonomy later in life can be acquired only through a kind of founding submission to a situation of dependency and attachment.

Such an account of the journey of the subject, although somewhat stylized, is at variance with perspectivist assumptions. Egaando are indeed considered to be alive, to possess animal or vegetal souls (or both) as well as a Mother/Owner, yet such attributions would seem almost incidental to their gradual positioning as subjects. The ability to occupy a "point of view" does not guarantee or index personhood, and their changing subjectivity relies not on a soul or body but on shifting relations to Owners or Mothers. This opens up important questions of variation foreclosed by the perspectivist recourse to overarching inversions: How and why, for example, are animism and perspectivism not unilaterally applied to nonhumans, and how and why may they often be restricted to particular species—"those which perform a key symbolic and practical role" (Viveiros de Castro 1998:471)? A consideration of such questions of variation suggests an alternative conceptualization of the Mother/ Owner figure, whom Eduardo Viveiros de Castro has claimed functions as a hypostatization of the species with which it is associated, creating an "intersubjective field for human-animal relations" (Viveiros de Castro 1998:471; see also Fausto 2007:509, n. 24). Such a formulation conflates rather than problematizes the relation between the individual, its species, and its Mother or Owner. If the egaando and its Mother/Owner are referred to interchangeably when the egaando is still in the river, this is patently not the case once it is extracted, at which point the egaando alone is addressed directly.

In Urarina thought, anything with "power" or "force" of some kind, whether to smell sweetly or burn fiercely, cause harm or inebriate, typically has a Mother or Owner with which this power is principally associated or identified. But despite this ostensibly offensive role, the Mother/ Owner is often described as an entity's "defense," the power on which it depends for continued existence. The Mother/Owner might more accurately be figured as a simultaneous hypostatization of the power or "voice" of authority that is the *condition* of subjectivity, constituted in a relationship, and an individual's incipient conscience, for these are at first necessarily indistinguishable from each other.[3] The taming of the egaando is the occasion for the definitive conversion of the power of authority into the egaando's individual conscience, which occurs as the shaman assumes full control and ownership. The category of the subject emerges here less as a location or "point of view" than as a kind of "transfer point" of attachments and dependencies. Shifts in attachments and dependencies—often, though not always, expressed in bodily modifications or transformations—would go some way in accounting for the variable and sometimes transient nature of subjectivity. The Amazonian concern with establishing individual rights of ownership over everything—including their "quest for non-overlapping mastership" (Erikson, this volume)—is evidently bound up in the equally characteristic "radical subjectivization" (García Hierro and Surrallés 2004:15) of nonhumans, and each in a sense implies the other.[4]

A few observations concerning gender are apposite here. Insofar as the hammock and egaando are conceived by the Urarina as agents for the instruction and transformation of humans, the objects' agency manifests itself as feminine and masculine respectively. The hammock materializes a mother's love for her baby, along with her relations with female kin and their collective desires for the baby's future identity, and it connects the baby and mother in a manner reminiscent of the placenta. Through the assembly of items of diverse origin into a single, harmonious whole, the hammock's use "normalizes" the child and incorporates it into social life. Women's labor is often similarly integrative in nature, and women themselves play an integrative role in the uxorilocal structure of Urarina society, consolidating the domestic unit and incorporating incoming men into the household. The hammock assumes a motherly and caring role, literally forming the child's body as it nurtures, protects, and regulates. Its use emphasizes the importance of integrative change in the establishment of social relations, of proximity and mutual dependency over individuality and hierarchy, and it reproduces the authority of women in the domestic spheres of bodily and child care. Men rarely touch—let alone swing—a hammock and claim to have little or no knowledge of their own child's rattle or its origins, deferring all questions on the matter to their wives.

Use of the egaando implies techniques of empowerment of a masculine nature. It is not manufactured or assembled, but found fully formed, in the shape of peccary testicles, albeit in a "wild" state and in need of taming. Men are said to have to "tame" their wives at the outset of marriage, in order that they assume a new, domestic identity as wives—a task further assisted, on occasion, by forms of ritual discourse. The egaando emphasizes relations with alterity over domesticity, the power of change through discipline and internal transformation, and it is individuating and differentiating in nature, enhancing a man's social status and promoting the singularity proper to shamans and to men in general. Through ways of dressing, naming practices, forms of address, and a variety of behavioral norms, women are symbolically homogenized in daily life, whereas men actively differentiate themselves. Urarina theories of gestation state that men contribute the "uniqueness" of a fetus, those features that distinguish it from others, while women provide the vessel for growth and formation.

In short, the two objects—the hammock and the egaando—are implicitly gendered as they are socialized. This suggests possible limits to the perspectivist definition of humanity solely in contradistinction to animality, which fails to differentiate between the male and female person (Rival 2007). Of course, gender is also an indispensable conceptual and analogic tool for imagining other forms of relation (see Hugh-Jones, this volume; Strathern 2001). The gendered agentivity of these two things, which captures or reiterates that of its makers or owners, further highlights the intimate connection between autonomy and dependency, or between the power that acts on a subject and brings it into being and that which the subject in turn enacts.

Notions of personhood form part of the ways by which actors legitimize their own actions in relation to others (Conklin and Morgan 1996:658). As vested interests inform the full or partial recognition as persons of things in specific contexts, use of the hammock and egaando serve to further the authority of women and men in distinct spheres of action. They may be understood as partaking in, and promoting, contrastive and co-existing models of personhood and agency. The selective application of such models to nonhumans recalls the concept of "nature regimes" (Escobar 1999), which are further articulated in opposition to the naturalistic and capitalist "natures" imported from elsewhere. Yet beneath the differences lie significant commonalities, and each model demonstrates above all the importance assigned to things in the work of producing persons. Things, like persons, may inhabit an autonomy born of dependency, an often ambiguous form of relationality perfectly encapsulated by the image of the hammock as placenta. This is envisaged, not as a property of the body, but as a potential of the spirit or shadow soul. What is being strived for, it seems, is not the identity of kinship but a kind of similarity or proximity, dyadic in nature, grounded in irreducible difference. While the Urarina theory of materiality manifests a sense of ownership or mastery as being of central importance in relations with things, it simultaneously holds that fabrication, even when symbolically equated with filiation (see Lagrou, this volume), is not the only means for its establishment, nor that of an equally important intimacy. Neither the baby nor the shaman themselves manufacture the objects with which they become entangled, though they are deeply involved in their creation as person-like companions. Things and persons may be mutually constituted, but it is through subjection, so often under the guise of companionship, that subjects form and endure.

Notes

1. Foreign goods such as radios or shotguns are not exempt from this logic, though they are sharply distinguished from locally manufactured items in at least one aspect: their Mother and Owner, source and ultimate destiny, is Moconajaera, a figure today equated by the Urarina with the devil, and who is said to burn souls in the celestial fire in order to purge them of sins and in accordance with the quantities consumed of "his" goods.

2. In Louis Althusser's (1971) well-known, allegorical example, a policeman hails a passerby on the street, calling, "Hey, you!" As the passerby turns, in that instant recognizing himself as the one who is addressed, interpellation—the discursive production of the social subject—takes place. Recognition by the law is proffered and accepted, and an identity is won by accepting the subordination and normalization effected by that "voice" (see also Butler 1997).

3. As Judith Butler (1997) has pointed out, there must be an irreducible ambiguity between the "voice" of conscience and the "voice" of the law if models of ideological interpellation are to avoid assumptions of any prior subject who performs the allegorical "turn" toward the voice that hails it. An antecedent complicity with authority—such as that potentially encapsulated in the Mother/Owner figure—is needed to explain why the individual responds at all.

4. Urarina are, of course, both masters and subjects in this matrix of symbolic control. Incidentally, one Urarina word for Mother/Owner, *ijiaene*, is virtually identical to that for mestizo, *ijiaaen*, a mutually reinforcing assimilation which may reflect not simply an earlier sense of mestizos as spirits, but their originary and continuing presence in Urarina territory in structural positions of authority and ownership. It is tempting to speculate that the continuing and often seemingly voluntary assumption by the Urarina of subordinate roles in relation to mestizos—in the still-pervasive system of *habilitación*, for example—further reflects not merely force of habit but yet another "passionate attachment" to subjection.

References

Althusser, Louis. 1971. Ideology and Ideological State Apparatuses. In Louis Althusser, *Lenin and Philosophy and Other Essays*, pp. 121–73. New York and London: Monthly Review Press.

Butler, Judith. 1997. *The Psychic Life of Power: Theories in Subjection*. Stanford: Stanford University Press.

Conklin, Beth. 1996. Reflections on Amazonian Anthropologies of the Body. *Medical Anthropology Quarterly* 10:347–72.

Conklin, Beth, and Lynn Morgan. 1996. Babies, Bodies, and the Production of Personhood in North America and a Native Amazonian Society. *Ethnos* 24(4):657–94.

Descola, Philippe. 1992. Societies of Nature and the Nature of Society. In Adam Kuper (ed.), *Conceptualizing Society*, pp. 107–26. London and New York: Routledge.

———. 1994. *In the Society of Nature: A Native Ecology in Amazonia*. Cambridge: Cambridge University Press.

———. 1997. *The Spears of Twilight: Life and Death in the Amazon Jungle*. London: Flamingo.

Escobar, Arturo. 1999. After Nature: Steps to an Antiessentialist Political Ecology. *Current Anthropology* 40:1–30.

Fausto, Carlos. 2000. Of Enemies and Pets: Warfare and Shamanism in Amazonia. *American Ethnologist* 26(4):933–56.

———. 2007. Feasting on People: Eating Animals and Humans in Amazonia. *Current Anthropology* 48(4):497–530.

García Hierro, Pedro, and Alexandre Surrallés. 2004. Introducción. In Alexandre Surrallés and Pedro García Hierro (eds.), *Tierra adentro: Territorio indígena y percepción del entorno*, pp. 8–23. Copenhagen: IWGIA.

Gell, Alfred. 1998. *Art and Agency: An Anthropological Theory*. Oxford: Clarendon Press.

Gow, Peter. 2000. Helpless: The Affective Preconditions of Piro Social Life. In Joanna Overing and Alan Passes (eds.), *The Anthropology of Love and Anger: The Aesthetics of Conviviality in Native Amazonia*, pp. 46–63. London and New York: Routledge.

McCallum, Cecilia. 1996. The Body That Knows: From Cashinahua Epistemology to a Medical Anthropology of Lowland South America. *Medical Anthropology Quarterly* 10:347–72.

Nietzsche, Friedrich. [1887] 1956. *The Genealogy of Morals*. New York: Doubleday Anchor.

Pollock, Don. 1996. Personhood and Illness among the Kulina. *Medical Anthropology Quarterly* 10:319–41.

Rival, Laura. 2007. Proies meurtrières et rameaux bourgeonnants: Masculinité et féminité en terre Huaorani (Amazonie équatorienne). In Claude-Nicole Mathieu (ed.), *Une maison sans fille est une maison morte: La personne et le genre en sociétés matrilinéaires et/ou uxorilocales*, pp. 125–53. Paris: Éditions de la Maison des Sciences de l'Homme.

Strathern, Marilyn. 2001. Same-Sex and Cross-Sex Relations: Some Internal Comparisons. In Thomas Gregor and Donald Tuzin (eds.), *Gender in Amazonia and Melanesia: An Exploration of the Comparative Method*, pp. 221–44. Berkeley: University of California Press.

Taylor, Anne-Christine. 2001. Wives, Pets, and Affines: Marriage among the Jivaro. In Laura Rival and Neil L. Whitehead (eds.), *Beyond the Visible and the Material: The Amerindianization of Society in the Work of Peter Rivière*, pp. 45–56. Oxford: Oxford University Press.

Vilaça, Aparecida. 2002. Making Kin Out of Others in Amazonia. *Journal of the Royal Anthropological Institute* 8(2):347–65.

Viveiros de Castro, Eduardo. 1998. Cosmological Deixis and Amerindian Perspectivism. *Journal of the Royal Anthropological Institute* 4(3):469–88.

———. 2001. GUT Feelings about Amazonia: Potential Affinity and the Construction of Sociality. In Laura Rival and Neil L. Whitehead (eds.), *Beyond the Visible and the Material: The Amerindianization of Society in the Work of Peter Rivière*, pp. 19–44. Oxford: Oxford University Press.

Žižek, Slavoj. 2000. *The Ticklish Subject: The Absent Centre of Political Ontology*. London: Verso.

II
Subjectivized Materialities

4

From Baby Slings to Feather Bibles and from Star Utensils to Jaguar Stones

The Multiple Ways of Being a Thing in the Yanesha Lived World

Fernando Santos-Granero

> Don Juan Tuesta claims that things are not as they are, but as what they are. (César Calvo, *Las tres mitades de Ino Moxo*)

> "Things have a life of their own," the gypsy proclaimed with a harsh accent. "It's simply a matter of waking up their souls." (Gabriel García Márquez, *Cien años de soledad*)

Many Amerindian peoples would agree with Juan Tuesta, the wise but unassuming *ribereño* shaman of César Calvo's novel, that "things are not as they are, but as what they are." They would also agree with Melchiades, the gypsy merchant of *One Hundred Years of Solitude*, that "things have a life of their own." More importantly, however, they would concur with him that the animacy of things is not necessarily a permanently manifested condition. Things—objects—might have souls, but their souls are not always active. Indeed, things differ in terms of the degree of animacy they possess, which depends on the kind of "soul stuff" that animates them. The subjectivity of some things—particularly those that do not possess powerful souls—must be "awakened" in order to reveal itself. From an Amerindian point of view, things are not all equally animated and thus are not agentive to the same degree. In fact, from this point of view, some objects are just plain objects—they are not endowed with souls.

This chapter explores the notion of materiality among the Yanesha of eastern Peru. It suggests that the Yanesha theory of materiality is multi-centric, based on the notion that there are multiple ways of being a thing. The bottom line of this indigenous theory is that most objects are endowed with souls but that subjectivized objects do not possess the same degree of animacy and agentivity. Defined as "the paradigm instance . . . in which an animate entity, X, intentionally and responsibly uses its own force, or energy, to bring about an event or to initiate a process; and the paradigm instance of an event or a process . . . that results in a change of the physical condition or location of X or of some other entity, Y" (Lyons 1977:483), the notion of "agentivity" comprises that of power. Thus, the Yanesha claim that objects possess different degrees of animacy and agentivity is tantamount to saying that they have different degrees of power. This power depends on, and can only be ascertained by, their particular ontological trajectories, social histories, and/or personal biographies.

The Multiple Ways of Being a Thing

In Western societies, the term "thing" refers broadly to "an entity of any kind" and includes both animate and inanimate beings. In one of its more narrow meanings, however, it designates "a being without life or consciousness: an inanimate object" (*Oxford Universal Dictionary Illustrated* [1974]). The Yanesha have a term—es—that has the same connotation as the Western broad meaning of "thing." But the range of entities within this category that the Yanesha deem to be "inanimate" is much smaller than in Western societies. In contrast, the diversity of things that we conceive of as objects and the Yanesha people consider as being animated is quite high.

The Yanesha discern at least five different classes of things that we would describe as "inanimate objects": (1) objects that have originated through self-transformation, (2) objects that have originated through metamorphosis, (3) objects that have originated through mimesis, (4) objects that have originated through ensoulment, and (5) plain objects. These categories are not named, but their existence can be deduced from the different ontologies the Yanesha ascribe to them. In some cases, they can also be deduced from the use of particular linguistic markers. This is not, however, an exhaustive, objectivist classification of Yanesha "things." There might be other classes of objects that I am not aware of at present. The aim of this categorization is thus, above all, to stress the point that among the Yanesha, there are many different ways of being a thing. A brief description of the origin of these different classes of things will provide the basis for a more thorough discussion on their animacy, agentivity, power, and perspectival perception.

Objects that have originated through self-transformation are mostly natural objects—such as the sun, moon, and stars—or geographical formations—such as waterfalls, lakes, and hills. The Yanesha consider this class of objects to be the material expression—they would say the "body"—of ancient divinities, who transformed themselves at the end of the second of the three eras into which the Yanesha divide their history. Prior to their self-transformation, the divinities lived on this earth side by side with other spirits and the primordial human forms of present-day humans, animals, plants, and objects. When Yompor Ror, Our Father Flower, decided to ascend to the heavens, he self-transformed into the sun. He was followed by many other divinities, who transformed themselves into the main celestial bodies and natural phenomena (Santos-Granero 1992:68).

A few among the divinities who transformed themselves into stars were artifacts or were associated with key artifacts, particularly musical instruments but also domestic utensils. These artifacts are nowadays conceived of as being the actual or metonymical extension of the ancient divinities. Yompor Ror, the sun, is associated with the playing of *requërcanets*, the five-tube panpipes that are now thought to be animated by his vital breath. Yompor Pencoll, who used to play the side-blown, three-holed flute known as *pencoll*, self-transformed into what we know as Orion's belt—the three stars of this constellation embodying the three holes of his flute. Yompor Oncoy, a somewhat mean divinity, ascended to the heavens playing his drum (*con*) in the company of numerous followers; they self-transformed into the Pleiades. Yompor Oresem is associated with the playing of the *pallot*, a small, end-blown flute with two or three holes, made of deer bone or a thin section of white cane. He climbed up to the heavens playing his little flute and is now visible as a bright star (unidentified). Other object-divinities that ascended with Yompor Ror and self-transformed into stars were Maize Mortar (Corona borealis), Fire Fan (the Orion Nebula), and Small Knife (Altair of Aquila and Sagitta). Thus, members of the class of objects that originated through self-transformation often have a double objective existence, present both as heavenly bodies *and* cultural artifacts.

Some of the major landmarks of the Yanesha territory also belong to this category of objects (Santos-Granero 1998, 2005). At the time of Yompor Ror's ascension, many ancient divinities self-transformed into the geographic formations that are visible nowadays. Yato' Caresa transformed himself and his followers into a lake to escape from the cannibalistic Muellepen. Yato' Ror transformed himself into the waterfall Sa'res, which has the property of prolonging the life of those who bathe in it. Most *mellañoîeñ* spirits—powerful spirits closely associated with human life—"hid" in rocks, ponds, fishing pools, and salt springs, becoming the guardians of these particular sites and animating them in the process. The most important skymarks and landmarks in Yanesha tradition have the character of objects born through self-transformation.

Objects that have originated through metamorphosis or other-transformation are those that were originally people who were transformed by the divinities into objects at the end of the second era of Yanesha history or early in the present-day era. Among them, the most important are what we could call "mineral people." Posona', or Salt Man, was sent by Yompor Ror so that his human creatures would have something to flavor their food with. He was transformed into salt (*pos*) through the intervention of Achaquë'llem, or Sharpening Stone. Yachor Aser was transformed into iron by Yompor Santo, the divine emissary, so that his followers would have the raw material to make machetes, needles, axes, and knives. And limestone (*eshoc*), used to precipitate the minute amounts of cocaine present in coca leaves, originated in the sperm of Yompor Ror and was transformed by the divinity for the benefit of his creatures. All these minerals are conceived of as the actual or metonymical expression of the bodies of the primordial persons from which they originated.

Within this class of metamorphosed or transformed objects are also many of the landmarks created by Yompor Ror and other higher divinities immediately before their ascension to Yomporesho, their celestial abode. It is believed that on his way to the mountain from which he climbed up to the heavens, Yompor Ror transformed into landmarks many of the people he found on his way, an action done out of anger for their inappropriate behavior. Some of these subjectivized landmarks became important pilgrimage sites after the advent of the present era, their original subjective nature being remembered by both the old and the younger people (Santos-Granero 1998). In this class of things are also several magical objects that were originally human but were transformed into animals at the time of Yompor Ror's ascension to heaven and, later on, were transformed into objects. The most outstanding among them are "jaguar stones," the shamanic stones that embody familiar spirit jaguars.

Objects that originated through mimesis are replicas of foreign objects—generally associated with white people—that capture the powerful subjectivities believed to reside in the originals (Taussig 1993). This class of objects was more common in earlier times, particularly in those periods of Yanesha history characterized by heavy missionary presence. The objects replicated were generally linked to Christian liturgy, festivities, or religious items of clothing. The most well known of these objects was a feather Bible made by the priestly leader of the ceremonial center of Palmaso in the early 1900s (Bailly-Maitre 1908:623). In contrast to the previous two classes of objects, mimetic objects are not the result of an actual transformation, but of the appropriation through magical means of the power of the Other—a mimetic appropriation that produces a different class of subjectivized objects.

Objects that originated through ensoulment are objects that have become subjectivized through direct contact with a subject's soul or vitality in accordance to what James G. Frazer (1996:12) called the "Law of Contact or Contagion." Yanesha people assert that human beings have two kinds of souls: *yechoyeshem*, "our shadow"—a kind of soul that is inert and permanently attached to the body until death—and *yecamquëm̃*, "our vitality"—a kind of soul possessed of sensory faculties and that can detach from the body under certain circumstances (Santos-Granero 2006). All "vitalities" are believed to be a manifestation of the vital breath/strength (*camuequeñets*) of the creator divinities. Being made of breath/strength, they are believed to lack corporality and physical boundaries. This condition allows vitalities to diffuse into those objects that are in closest contact with a given person. This is particularly true of personal ornaments and other objects of daily use. Thus ensouled, or subjectivized, these personal possessions become as it were an extension of their owners' bodies.

Finally, the Yanesha view certain objects as plain objects, that is, objects that were never subjects and have little chance of ever becoming subjectivized—although this is always a possibility. Among them are included sand, water, air, dirt, and most stones. However, whereas in their generic dimension these natural objects are considered to be plain objects, in their particular manifestations they are sometimes conceived of as objects that originated through self-transformation or metamorphosis. Thus, air in general is considered to be inanimate, but strong winds are believed to be ancient people, *huomenquës'*. Water is an object, but specific ponds, lakes, waterfalls, and salt springs are self-transformed divinities. Stones are generally inanimate, but some are ancient people transformed into stone and others are the hiding places of particular mellañoteñ spirits.

Most alien objects are also considered to be plain objects devoid of subjectivity. There are, however, certain exceptions. "Small Knife," the prototype of present-day small knives, is considered to be an ancient person self-transformed into a constellation. This is also probably true of other iron utensils. The explanation for these exceptions is that for at least one century (1742–1847), Yanesha people produced their own iron tools in ironworks associated with their ceremonial centers (Santos-Granero 1988). Appropriation of metallurgic techniques and direct production transformed soulless alien tools into soulful native utensils. Other alien objects, such as pans, plastic tableware, watches, radios, flashlights, batteries, and so on are considered to be so alien that even if they are used on a daily basis they do not have the capacity of becoming ensouled. Briefly, both generic natural objects and generic alien objects are considered to be intrinsically lifeless and impregnable by the vitalities of the individuals with whom they come into contact.

Variations in the Theme of Animacy and Agentivity

Western ontologies are based on a series of distinctions that always have an anthropocentric quality. At the more general level, the main distinction is that between inanimate and animate entities. At the level of animate beings, the most important opposition is that between animality and humanity. At the level of humanity, the main oppositions are those that distinguish between higher and lesser forms of humanity—e.g., those resulting from debates centered on racial theories—or between higher and lesser forms of personhood—e.g., those resulting from debates centered on the status of human embryos. Thus, the greatest concern in Western thought is the issue of humanity and personhood, namely: What is it that distinguishes humans and persons from all other beings and entities? In contrast, in Amerindian societies—where most beings and entities are believed to have a human-shaped soul—the main philosophical concern is not so much what distinguishes humans from other states of being, but rather how the host of animate beings differentiate themselves.

In effect, native Amazonians have no doubt that most entities in this world are animated or that they possess a human-shaped soul. Most Amerindian mythologies mention a time in which all beings were human and narrate the causes that led to their transformation into the animals, plants, natural phenomena, spirits, and objects that exist today. They thus understand that although not all beings are human, all of them are persons. Amerindians recognize, however, that the difference between these diverse types of persons is not only one between "human persons" and "other-than-human persons," as Alfred Irving Hallowell (1975) and Kenneth M. Morrison (2000) have proposed, but also a difference in terms of beings' respective degrees of animacy, agentivity, and consciousness. Distinctions such as this one, as I have suggested elsewhere (Santos-Granero 2006), seem to derive from the different constitution of beings' souls and bodies.

It has been argued that in the "multinaturalist" Amerindian ontologies, all beings share a similar human-shaped soul and differ in terms of their bodies, understood as "bundle(s) of affects and capacities" (Viveiros de Castro 1998:470, 478). This notion has been contested by Carlos Londoño Sulkin (2005), who suggests that souls and bodies are shaped by the substances of which they are made, rendering them more or less moral, as well as by Dan Rosengren (2006), who argues that souls are not generic but are highly personalized as the result of the particular experiences and influences to which they have been exposed. I have argued, in addition, that without a careful examination of the sensorial capacities that native Amazonians attribute to the souls and bodies of different kinds of persons, it is impossible to understand certain asymmetrical aspects inherent in Amerindian notions of perspectivism, such as the lack of awareness in animals, spirits, and plants of the perspectival nature of perception (Santos-Granero 2006).

Here, I propose to explore these issues through a series of anecdotes that occurred to me during my fieldwork among the Arawak-speaking Yanesha. At the time, I did not pay too much attention to those events, concerned as I was with gathering information for my proposed subjects of research—so I have had to reconstruct these events by resorting to the few field notes that I quickly scribbled at the time and to my own reminiscences. Thus, rather than field reports, the following vignettes must be read as field memories.

Musical Awakenings

That morning, when I got up at dawn, I saw Matar sitting next to the fire, chewing coca leaves. After a while, he climbed up on a stool and took down from the rafters above the kitchen fire a large number of panpipes that were partly hidden under the thatch. This did not surprise me, since I knew that he was holding a drinking party that night and at some point guests would want to sing and dance to the rhythm of *coshamñats* sacred music. With a thin stick, Matar started cleaning the panpipes one by one, sticking it into each panpipe's five cane tubes to clean out mud wasp nests, dead cockroaches, and other pests. He was especially meticulous while cleaning the two shorter panpipes—the leading panpipes. Then he proceeded to clean the longer ones. Since he had eight of these, cleaning them took some time. When he finished cleaning all the panpipes, he took a bowl of manioc beer and poured a little bit into the tubes of each panpipe, all the while muttering something under his breath. When I asked him what he was doing, he said that he was soaking the tubes so that they would expand and tighten and, thus, produce a finer sound. Then he put into his mouth a new wad of coca leaves and asked me for a cigarette. He lit it and started smoking. After a while he started blowing smoke into the panpipes to appraise—he told me—how they sounded. When the sound was wrong, he stuck the little twig into the tube that was out of tune to further clean it, often finding some more dirt stuck in its bottom. When he was satisfied that all panpipes were tuned, he hid them again under the rafters.

At the time I saw Matar cleaning his panpipes, I was satisfied with the idea that he was merely cleaning and tuning them. His matter-of-fact answers to my questions—which sounded sensible—and his down-to-earth behavior deflected my attention from what he was really doing. It was only much later that I understood that the "cleaning" of the panpipes was only one of the many ritual actions intended to "awaken" the vitality vested into *requёrcanets* panpipes, which is none other than the power of the creator divinity, Yompor Ror (see fig. 4.1). The pouring of manioc beer is always a ritual act (*a'mteñets*). Men and women pour a little manioc beer on the ground before drinking as an offering to the divinities who so generously share with their human creatures their strength and vitality. They also pour manioc beer on the ground prior to the opening of a

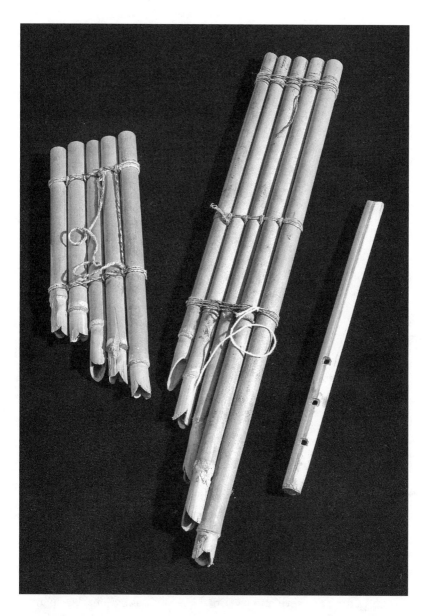

Figure 4.1. *Requërcanets* panpipes and *pallot* flute. *Photo*: Marcos Guerra, 2006.

new garden or the building of a new house. In all cases, the offering is accompanied by silent thanksgiving prayers.

Coca leaves and tobacco smoke are also central to a'mteñets ritual offerings. When I saw Matar tuning the panpipes, I barely noticed that each time he tried one, he blew tobacco smoke—as well as his coca-perfumed breath—into them. This is exactly what Yanesha hunters and fishermen do when divining the best place to hunt or fish. They blow tobacco smoke and spray coca juice in all directions as an offering to the masters of animals or the mellañoteñ spirits that guard particular fishing pools and salty waterholes so that these spirits will allow some of their wards to be hunted or fished.

Manioc beer, coca, and tobacco are the main nourishment of super-natural beings. By pouring manioc beer and blowing coca juice and tobacco smoke into the panpipes, Matar sought to nourish the souls of the panpipes so as to activate them. As in the ritual offering of manioc beer to the solar divinity, this act triggers, in turn, the vitality inherent in the panpipes—a vitality that, when the panpipes are played in honor of the divinities, is disseminated to all those present in the celebration. Briefly, although the Yanesha do not consider panpipes sacred, they conceive of them as endowed with a kind of power/vitality that can be awakened through the proper ritual gestures and substances. The panpipes acquire their maximum degree of animacy and agentivity, that is, their highest degree of personhood, when being played in honor of the divinities. In such a context, the two short panpipes, always played in a sort of canon, are called "leader" (*arequercañ*) and "helper" (*panmapuer*) respectively; the longer panpipes, which mark the rhythm by following the second leading panpipe, are called the "pursuers" or "followers" (*actañ*). The use of such terms recognizes the highly personified nature of requërcanets panpipes, especially when they are being played.

Shamanic Transmutations

When he finally showed it to me, I took it as a personal, albeit fleet-ing victory. For several days, I had been harassing Jeñari, a shaman renowned for his healing and bewitching powers, his many wives, and his insatiable appetite for meat, to show me his jaguar stone. At first, he denied possessing one, arguing that only the greatest shamans had such stones. But I knew that Jeñari was considered one of the most powerful living shamans among the Yanesha—a *pa'llerr etso'ter* or "shaman with supreme mastery." And I had been told that he possessed at least one jaguar stone. Later on, he smiled slyly each time I made oblique references to his famous jaguar stone, neither denying nor admitting its existence. It was only after I asked him to cure me of a chronic back pain that had been bothering me since before going into the field that he opened up. I can still feel his penetrating eyes searching mine when he asked me if I believed that he could cure me and I said yes. Truth be said, at the time, I was not all that sure that he could, but I must have looked very firm in my conviction because Jeñari agreed to treat me. The cure was a combination of bodily manipulations—resembling a Thai massage—a spraying of tobacco juice, and sucking of sorcerous objects from the affected part. That night, somewhat relieved by his treatment while we chewed coca and smoked in the darkness of the male section of the house, he opened his fist and showed me a small stone in the form of a jaguar's paw, asking: "Is this what you wanted to see?" After saying this, he closed his fist and put the stone back into his shoulder bag. He then fell silent and despite my many attempts to entice him to talk, he did not say a word until we went to bed. Postscript: My chronic back pain disappeared and did not come back until many years later.

Jaguar stones, sometimes referred to as *ma'yarromapue'*, are rare and prized gifts bestowed by Yato' Yemats, Our Father Tobacco, upon diligent shamans or would-be shamans. Yemats is considered to be the "owner" of all spirit jaguars. Shamanic apprentices strive to obtain familiar spirits (*pabchar*) through the practice of prolonged vigils, fasts, and sexual abstinence. But the key to obtaining such spirits is the intensive consumption of concentrated tobacco juice. In tobacco-induced states of consciousness, the apprentices hear the songs of different animals—generally fierce animals or animals of prey. If they are careful in distinguishing "true" from "false" animal spirits, they might befriend some of these spirits and engage them as their familiars or protectors.

The most powerful pabchar are jaguars. Indeed, the power of Yanesha shamans is often measured by the number of jaguar spirits they are said to possess. Yato' Yemats gives away his jaguars to worthy shamans either in dreams or while they are under the effects of the ingestion of tobacco juice. Some he gives away in their spiritual form; others he transforms into stone, telling the shaman where he can find them. These jaguar stones are thus the result of a double metamorphosis: they have been transformed from people into animals by Yompor Ror and from animals into stones by Yato' Yemats. It is said that Jeñari possessed eight jaguar spirits, only one of which was in the form of stone (see fig. 4.2).

In contrast to other jaguar familiars, with whom the shaman has established a relationship of friendship and who cannot be seduced to abandon him, the spirit jaguars contained in jaguar stones are trapped and do not have the kind of autonomy and agentivity of their spiritual peers. For this reason, they are carefully hidden and guarded against loss or theft. Otherwise, if the person who finds or steals one of them has the proper knowledge, he or she could animate it and make it do whatever they want. Shamans use their jaguar stones when fighting against a particularly strong sorcerer or to combat the downriver spirit jaguars that periodically attack the upriver communities in search of people to eat. Under such circumstances, they activate their jaguar stones by blowing tobacco smoke on them and reciting some magical chants—reminiscent of Wakuénai musical modes of materializing the occult (see Hill, this volume). Thus animated, the potent spirit jaguars summon all carnivorous animals and with their help fight off the intruders. Once the battle is over, the shamans recall their spirit jaguars and induce them back into their stone shape.

Devout Simulations

While Poniro was telling me in vivid terms his impressions of Berna's *puerahua*, I could imagine his excitement when he was nine years old, a child making his first visit to a ceremonial center. Berna was the last officiating *cornesha'*, or priestly leader, and his temple operated for only a few years, between 1956 and 1959. "When I walked into the puerahua, I was dazzled by the brilliant colors of the flower crosses woven into the thatch roof," Poniro said. "They changed the flowers every two days." The temple was a two-floor building with a rectangular plan and a thatch roof with rounded ends. It was completely walled. "On the second floor, Berna kept three images of saints, Saint Francis being the largest." The images were made of plaster. They were kept on a kind of altar. "No one was allowed onto this floor except Berna and his closest associates." During temple ceremonies, Berna passed the images around, saying: "Take it, hold our god." Then, he would pick up the image of Saint Francis and show it to all the celebrants gathered on the ground floor. "When he shut

Figure 4.2. Master shaman Jeñari possessed seven spirit jaguars and one jaguar stone. *Photo*: Fernando Santos-Granero, 1983.

down his puerahua, he took the images to his house. One night, during a party, some youths broke the head of the Saint Francis. The headless image stayed around for a few years until one day it disappeared."

The Yanesha have a long tradition of mimetic appropriation of the power of the Other. This is especially true in relation to the Franciscan missionaries, who for several centuries were the main representatives of white society and power in the Selva Central region. The mimetic function applied to a large variety of things brought by the missionaries in colonial times: crosses, medals, and even the hoods of Franciscan robes. But the Yanesha also mimed some of the central legends of Catholic hagiography, such as the legend of St. Christopher and the Child Christ (Santos-Granero 2002). And they mimed the bonfires lit during the St. John's summer solstice festival, which in eighteenth-century Europe was as prominent in the Catholic calendar as Christmas.

The mimetic operator continued to be active in postcolonial times with the reentry of Franciscan missionaries into the region after more than one hundred years of absence. The most important mimetic agents at the time were the cornesha', or Yanesha priestly leaders. It is reported that the most important among them—the priest of Palmazu, a prestigious pilgrimage site that housed the stone images of Yompor Yompere—and his wife and classificatory son spent one year attending mass and catechism at the neighboring mission of Quillazu, after which time he started replicating in front of his "idols" many of the liturgical acts of the Catholic mass (Bailly-Maitre 1908:623). The most important of these acts was the solemn "reading" of a book made of feathers, which undoubtedly replicated the Bible, so prominently displayed in Christian celebrations. It is more than possible that the feathers used to make this mimetic Bible were those of Amazon parrots (of the *Amazona* genus), which are renowned for their capacity to talk. By using such feathers, the priest of Palmazu would have sought to appropriate the power of the foreign book—under the form of divine messages—through the communicative skills of native parrots.

Mimesis continued to be an important mechanism of cultural innovation in later times, as the decoration of Berna's 1950s puerahua suggests. It is not clear whether the plaster images Berna kept in his temple were originals or replicas, but even if they were originals, they acted as replicas insofar as they had not been adopted as Catholic saints but as Yanesha gods. Berna's was not a process of conversion but one of mimetic recreation. Through his devout simulations, Berna sought to acquire the power of the foreign gods for the benefit of his own people. As was the case with other Yanesha gods (Santos-Granero 1991:141–42), the appropriated images were nourished with manioc beer especially brewed by prepubescent girls. This especial brew was placed next to the images in the altar. It was believed that the gods extracted the vitality of the offered beer while at the same time infusing it with their own breath/strength (*a'īoreñets*), which was later shared by all those participating in the temple ceremonies.

Vital Connections

We were still a few hundred yards away from Muenaresa's house when we started hearing the racket, a cacophony of yelling adult women, screaming children, and crying infants. When we arrived in the broad clearing that surrounded the house, we were met by a scene of pandemonium. The older children were chasing two large pigs with sticks. The lady of the house shouted abuse at the pigs, at the children, and, particularly, at her eldest daughter, who was on all fours picking things from the dirt floor. A naked toddler lay abandoned on the ground of the impeccably clean patio, crying at the top of her lungs. In the middle of this was Muenaresa's mother, Huepo, sobbing quietly, her hands wrapped around her thin body. When Muenaresa asked what had happened, he was told, amidst shouts and sobs, that the pigs had eaten Huepo's *tse'llamets*, her decorated chest bands. As it happened, since we were in the middle of the rainy season and it had been a sunny day, Huepo had decided to dry in the sun her most cherished ornaments, a bundle of palm-fiber chest bands profusely decorated with fragrant seeds, the teeth and claws of diverse animals, and the bodies of many desiccated colorful birds. She had placed the chest bands on the thatched roof and had gone to the river to fetch water, not before asking her eldest granddaughter to keep an eye on her ornaments. When she came back, she found no one in the house, only the pigs trampling over the remains of her beloved chest bands. That's when she started chasing the pigs away and the whole racket began. Later on, that same day, Huepo fell ill with what seemed to be a cold. She stayed in bed, in a feverish state, for many days, crying intermittently, desolated by her loss.

Tse'llamets are the most important female ornaments among the Yanesha. They consist of numerous flat strips woven from palm fibers or of multiple strands of tiny wild seeds or colored glass beads that are worn across the chest, hanging from the right shoulder (see fig. 4.3). Often, palm fiber chest bands are decorated with seeds, little birds, and animal body parts that women collect in the forest or that are given to them by their husbands, sons, and grandsons. Tse'llamets are also used as baby slings and constitute a sign of womanhood. Prepubescent girls are not allowed to wear them until they have undergone ritual confinement. One of their main chores while secluded is precisely to weave a large number of tse'llamets that they will wear for their coming-out party. Older women, past the age of child bearing, take great pride in their highly ornamented chest bands, which they wear only on special occasions. This is why I thought Huepo was so upset when the pigs ate her chest bands.

Much later, I was to find out that her despair was not due to the loss of beautiful possessions, but because of the loss of something much more vital, namely, a part of herself. The Yanesha believe that things that are in permanent close contact with a person become gradually infused with that person's vitality (*yecamquëm̃*). Personal ornaments are particularly prone to be ensouled in such a way. The same is true of those objects that, because they are gender or role specific, stand in a metonymic relationship with their owners. A woman's loom, a man's bow, and a shaman's tobacco tube are all objects that through frequent use become infused with the soul of their owners and thus appear as if they are extensions of their bodies (see Erikson, Turner, Miller, and Walker, this volume, for similar notions among the Kayapo, Mamaindê, and Urarina).

The most important among these objects are tunics (fem. *cashe'muets*, masc. *shetamuets*), which in Yanesha thought are equivalent to a person's body. Because of the process of ensoulment, the relationship between bodies and tunics is not metaphorical but rather literal: bodies are tunics, as tunics are bodies (Santos-Granero 2006). This equivalence is linguistically marked by the use of the privative suffix "—vts" or "—ts" in the non-possessed forms of terms referring to body parts (e.g., *oñets* or "head"; *otats* or "hand"), immaterial aspects of the self (e.g., *camuequeñets* or "vitality/ soul"; *choyeshe'mats* or "shadow soul"; *noñets* or "words"), and items of personal use (e.g., "cashe'muets" or "tunic"; "tse'llamets" or "chestband"; *serets* or "glass beads")(see Duff-Tripp 1997:31). Thus, the Yanesha and other Amerindian peoples conceive of bodies as including the objects

Figure 4.3. Huepo wearing a bundle of *tse'llamets* decorated with fragrant seeds. *Photo*: Fernando Santos-Granero, 1983.

more closely linked to a person through frequent use. Such contiguity between bodies and personal possessions is particularly stressed in myths describing certain animal body parts as being former objects, such as beaks that were axes and armors that were straw mats.

Objects that become subjectivized through ensoulment do not have much agentivity, but because they are animated by the vitality of their owners, they become part of their owners and can thus be used to inflict harm on them. One of the most powerful ways of ensorcelling a person is by "working" an evil charm on one of his or her personal possessions. The closer the possession is to the victim, the more difficult it is to counter the sorcerous charm. This is why Huepo was so distressed. And this is why she fell ill that same day. From her point of view, the fact that she became sick after her chest bands had fallen to the ground and were eaten by pigs was not a mere coincidence. It was the result of the sorcerous actions of someone who wished her ill.

For this reason, whenever someone gives away a personal possession, they first de-subjectivize it through ritual cleansing in order to prevent the object from being used to cause them harm. This is what Jeñari did when he gave me his tobacco tube as a present—after much begging on my part, I should add (see fig. 4.4). Tobacco tubes are among a shaman's most important possessions. They are constantly replenished with tobacco syrup and shamanized by blowing tobacco smoke over them. Before he gave it to me, Jeñari spent a long time in the river scrubbing the inside of the tube so that not even a drop of tobacco was left in it. Only after being thoroughly washed and dried in the sun was the tube ready to be presented as a gift.

For a similar reason, Yanesha destroy or burn all the possessions of a dead person. Because such possessions are infused with the residual subjectivity of their owner, the deceased continues to be attached to them. If they are not destroyed—that is, de-subjectivized—the vitality and the shadow soul of the deceased continue to linger on this earth instead of severing their links with the living and going to the diverse places where they gather after death (see Turner, this volume, for a more detailed discussion of this practice among the Kayapo). This may pose important threats to the living, since dead people always want to take with them some of their relatives so as to have company in the afterworld. By destroying the possessions of the deceased, his or her relatives contribute to accelerate the process of de-facement and re-facement of the deceased's former self, thus ensuring their own safety (Caiuby Novaes 2006).

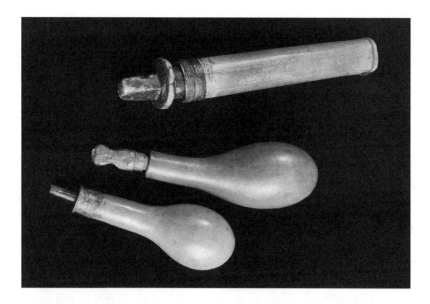

Figure 4.4. Tobacco tube and lime gourds. *Photo*: Marcos Guerra, 2006.

Conclusions

Juan Tuesta's assertion that "things are not as they are but as what they are" seems to point to the dichotomy between the "appearance" and "essence" of things. What it ostensibly suggests is that things are not as they look but as they appear to the eyes of those who can see their "true" spiritual dimension, namely, as people. But although most Amerindians would agree with this notion, I do not think that this is what Tuesta had in mind. I would suggest, instead, that what he meant is not that things are what they "really" are, but that they are what their degree of animacy allows them to be. Thus, the emphasis would be not so much on the human essence of all beings but rather on their different capacities for action in the lived world. All beings might have or share a human-shaped soul, but not all human-shaped souls have the same capacities.

This is something Philippe Descola (1996:375) noted when discussing Achuar cosmology: "Contrary to the naïve Platonism sometimes imputed to the Jivaros, in which the true world of essences . . . is opposed to the illusory world of daily existence, it seems to me," he argued, "that the

Achuar structure their world on the basis of the type of exchange that they can establish with all its diverse inhabitants, each of which is invested with a greater or lesser existential reality *according to the kind of perception to which it lends itself and with which it is in turn credited*" (my emphasis). Since almost all entities in the Jivaro lived world are endowed with a *wakan* soul, cosmological relations are always intersubjective. Nonetheless, intersubjectivity between the various living beings varies in quality and depth as a consequence of the fact that perceptive skills and the capacity for communication are unequally distributed. Therefore, Achuar cosmology does not discriminate between humans and nonhumans but rather between persons possessing different communication skills.

Descola does not dwell on what causes this differential distribution. Other authors have suggested, however, that the capacity for communication varies in relation to the degree of animacy. In her pioneering discussion on Kalapalo categorization of beings, Ellen B. Basso (1985:65) asserts that the Kalapalo distinguish five classes of beings according to their degree of animacy, to wit, from lower to higher: (1) inanimate objects and body parts, (2) inalienable organs of the body, (3) independent animate beings, (4) human beings, and (5) powerful beings. Each of these classes is set apart by particular forms of communication and the fact that their members can act only upon members of the same class or of classes with a lower degree of animacy.

The Yanesha—and, I suspect, many other Amerindian peoples—entertain similar ideas. Radical versions of perspectivism, with their emphasis on the uniformity of souls, their assumption that all souls are endowed with similar sensorial capacities, and their stress on the notion that all perspectives have equal value, have tended to downplay this crucial aspect of Amerindian cosmologies. This tendency has been aggravated by an almost exclusive focus on the perspectival relationship between humans and animals, a narrow focus that has been justified on the basis that "the spiritualization of plants, meteorological phenomena or artifacts seems . . . to be secondary or derivative in comparison with the spiritualization of animals" (Viveiros de Castro 1998:472). Even if this were true, the only way of attaining a more comprehensive portrayal of Amerindian perspectivism is by taking into consideration other beings such as plants, meteorological phenomena, and artifacts.

Once we introduce such beings into the equation, it becomes clear that differences in animacy and agentivity—measured in terms of capacity for goal-oriented thought and action, motion, and feelings (Basso 1985)—are not only crucial to understanding different ways of "being in the world" but also to understanding crucial differences in terms of perspectival capacities. In Yanesha thought, subjectivized or personified objects have a lesser degree of animacy than any other animate being. Within this broad category of objects, ensouled objects are the ones that have the least agency of all, followed by objects originating through mimesis, objects originating through metamorphosis, and objects originating through self-transformation. Although all these objects are capable of intentionality, their agentivity is always dependent on human intervention. In order to be able to act upon the world, objects must be ritually awakened—the Yanesha would say "raised," "revived," or "resurrected" (*tantaterran*)—through offerings, chants, and prayers (see Chaumeil 2007:269 for similar practices in other Amerindian societies). Thus, the existence of subjectivized objects alternates between agentive and nonagentive phases.

The Yanesha explain the low degree of animacy and agentivity of objects as the consequence of the objects' lack of proper souls and fully sentient bodies. Ensouled objects do not have proper souls—they just partake of the vitality of their owners. Mimetic objects are not animated by independent souls; they are magical creations insufflated with vitality stolen from their originals. Objects originating through metamorphosis have powerful souls, but they have been condemned by their creators to a life of sensory deprivation. Finally, objects existing through self-transformation, with their double physical existence, have extremely powerful souls as stars but weaker vitalities in the shape of musical instruments or utensils. For these reasons, objects lack the sensory faculties indispensable to act independently in the world and the kind of perspectival perception characteristic of other beings. Intersubjective relations with objects depend mostly on human initiative. Objects may be far more powerful than the human beings that possess them, but they are subject to the personal whims of their owners, who can choose to stimulate or suppress their potential by activating or deactivating their subjectivities. Thus, while objects are always persons, they are not always active subjects, coming in and out of active subjectivity in accordance with their owners' will.

References

Bailly-Maitre, Luis. 1908. Viaje de estudios del estado mayor general del ejército entre Huánuco y el Mairo. In Carlos Larrabure i Correa (ed.), *Colección de leyes, decretos, resoluciones y otros documentos oficiales referentes al departamento de Loreto*, vol. 14:593–635. Lima: Oficina Tipográfica de La Opinión Nacional.

Basso, Ellen B. 1985. *A Musical View of the Universe: Kalapalo Myth and Ritual Performances*. Philadelphia: University of Pennsylvania Press.

Caiuby Novaes, Sylvia. 2006. Bororo Funerals: Images of the Refacement of the World. In Fernando Santos-Granero and George Mentore (eds.), In the World and about the World: Amerindian Modes of Knowledge. Special Issue in honor of Prof. Joanna Overing. *Tipití: Journal of the Society for the Anthropology of Lowland South America* 4(1–2):177–98.

Calvo, César. 1981. *Las tres mitades de Ino Moxo y otros brujos de la Amazonía*. Iquitos: Proceso Editores.

Chaumeil, Jean-Pierre. 2007. Bones, Flutes, and the Dead: Memory and Funerary Treatment. In Carlos Fausto and Michael Heckenberger (eds.), *Time and Memory in Indigenous Amazonia: Anthropological Perspectives*, pp. 243–83. Gainesville: Florida University Press.

Descola, Philippe. 1996. *The Spears of Twilight: Life and Death in the Amazon Jungle*. Glasgow: HarperCollins Publishers.

Duff-Trip, Martha. 1998. *Gramática del idioma Yanesha' (Amuesha)*. Lima: Instituto Lingüístico de Verano.

Frazer, James G. 1996. *The Golden Bough: A Study in Magic and Religion*. New York: Simon and Schuster.

García Márquez, Gabriel. 2006. *Cien años de soledad*. Madrid: Plaza y Janes.

Hallowell, A. Irving. 1975. Ojibwa Ontology, Behavior, and World View. In Dennis Tedlock and Barbara Tedlock (eds.), *Teachings from the American Earth*, pp. 141–78. New York: Liveright.

Londoño Sulkin, Carlos. 2005. Inhuman Beings: Morality and Perspectivism among Muinane People (Colombian Amazon). *Ethnos* 70(1):7–30.

Lyons, John. 1977. *Semantics*. Cambridge: Cambridge University Press.

Morrison, Kenneth M. 2000. The Cosmos as Intersubjective: Native American Other-than-Human Persons. In Graham Harvey (ed.), *Indigenous Religions: A Companion*, pp. 23–36. London and New York: Cassell.

Rosengren, Dan. 2006. Matsigenka Corporeality: A Non-Biological Reality: On Notions of Consciousness and the Constitution of Identity. In Fernando Santos-Granero and George Mentore (eds.), In the World and about the World: Amerindian Modes of Knowledge. Special Issue in honor of Prof. Joanna Overing. *Tipití: Journal of the Society for the Anthropology of Lowland South America* 4(1–2):81–102.

Santos-Granero, Fernando. 1988. Templos y herrerías: Utopía y re-creación cultural en la Amazonía peruana, siglo XVIII. *Bulletin de l'Institut Français d'Etudes Andines* 17(3–4):1–22. Lima.

———. 1991. *The Power of Love: The Moral Use of Knowledge amongst the Amuesha of Central Peru.* London: Athlone Press.

———. 1992. The Dry and the Wet: Astronomy, Agriculture, and Ceremonial Life in Eastern Peru. *Journal de la Société des Américanistes* 77–78:107–32.

———. 1998. Writing History into the Landscape: Space, Myth, and Ritual in Contemporary Amazonia. *American Ethnologist* 25(2):128–48.

———. 2002. St. Christopher in the Amazon: Child Sorcery, Colonialism, and Violence among the Southern Arawak. *Ethnohistory* 49(3):507–43.

———. 2005. Arawakan Sacred Landscapes: Emplaced Myths, Place Rituals, and the Production of Locality in Western Amazonia. In Ernst Halbmayer and Elke Mader (eds.), *Kultur, Raum, Landschaft: Zur Bedeutung des Raumes in Zeiten der Globalität*, pp. 93–122. Frankfurt am Main: Brandes and Apsel Verlag.

———. 2006. Sensual Vitalities: Noncorporeal Modes of Sensing and Knowing in Native Amazonia. In Fernando Santos-Granero and George Mentore (eds.), In the World and about the World: Amerindian Modes of Knowledge. Special Issue in honor of Prof. Joanna Overing. *Tipiti: Journal of the Society for the Anthropology of Lowland South America* 4(1–2):57–80.

Taussig, Michael. 1993. *Mimesis and Alterity: A Particular History of the Senses.* New York and London: Routledge.

Viveiros de Castro, Eduardo. 1998. Cosmological Deixis and Amerindian Perspectivism. *Journal of the Royal Anthropological Institute* 4(3):469–88.

5
The (De)animalization of Objects
Food Offerings and Subjectivization of Masks and Flutes among the Wauja of Southern Amazonia

Aristóteles Barcelos Neto

The illness-shamanism-ritual system emerged as one of the classical themes of South American ethnology in the 1970s. One of its main landmarks was the ethnography *The Shaman and the Jaguar* by Gerardo Reichel-Dolmatoff (1975). Since that work was published, numerous insightful texts have been produced on this theme. Yet despite the impressive richness of all this material, there has been little analysis of the social roles played by objects in this system or the potential questions they raise for the subject/object divide.

Most South American indigenous ontologies show special interest in the differential capacities for agency of objects and humans. Speaking of objects' capacities for agency, I do not mean their instrumental value as tools and implements, but rather the apprehension of their technological and aesthetic characteristics—whether or not the objects in question are native—as magical and/or lethal in kind (Albert 1988; Barcelos Neto 2006a). According to Amazonian ontologies, some objects are *always* capable of doing certain things—for example, killing or curing—that humans can do only when they experience a temporary transformation (in general, shamanic). In the case of killing, this occurs either when humans occasionally break some moral rule or when they enter a cycle of revenge, as with warfare. Shamanism and predation are the main conceptual terrains traversed by South American indigenous objects. From the viewpoint of various Amerindian ontologies, objects are less than or more than human. The states of synergy created between objects and humans basically occur in ritual contexts in which objects, performers, and specialists produce a transformation in themselves and/or in others.

How do living and nonliving systems acquire certain states of synergy and mutually affect each other? Why are objects attributed with intention and agency? Following Alfred Gell (1992; 1998), what should be observed from the outset is a methodological separation between action and event. The action should be situated at the level of prior intentions and originates from conscience, whereas the event originates from physical laws. This separation avoids encouraging the assumption that native notions of causality are mistaken. Shamanism, magic, and sorcery are not "a tragic misunderstanding of the nature of physical causality, but a consequence of epistemic awareness itself" (Gell 1998:100). According to Gell, natives know that stones are not alive. However, for native peoples, physical statements have less importance than cognitive statements, since the latter are invested with a relational salience capable of (re)producing people and replicating effects that can be controlled. Shamanism—that is, the capacity to exchange points of view and travel between multiple worlds—is the central epistemological operator in this control. In the case of indigenous Amazonia, it can be asserted that:

> We are faced by an epistemological ideal that, far from seeking to reduce the "ambient intentionality" to zero in order to attain an absolutely objective representation of the world, takes the opposite decision: true knowledge aims to reveal a maximum of intentionality . . . a good shamanic interpretation is one that manages to see every *event* as, in truth, an *action*. (Viveiros de Castro 2002a:359)

In this chapter, I explore the production of artifactual subjectivities in the illness-shamanism-ritual system of the Wauja, an Arawakan people of the Upper Xingu. One of the central ideas of Wauja shamanic philosophy is the existence of multiple nonhuman entities (basically, masked beings in animal and monstrous forms) endowed with their own intentions and points of view. These entities, called *apapaatai*, lie at the origin of illnesses and cures alike. The Wauja translate "apapaatai" into Portuguese as *bichos* ("animals, beasts") and *espíritos* ("spirits"). These beings synthesize a prototypical alterity whose ontological background is a continuum of transformations that includes both these artifacts and the Wauja themselves. The transformations are effects of very precise actions (such as eating raw food, manipulating certain substances, being exposed to an eclipse, or breaking taboos). Of especial interest to us here is the idea that the apapaatai can be converted from the position of pathogenic agents ("animals") to the position of ritual figures ("objects").

For the Wauja, every serious illness corresponds to multiple and successive captures of fractions of the sick person's soul by various apapaatai.[1] Once in the company of the apapaatai, the soul (or fractions of it) will begin to consume "animal" food—raw or rotten meat, blood, grass, leaves, feces, larvae. The radical change in diet and the new day-to-day life among the apapaatai unleash a process of alteration in the sick person's points of view: he or she begins to see the world as the apapaatai see it. The cure—that is, the recovery of the point of view that differentiates humans from the apapaatai (Viveiros de Castro 2002a)—can only be achieved by the *yakapá*, the visionary-divinatory shamans, who use secret songs and musical instruments (mainly the maracá and bamboo flute) to remove from the sick person's body the pathogenic substances that provoked his or her transformation into an "animal." The completeness of the cure depends, however, on ensuring that the apapaatai are adequately fed. In order to achieve this, ritual specialists known as *kawoká-mona* must make the apapaatai in the form of masks, flutes, and/or other objects. The ill person—or formerly ill person, if his or her state of health has normalized—assumes the status of *nakai owekeho* or "owner" of the ritual. As such, he or she must look after and feed the apapaatai.

By mapping the circulation of a series of domestic and high-status objects, I was able to discover the existence of extensive networks of ritual payments among the Wauja. I noted that objects such as manioc diggers, spatulas for flipping over manioc flatbread, pans larger than sixty centimeters in diameter—indispensable for cooking the poisonous manioc juice (see fig. 5.1)—large pestles used to grind flour and animal meat, and large carrying baskets were not, in most cases, fabricated by the residents of the houses where they were used. Instead, they came from other households and were offered as ritual payment. During my survey, I obtained information indicating that particular sets of objects could be traced to the apapaatai—in other words, to a past state of sickness and a ritual performance that had generated a range of specific payments in objects. Thus, the carrying baskets had been made by jaguars,[2] the flatbread spatulas and manioc diggers by larvae, the large pestles by *Yamurikumã* (groups of apapaatai women), and so on. In effect, the objects formed a system that corresponded to two wider systems: (1) that of the cultural attributes of the apapaatai, and (2) that of rituals of curing/production based on shamanic divinations into the origin of a particular sickness.

Figure 5.1. Decorated *kamalupo* pot used to process large quantities of bitter manioc. It is one of the most distinctive objects used as ritual payment among Xinguano Indians. *Photo*: Aristóteles Barcelos Neto, 2000.

Food Offerings and Ritual Modes of Transformation

When someone is seriously ill, the apapaatai are said to be "killing" him or her, and the person is described as "dead" (*kamãi*). As soon as the apapaatai killing the sick person are revealed, one of the co-resident women arranges for the distribution of cold manioc porridge (*usixui*) from various small cauldrons, the number of cauldrons matching the number of apapaatai who kidnapped the sick person's soul(s). These pots are taken to the *enekutaku* (the patio in front of the flute house in the central plaza) by the *akatupaitsapai* (the person looking after the patient—usually a consanguine and coresident kin, normally responsible for contracting the yakapá for the patient). Then, in a voice loud enough for the entire village to hear, the akatupaitsapai cites the names of the people who must consume the porridge. The invariant phrase on these occasions is: *Mana patuwata apapaatai*, which means, "Come and bring apapaatai." The person convoked walks across to the enekutaku and asks

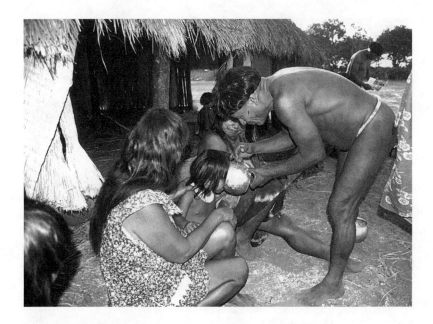

Figure 5.2. A group of *kawoká-mona* redistributes porridge in front of the flutes' house. *Photo*: Aristóteles Barcelos Neto, 2000.

the akatupaitsapai: *Katsá apapaatai natuwiu?* Or, "Which apapaatai am I?" He or she is told the answer and then given a small pot of porridge to gulp down on the spot (see fig. 5.2).

Once all the porridge is consumed, the convoked persons assume the identity of the different apapaatai by taking and presenting them to the ill person. This entails bearing improvised adornments, insignias, and/or objects characteristic of their particular apapaatai—such as a tuft of straw placed on the head, a cord tied around the waist, or a manioc stalk—and chanting the songs that belong to that apapaatai. The only instance in which an improvised adornment is not used and chanting does not occur is when the apapaatai affecting the sick person is Kawoká, the most powerful and dangerous spirit in Xinguano cosmology, who is conceived of in the form of a trio of wooden flutes. In this particular case, the insignia used is the *Kawoká otãi* flute (literally, "the son of Kawoká"), and the action of taking/presenting is expressed through the musical instrument alone.[3] The summoned participants perform the music and dance choreography on the path from the enekutaku to the patient's house and on their way back.

The ritual of "bringing apapaatai" (*mana patuwata apapaatai*) is an extreme and urgent measure that has three closely related components. The first component is the familiarization of the apapaatai. This begins with the consumption of a thick gruel made from soaked manioc bread, taken to the enekutaku by the akatupaitsapai. The feeding amounts to a reversal, since during the critical phase of the illness it was the apapaatai who familiarized the victim with their offers of raw meat and blood. In the ritual for "bringing apapaatai," it is instead the parents of the sick person who familiarize the apapaatai by offering it manioc bread porridge. The logical operation involved produces an opposition between a carnivorous and raw diet (implying hunting and hematophagy) and a vegetarian and cooked diet (implying agriculture and fire), with a sociocosmic outcome of the production of kinship. As Carlos Fausto observes: "Eating *like* someone and eating *with* someone is a strong vector of identity, in the same way as abstaining for or with someone. Sharing food and the culinary code thus fabricate people of the same species" (2002:15).

The concept of offering food leads to other questions and issues. Peter Rivière refers to a Trio myth in which humans proffer food to white-lipped peccaries in order to establish an exchange relationship whose "terms are cultivated foods and respect on one hand, and a moderate supply of game on the other" (2001:47). As we shall see below, the Wauja provision of cooked food to the apapaatai (see fig. 5.3) also implies a relation of negotiated reciprocity.

Alimentary forms comprise one of the most important modes of transformations in Amerindian cosmologies. The difference between raw and cooked evokes not only the Nature/Culture distinction and the passage from one state to the other but also affections and transformative possibilities. In a pioneering text, Rivière (1995) quotes another Trio myth in which a boy puts on jaguar "clothing" and licks the raw blood of killed game: "[A]s a result, he was no longer able to remove his clothes: they stuck to him and he turned into a jaguar, not just in appearance but in reality" (196). This implies that by eating food like a jaguar (raw), one becomes a jaguar.

The cooked food offered by the Wauja to the apapaatai, made in the form of ritual objects, minimizes the ferocity of these beings, enabling them to be de-animalized. However, the animal nature of these objects is not completely annulled: they remain hybrids, linked to their supernatural

Figure 5.3. The *apapaatai* Sapukuyawá Yanumaka (Jaguar) receiving food (smoked fish rolled in cassava bread) from Itsautaku, his ritual "owner," who also gave the Sapukuyawá a cotton waistband, which can be seen rolled up next to the feather diadem. *Photo:* Aristóteles Barcelos Neto, 2000.

prototypes or, as the Wauja say, to their apapaatai "owners." When these objects are abandoned or during eclipses, these animal "parts" may leave them and flee from the village to reunite with their "owners," whether as animals or as monster-artifacts (see fig. 5.4).

The second key component of the rituals is the recognition of the apapaatai visitors as powerful ritual figures, a topic that I examine in the next section. The third component is the reintegration of the sick person's soul(s) with his or her body. Each visiting apapaatai returns to the kamãi the fraction of soul it had captured earlier. By blowing and rubbing tobacco on the kamãi's body, the visitors induce the reintroduction of the patient's soul-fractions, fractions of his or her vital substance. If the kamãi's health shows clear signs of improving over the next few days, the therapy is assumed to have been concluded. However, if the patient relapses, the performance of a more "complex" ritual for rescuing his or her soul(s) becomes necessary: this is called *Pukay*.[4] Should the patient fail to improve, the ritual for bringing apapaatai cannot be repeated with

Figure 5.4. Two monstrous manioc digging sticks. Drawing by Ajoukumã Wauja, 1998.

those apapaatai who visited previously, since these have already returned the sick person's soul(s) and promised to refrain from causing any more harm. Thus the ritual will be re-performed only if new apapaatai kidnap the victim's soul(s). If the illness recurs, the apapaatai-bringing ritual is never said to have "failed," since its objective is always attained. In such cases, the patient's failure to recover is attributed either to the fact that some soul-fraction is still at large and its location is as yet unknown to the yakapá, or to the fact that the person's "death" is actually being caused by sorcerers (Barcelos Neto 2006a).

When the apapaatai visit the sick person and return his or her soul, they become *kawoká*—shamanic spirits who are able to protect the ex-patient against future attacks by apapaatai. As we have seen, this visit is always performed by a group of people from the village who thereby acquire the status of kawoká-mona—ritual specialists who perform the Manapatu-wata Apapaatai as ritual figures. Such a visit personifies a relationship with the apapaatai, one that was previously experienced *only* as a "death" or journey. In a narrow sense, the kawoká-mona mediate a relationship, but in a wider sense, they correspond to an extension and distribution of the apapaatai person.

In becoming kawoká, the apapaatai enter a special condition that can be recognized by the following signs: (1) the offering of cooked foods by humans and their consumption by the apapaatai—in this case, the kawoká-mona; and (2) the familiarization of the apapaatai as a "supernatural protector" of the ex-patient, or more precisely, the person who offers the food. These signs of recognition are reciprocal: the apapaatai see humans as providers of cooked foods, whereas humans see the apapaatai as protectors against the assaults of other apapaatai. Atamai, an "ex-dead person," feeds Tankwara Yanumaka (Jaguar) by sponsoring the latter's ritual, performed by a quintet of clarinetists, his kawoká-mona, who play the Tankwara clarinets. It is Tankwara, as a nonhuman person and a *kumã* being (a shamanic subject), who protects Atamai. And it is Atamai, as a human person capable of mobilizing ritual specialists (originally presented as shamanic visitors, kawoká-mona), who enables what was previously a subtraction of his soul to become an addition of new ritual subjects—the apapaatai. Here, the most original aspect of Wauja shamanism comes to light, namely, the way it links curing to specialization in ritual performances that identify each apapaatai one by one.

But the Kawoká and kawoká-mona entities imply a further conceptual dimension. A brief comparison can be made with the Yawalapíti, whose own term for apapaatai is *apapalutápa*. The word *Apapálu* refers to the Kawoká flutes (known as *Jakuí* in Kamayurá and *Kagutu* in Kuikuro/Kalapalo)—"instruments that are, in effect, the quintessential manifestation of Upper Xingu spirituality" (Viveiros de Castro 2002b:34). This suggests that Kawoká, the spirit in the form of a trio of flutes, is the supreme model (-*kumã*) of apapaatai spirituality, and kawoká is its actualization on the ritual plane. Indeed, the Wauja explicitly confirm that Kawoká is the "chief of all apapaatai," the "strongest" among them, whose lethal power when "very angry" proves to be equal or superior to that of sorcerers. However, Kawoká also possesses one of the greatest therapeutic powers. Kawoká "kills" and cures. The kawoká-mona are the actualization of this archetype of curing.

To attain a clearer understanding of the notions of Kawoká and kawoká-mona, we can turn to Eduardo Viveiros de Castro's (2002b) analysis of the modifying affixes (-*kumã*, -*ruru*, -*mína*, -*malú*) forming the base concepts of Yawalapíti ontology.⁵ Viveiros de Castro (2002b:34–35) argues that the suffix -*mína* (-*mona*) functions as an embodier of substances. The Wauja material lends strong support to his analysis, which contrasts -*kumã* and -*mína*, associating the morphemes with the conceptual senses of *soul* and *body* respectively. In Viveiros de Castro's formulation, -*kumã* is a spiritual condition of the body and -*mína* a bodily condition of the spirit. The kawoká-mona are precisely those that *bring* the "spirit" into a body. This explains the logic of undertaking the Manapatuwata Apapaatai ritual as a means of therapy.

All the apapaatai exist in a kumã state—prototypical, powerful, invisible, and pathogenic. The only situations in which we humans may have a nonpathogenic/nonlethal experience with such kumã-beings is when we dream of them or when they are "reduced" to a *mona* nature—diminished from spirit to body, in other words. This implies that a human being who is awake and whose body-soul unity is intact—that is, in a normal state of health—should not approach a *Monkey*, a kumã-being par excellence, whose body or "clothing" is potentially pathogenic. On the other hand, a human may approach a monkey, that is, an *apapaatai-mona*. As Viveiros de Castro (2002b) has pointed out, the modifying suffix -*mona* indicates an actualization of the prototype marked by a lack, in this particular case corresponding to its shift from a cannibal position to a commensal position vis-à-vis humans.

Most adult Wauja have some extensive shamanic knowledge, but very few among them will become a yakapá—a "paramount specialist." The majority of Wauja profit from their shamanic knowledge when they are asked to be kawoká-mona ritual specialists for someone who is seriously ill. The kawoká-mona actualize a shamanic capacity conferred to them when they agree to take apapaatai to the sick patient. The kawoká-mona have the power to cure because they can actualize in a "corporeal" state a being that is in a "spiritual" state. This actualization—akin to the "materialization of the occult" mentioned by Jonathan Hill (this volume) for the Wakuénai—is made possible only through musical-choreographic performance combined with specific insignias/decorations/objects. In sum, the cure here involves the curer becoming specialized in the performances that identify each apapaatai individually.

Wauja shamanism is a two-way flow of transformations. Kin become apapaatai (as kawoká-mona) and apapaatai eat cooked food and become "kin" (or familiars, at least) in a simultaneous double movement that dissolves self-identities. Preservation of the human—the reversal of the patient's transformation into an apapaatai—is achieved by an anti-preservation of the human—that is, kin turn into kawoká-mona in order for the patient to regain his or her soul(s). The very condition of shamanism is the dissolution and inversion of self-identities.

Finally, the yakapá, a "mixed" subject with a body full of extra-human substances, is there to manage this inversion and the correct allocation of human and nonhuman subjectivities within the cosmos. Were it not for the yakapá, all those who become seriously ill would turn into apapaatai. This may well be a classic Wauja mode of explicating the swampy terrain of identities: the yakapá is slightly nonhuman in order for other Wauja to stay human.

Raw Materials and Hierarchy of Ritual Objects

The ritual form assumed by the apapaatai depends, directly and exclusively, on the form in which they appear to the yakapá during the divinatory trances that initiated the cure of a particular patient. Once the phase of shamanic diagnosis is complete, the decision about whether or not a particular ritual will take place in the center of the village falls primarily to the kawoká-mona of the cured person (or sick person, if his or her state of health is still not normal). Thus, the figure of the yakapá shifts into the background following the diagnosis. His divinatory skills will be required one last time on the day of the mask painting, when he provides the kawoká-mona with a description of the mask paintings of the apapaatai that he identified in his trances and/or dreams. The kawoká-mona must execute these paintings as faithfully as possible, or else an apapaatai other than the one that made the subject sick will be produced by the ritual therapy. What matters, therefore, is not only the knowledge of the iconographic repertoire but also the singular way in which the graphic motifs must be employed in order for the apapaatai to be individualized as ritual figures. This can be established only by the yakapá.[6]

The mask ritual form is by far the most frequently used, being responsible for generating the largest number of small rituals. Next in importance are the clarinets, the wooden flutes, and the Yamurikumã (female choirs). The ritual forms of the apapaatai are hierarchically organized around the central position occupied by the wind instruments in this system.

After the ritual terminates, the objects that personify the apapaatai are not immediately discarded. The Wauja retain these objects for various months, years, or decades. The permanence of the objects over a long time span obviously does not imply the uninterrupted continuation of the rituals, but it does support the idea of making the conditions for their realization permanent—and with it, that of the persona of the apapaatai, now familiarized, among the Wauja. In this post-ritual phase, relations are basically marked by the offer of cooked foods and new objects, especially ceramic pots and carrying baskets.

Indeed, an apapaatai ritual is maintained through the exchange relations between the nakai owekeho (the ritual's "owner") and his or her kawoká-mona. It is the ritual tasks executed by the "hard object" performers, especially flautists, that ensure the production of the foods that will be offered by the nakai owekeho to these same flautists and their families. The permanence of the apapaatai has a profound impact on Wauja sociality. As Viveiros de Castro asserts: "The ceremonial system activated by the illness takes the place of ceremonial or kinship groups that elsewhere would provide the mediation between 'individual' and 'society,' non-existent in the Xinguano social constitution" (2002b:81).

The Xinguano ceremonial groups are precisely the kawoká-mona groups, each one officiating one or more types of apapaatai ritual forms. Depending on their abilities, the kawoká-mona may take part in more than one ceremonial group and assume more than one type of ritual figure.

My hypothesis is that the actions performed by these ceremonial groups are imbued with political meaning vis-à-vis humans and apapaatai alike. The founding idioms of this politics relate both to control and power—basically manifested through moral constraints and privileges expressing ritual knowledge—and to aesthetics. These idioms are like dense bodies attracting each other. The "symbolic economy of power" (Heckenberger 1999) and the "political economy of beauty" mutually compete to produce Wauja sociality. These "models" are two-way constructions: made by the apapaatai (as donors of paintings, objects, images, music, cures, and dances) for humans, as well as by humans (as donors of cooked foods and the conditions for sharing states of joy) for the apapaati. Power and beauty are the basic Wauja sociocosmological idioms, especially in the arena of relationships between *amunaw* (chiefs/aristocrats), kawoká-mona (ritual specialists), and yakapá. And there is one important detail: because of their kumã nature, most of the apapaatai are all of these three things at one and the same time.

The conjunction of the symbolic economy of power and the political economy of beauty results in a proliferation of objects that carry and distribute the persona of the apapaatai (concretized as the production of swiddens, pots, canoes, houses, pestles, and so on) and in exchanges of moral pronouncements: respect (*monapaki*), shame (*aipitsiki*), generosity (*kamanakaiyapai*), and jealousy/envy (*ukitsapai*). In fact, the ukitsapai exerts a "counter-power" force and lies at the base of conceptual images of sorcery and challenges to the legitimacy of chiefs (amunaw) (Barcelos Neto 2006a).

Elsewhere (Barcelos Neto 2002) I have stressed the instrumental/lethal value of the apapaatai's "clothing." Following the Wauja's lead, I claimed that the apapaatai are like machines (helicopters, submarines, aircraft, etc.) whose capacities for action are determined by various degrees of pathogenic power. The effect of this gradation is transposed to the hierarchical organization of ritual objects, which are divided into the basic types of wind instruments (flutes and clarinets), female choirs (Yamuri-kumã), masks, bullroarers, and "assorted objects" (flatbread spatulas and manioc diggers).

In order to understand the plane of permanence of the apapaatai and the productive organization of their rituals, we need to turn our attention to the raw materials making up each ritual figure. The materials and substances are the vehicles for transmitting and manifesting the pathogenic and therapeutic powers of the apapaatai. Some emetics, such as *totu* (an unidentified species of bush), are capable of transferring particular physical and psychic properties of their "owners" to the bodies of those that consume them. Hence, totu, whose "owner" is the Jaguar, may be consumed by a young man in reclusion with the aim of strengthening him and turning him into a *kapiyekeho* (wrestling champion), since the Jaguars are the prototypical kapiyekeho. Clay, for its part, carries the pathogenic potency of its "owner," the mythic snake Kamalu Hai,[7] being as it is the snake's feces. If handled by potters with small children—that is, infants who have yet to walk—the clay's potency will be transferred to them in the form of skin or respiratory infections.

The ritual making of the apapaatai necessarily implies the use of materials. In the specific case of ritual objects, the meaning of power is rooted in a homology between the material's hardness and the object's permanence. Along with the shells in necklaces and waistbands, the *yalapanã*[8] wood used to manufacture the Kawoká flutes is the hardest raw material employed in Wauja material culture. Following the order of hardness of the materials, after the flute comes the trocano or Pulu-Pulu,[9] a drum made from the whole trunk of a tree of the same name. This is followed by the Yakui masks, made from a slightly softer wood. The female choirs (Yamurikumã) also make up part of this system. At first, it might seem strange that these choirs belong to a system whose logic is based on a gradation between hard and soft materials. However, it does not seem to me that the voice of the Yamurikumã choirs is the object of classificatory interest in this context; instead, I believe it is an object made in the Yamurikumã ritual, the pestle. During the biographic cycle of a Yamurikumã ritual, the pestles are alternately produced and destroyed (by the flames of the bonfire) when they have already attained an advanced state of wear. The replacement of the pestles by the Yamurikumã is a signal of the renewal of the exchange commitments between the owners of the ritual and their kawoká-mona.

The meaning of the hierarchical schema premised on hardness—configured by flutes, drums, pestles, and Yakui masks, in this order—is linked to the *durability/longevity* of the ritual objects. Ideally, therefore, the more durable the object, the longer its ritual can be maintained. The pestle is an interesting example of the fact that we cannot reduce Wauja ritual objects to the "musical instrument/mask" paradigm. Other examples that reinforce this idea are flatbread spatulas and manioc diggers, objects manufactured in the Kukuho ritual (named after a larvae spirit that "owns" the manioc) and with which the Wauja sing and dance, turning these two types of objects into bona fide ritual figures.

Situated at an intermediate level between the Kawoká and the straw Yakui masks are the Kuluta and Kawoká Otãi flutes (see fig. 5.5) and the Tankwara and Talapi clarinets, all four of which are made from bamboo. Masks are not objects made to last. They must be burned some months or years after their ritual, putting an end to the obligations of the masks' owner to provide food for his or her kawoká-mona and for the kawoká-mona to repay the owner with work and/or objects. Ideally, the wooden flutes and clarinets are not destined for the fire, since the image of durability associated with them assure the permanence of their ritual form. The ritual performance for the masked apapaatai of a specific "owner" is held just once, while the performances of the Kawoká flutes and/or Tankwara clarinets may be repeated various times until the end of their "owner's" life, or they may even continue in the care of his or her heir(ess), should the heir(ess) so wish.

Although Yamurikumã female choirs make no use of masks during their ritual performances, they are still masked. It is their songs that give the transformative meaning of masking: the Yamurikumã wear "verbal masks" (Pollock 1995). The myth of the Yamurikumã is homologous to

Figure 5.5. Kaomo plays Kawoká Otãi inside the flutes' house.
Photo: Aristóteles Barcelos Neto, 2000.

the myth of the emergence of the apapaatai—that is, the fabrication of animal or monster "clothes" by the male Animals.[10] According to the myth, while the men were making "clothes" and flutes in order to turn into "animals" in a remote fishing camp, the women were left hungry in the village, waiting for their husbands, fathers, brothers, and sons to come back from the fishing trip. The women felt scorned with the delay of their husbands and the news that they were turning into "animals." Indignant, they decided to do the same, transforming into Yamurikumã and running off with the apapaatai-men in reprisal.

Shamanic Visions of Others and Other Visions of Hierarchy

As I mentioned above, only shamanic divination (diagnosis) can determine which apapaatai will penetrate the Wauja social domain and which ritual forms they will assume. According to Emilienne Marie Ireland:

While we cannot presume to know all the factors in the chief's[11] mind determining which spirits he names in a given case, there are nevertheless certain predictable patterns in his diagnosis. Usually wealthy and generous individuals are diagnosed as afflicted by spirits requiring expensive and elaborate ceremonies that provide much food and entertainment for the community and prestige for the sponsor. In contrast, it seems to be primarily children and adults with few assets who are found to be troubled by spirits associated with less elaborate ceremonies. (Ireland 1985:13)

By producing a map of the current apapaatai ritual sponsors and comparing this with the diagnoses of people who became seriously ill during my research trips, I was able to observe that the pattern suggested by Ireland is at the base of the socioeconomic organization of the apapaatai rituals. In effect, shamanic divination involves a controlled distribution of the consumptive and productive potential of the apapaatai. It is the yakapá who designs the sociological framework associating humans and apapaatai. The framework's construction, effected by the engagement of the "community" in ritual tasks, seems to be aimed toward the creation of political and prestige-based distinctions. Keeping this in mind, it is not surprising that it is rare for a yakapá to diagnose Kawoká as the cause of a baby's sickness, while he may more easily do so in the case of an adult, whose family structure allows this particular apapaatai's festival to be held. If a yakapá diagnoses an apapaatai that demands expensive rituals for a kamãi who owns few resources, this will cause confusion and imply deception, since this person and his or her family will be unable to fulfill the therapeutic requirement to make the apapaatai and subsequently feed it. If this situation happens frequently, the yakapá runs the risk of losing his community's trust. Much of his prestige derives from the confidence that the community places in him—that is, his capacity to organize and distribute the apapaatai's potential agency among the Wauja in an appropriate form.

What make an apapaatai expensive are the musical performances of flautists and female choirs—as well as the materials the performers use to fabricate the apapaatai. Before the performances themselves are paid for, the cost of fabricating the apapaatai has to be met. This cost may be extremely high, as in the case of Kawoká, or almost negligible, as in the case of Kagaapa, where the performers use straw skirts, therapeutic leaves of *epeyei* (an unidentified plant species), simple featherwork adornments, a bow, a gourd rattle, and a percussion stick.

It is important to note that the schema of durability of the ritual objects, which I described above, has a homologous relationship to the musical capacities of these objects and figures. The flute is a musical object par excellence. The high cost of a flute ritual is due to the payment required by the manufacturer of the flutes, which are luxury items, and to the cost to supply enough food to last during the lengthy cycle of this ritual—Kawoká is a very hungry apapaatai.

Located at the lower-cost end of this material-musical system are the masks: ritual figures with little music. Many of the mask songs are brief, while some masks do not sing at all, such as the Atujuwá, Atujuwátãi, and Yuma masks. Most shamanic diagnoses identify apapaatai as masks rather than flutes, so masks are the ritual objects most widely produced among the Wauja. Moreover, compared to the aerophone rituals, the mask rituals are cheap, since they do not require the contracting of renowned specialists in apapaatai music. The apapaatai made as masks sing very little, and perhaps for this reason also last for a very short time.

Dozens of people have various apapaatai manifested as masks waiting to be made in the future in a large ritual (the Apapaatai Iyãu ritual) so that they can dance under the command of Kawoká trios. In Piyulaga, there are more apapaatai, whether awaiting rituals or not, than there are humans. Several dozen apapaatai are already incorporated among the Wauja as groups of Jaguars, Fish, Monkeys, Fire, Stingray-Women (*Yamurikumã Yapunejunãu*), Turtle-Women (*Yamurikumã Ixunejunãu*), Frogs, Bats, and so on.

An important distinction between masks, flutes, and clarinets in terms of Wauja ritual resides in the productive capacities of each category of object. The Kawoká occupy the center of the ritual system since, among other things, they are responsible for the production of a series of other objects of lesser hardness/durability. The Kawoká, due to their condition of physical durability and long retention of personhood, are capable of mobilizing a productive chain spanning from the planting of a swidden to the building of a house and its storage silos for flour produced from the swidden in question. However, there are situations in which the Kawoká should intensify or suspend their ritual work. The first such situation involves Kawoká flutes from other Xinguano villages within the Yeju and Huluki inter-village rituals, while the second involves the ascension of other Kawoká from the village itself in the context of disputes over political prestige.

The Kawoká population offers us a clear idea of these problems. In 2002, there were five manufactured Kawoká trios in the Wauja village, four of which were operating, that is, they were performing ritual tasks in compliance with a more or less regular program. Another two "owners" declared that they would like to fabricate their trios before dying. The lack of operation of one of the trios was basically due to the mourning of its "owner." The ancient ritual privilege of its Kawoká was rapidly occupied by a younger "owner" who was "waiting his turn." Hence, we can perceive that the Wauja village works at its maximum capacity in its ritual care of the Kawoká. No other village of the same size in the Upper Xingu possesses more than two Kawoká trios, and many of them possess just one, such as those of the Matipú, the Nahukwá, and the Kalapalo.[12]

Although the Kawoká flutes occupy the highest position in the ritual's hierarchical organization, their ritual groups rarely exist or act in isolation. There is clear cooperation between the apapaatai fabricated as flutes and those fabricated as masks. Thus, if the "owner" of an aerophone ritual also possesses kawoká-mona of masked apapaatai, the masked apapaatai should help the aerophone kawoká-mona in their ritual work. However, the inverse does not apply. Once again, this confirms the central and superior position of wind instruments in this system.

According to some of the Wauja, since the mid-1990s this hierarchical ordering—based on a logic of the sensible (sound and matter) that places the Kawoká flutes in a privileged position—has been in the process of being "subverted." There are individuals who are ritual "owners" of Kawoká but who have continually received services and goods of a lower value than that received by a ritual "owner" of Tankwara. This fact has been an object of some disagreement in the Wauja political field since, ideally, clarinets cannot be equivalent or superior to wooden flutes in terms of their ritual productivity. The disequilibrium between the "wood-capacity" and the "bamboo-capacity" provides evidence of a conflict (or perhaps inconstancy) in the Wauja ritual structure itself. Whether the structure is in the process of changing or whether the ideal equilibrium will be re-established, only observation of the conflict over the following years will be able to tell.

The idea of durability represented by the Kawoká is indeed profound. An interesting example is provided by the subaquatic holes (*memulu*) made to store the Kawoká and wooden masks (*Yakui*) for periods of mourning or any another reason for temporarily suspending the ritual. These holes were used until the second large measles epidemic, which occurred in the mid-1950s. There are many Kawoká and Yakui abandoned in memulu. These ritual objects can no longer be recovered, however, since they have transformed forever into extremely dangerous beings, capable of killing whoever touches them. Their lethalness emerged due to the long time they remained without cooked food and ritual care.

The Wauja say that "in the past," there were people who, out of pure spite, abandoned their ritual objects in the lakes, leaving the apapaatai to become aggressive and consequently infesting the lakes with dangers. The stories of the memulu and the abandoned objects show that ritual items can definitively and irreversibly assume an uncontrollable kumã nature. A wooden flute is a hyper-resistant body that, once thrown in the memulu, tends to become ever harder and ever more monstrous.

The wooden flutes are one of the very few categories of ritual objects capable of being passed on through generations. The heir(ess) in question receives not only the Kawoká but also the kawoká-mona responsible for their ritual performance. When someone inherits a Kawoká trio from a parent, he or she immediately takes measures to ensure the conditions for feeding their kawoká-mona. If the heir(ess) realizes that he or she will be unable to meet the Kawoká's alimentary demands, he or she will decide to burn the flutes, offering a last ritual.

Final Words

From donning and removing "clothes" to being present in the location of an eclipse, there are few Wauja actions that occur outside the arena of a relationship between the apapaatai and the spiritual "owners" (*wekeho*) of things and beings. Even the simple jobs of de-husking manioc and handling clay place the subject of the action on the threshold of this type of relation. In addition, both in the case of serious illness ("death") and during the therapeutic process (the visitation of the kawoká-mona, especially), commensality founds a principle of transformation and identity/alterity.

Based on the ethnographic leads presented in this text, it does not appear to me that Wauja thinking concerning the subjectivation of things and beings implies a dissolution of the human into the animal or vice versa—or, in other words, that a zone of indistinction is generated. What can be said with a certain degree of confidence is that this regime of subjectivation modulates the degree and type. For example, there are Jaguars who are more Jaguar than other Jaguars, just as there are Wauja who are less Wauja than other Wauja, especially the seriously ill. However, although the "jaguarness" of the Wauja is of the same type as the jaguarness of Jaguars, both may certainly be different in degree. Therefore, there will always be a residue of difference. The speech of the "dead" who wander with the apapaatai in their dreams of transformation illustrates this point clearly: "I was with strange people; they were people, but not like the Wauja; they were ugly; they had the fingers of toads."

These ideas also have echoes in the field of ritual objects, where the jaguarness of a flute is not equal to that of a mask, and where a Jaguar cannot be a bullroarer or a bullroarer a Larva. Each ritual object gives a specific and singular body to distinct "species" of Jaguars, Fish, and Birds. Furthermore, the artifactual body confers shamanic powers that redefine objects hierarchically, meaning that a Jaguar made as a flute is more powerful than a Jaguar made as a mask. The objects are specific populations of beings marked by corporeal discontinuities with their "owners" (e.g., a flute body's separation from a human body) as well as spiritual continuities with their "owners" (e.g., both subjects' awareness and capacity for musical performance). The analysis that Tânia Stolze Lima (1999:47) proposes for the Juruna material—distinguishing what is human, divine, and animal in the class of humans, the class of animals, and the class of spirits—sheds an interesting light on these processes, allowing us to see each being in terms of a relational position and not as the effect and succession of an order or classes. In this sense, a flute may be a jaguar in the domain of humans, while a jaguar who plays a flute may be a spirit in the domain of animals.

Ritual objects, especially wind instruments and masks, are like a captive population of "supernatural" beings who must be cared for by the "ex-dead" (or "owners"). When properly fed via ritual specialists who execute their performance, these objects ensure that the "ex-dead" person does not "die" again—at least not soon. However, the offer of cooked foods to the ritual objects needs to be suspended only long enough for them to embody the pathogenic potential of their prototypical animalities-monstrosities. This is why the Wauja burn or abandon their ritual objects when unable to feed them. The masks, the standard apapaatai-objects, are the items that most frequently end up on the bonfire or, as a last resort, are left to rot. Here, an important and curious detail is that some of the masks made for craftwork shops were not given eyes, a mouth, and/or teeth—a strategy for de-subjectivizing them, preventing their monstrosity from emerging due to a lack of food.

On the other hand, durable objects whose existence lasts longer than the lifespan of a human being, such as the Kawoká flute trios, stay to eat among the Wauja for decades on end without being destroyed. By representing an exemplary spirituality (Viveiros de Castro 2002b), the Kawoká are more than human and more than apapaatai, ordinarily speaking. The Kawoká are the only objects-subjects in the Wauja cosmos that are truly hyper-retentive of personhood, both prototypical and actual. It is perhaps for this reason that their music conducts the corpses of Wauja chiefs/aristocrats—amunaw, other similarly personhood-retentive subjects—to their graves.

I finish with a speech given by Hukai Wauja, itself a synthesis of the continual Wauja desire to de-animalize the apapaatai-objects: "If my father or mother passes Kawoká on to me, I'm going to accept them, I'm going to carry on with Kawoká. Because Kawoká cannot be lost. They have to stay here, eating our food. Because Kawoká stay with our soul; we can't see them, but Kawoká are always there, in our houses, eating."

Acknowledgments

My fieldwork was financed by the government of the state of Bahia, Universidade Federal de Santa Catarina, Museu Nacional de Etnologia de Portugal, Fundação de Amparo à Pesquisa do Estado de São Paulo, and Musée du Quai Branly. Coordenação de Aperfeiçoamento de Pessoal de Nível Superior, Fundação de Amparo à Pesquisa do Estado de São Paulo, and Conselho Nacional de Desenvolvimento Científico e Tecnológico provided me with study grants during different stages of the research. I am grateful to the Wauja for teaching me so much. Lux Vidal, Maria Rosário Borges, Pedro Agostinho, Michael Heckenberger, Rafael Bastos, Bruna Franchetto, and Carlos Fausto contributed to my work with valuable comments and incentives for my research in the Upper Xingu. Some sections of this text have been taken from my 2008 work *Apapaatai: Rituais de máscaras no Alto Xingu*. This article was translated from Portuguese into English by David Rodgers.

Notes

1. The soul to which I refer here is the *upapitsi*, which can be translated literally as "the other body." This "other body" has a "spiritual" nature that is understood to mean "vital substance," "consciousness," or "mind."

2. The uppercase and lowercase letters used in the names of nonhuman beings register a crucial distinction between animal-people (hereafter Animal) and animal-animals (hereafter animal). For example, "jaguar" corresponds to the animal of the species *Panthera onça*, while "Jaguar" refers to a jaguar-person (Yanumaka). Words referring to "spiritual" objects (*kumã*)—for example, Tankwara, the clarinet, and Kawoká, the wooden flute—are also capitalized.

3. See Acácio Tadeu Piedade's dissertation (2004) on Wauja instrumental music.

4. Descriptions of this ritual can be found in articles by Robert Carneiro (1977) and Rafael José de Menezes Bastos (1984–1985).

5. In the Wauja language, these suffixes are: *-kumã*, *-iyajo*, *-mona*, and *-malu* (Barcelos Neto 2006b).

6. For an analysis of the relations between iconography and the attribution of the identities of the ritual masks, see Barcelos Neto (2004a and b).

7. This myth was published in Barcelos Neto (2002:156–58).

8. This wood is extracted from a homonymous tree of an unidentified species.

9. This is a kind of drum made from a hollowed-out tree.

10. Barcelos Neto (2006b) contains an analysis of the Wauja myths of the origins of humans and Animals.

11. Ireland refers here to Malakuyawá, a former chief (*putakanaku wekeho*, "owner of the village") and a great yapaká. The author is not saying that it is the *chief category* that identifies "spirits," but *one* chief in particular who, evidently, was also a yapapá. During the period of Ireland's research in the Upper Xingu (1981–1983), Malakuyawá was, in fact, the only Wauja yapapá.

12. Xinguano ritual objects such as masks and flutes are never exchanged. In fact, there is much interdiction involving these objects and their knowledge (for example, see Piedade 2004). We could say that Kawoká trio flutes are god-like objects, much connected to the empowerment of aristocrats. Because they are *kanupá* ("taboo"), exclusive, and expensive (they demand a huge amount of food and goods to be ritually operational), there is a complicated protocol that makes extremely difficult their circulation within the Upper Xingu and elsewhere. The only occasion on which Kawoká trio flutes travel is to pay homage to aristocrats of neighboring villages.

References

Albert, Bruce. 1988. La fumée du métal: Histoire et représentations du contact chez les Yanomami (Brésil). *L'Homme* 106–107:87–119.

Barcelos Neto, Aristóteles. 2002. *A arte dos sonhos: Uma iconografia ameríndia.* Lisboa: Assírio and Alvim / Museu Nacional de Etnologia.

———. 2004a. *Visiting the Wauja Indians: Masks and Other Living Objects from an Amazonian Collection.* Lisboa: Museu Nacional de Etnologia.

———. 2004b. As máscaras rituais do Alto Xingu um século depois de Karl von den Steinen. *Bulletin de la Société Suisse des Américanistes* 68:51–71.

———. 2006a. De divinações xamânicas e acusações de feitiçaria: Imagens wauja da agência letal. *Mana* 12(2):285–313.

———. 2006b. "Doença de índio": O princípio patogênico da alteridade e os modos de transformação em uma cosmologia amazônica. *Campos: Revista de Antropologia Social* 7(1):9–34.

———. 2008. *Apapaatai: Rituais de máscaras no Alto Xingu.* São Paulo: Editora da Universidade de São Paulo.

Basso, Ellen B. 1973. *The Kalapalo Indians of Central Brazil.* New York: Holt, Rinehart and Winston.

———. 1985. *A Musical View of the Universe: Kalapalo Myth and Ritual Performances.* Philadelphia: University of Pennsylvania Press.

Carneiro, Robert. 1977. Recent Observations on Shamanism and Witchcraft among the Kuikuro Indians of Central Brazil. *Annals of the New York Academy of Sciences* 293:215–28.

Fausto, Carlos. 2002. Banquete de gente: Comensalidade e canibalismo na Amazônia. *Mana* 8(2):7–44.

Gell, Alfred. 1992. *The Anthropology of Time: Cultural Constructions of Temporal Maps and Images.* Oxford and New York: Berg.

———. 1998. *Art and Agency: An Anthropological Theory.* Oxford: Oxford University Press.

Heckenberger, Michael. 1999. O enigma das grandes cidades: Corpo privado e estado na Amazônia. In Adauto Novaes (org.), *A outra margem do Ocidente,* pp. 125–52. São Paulo: Companhia das Letras.

Ireland, Emilienne Marie. 1985. Kwahahalu and Sapukuyawa Ceremonial Masks. Description of Artifacts Collected in the Waurá Village, Xingu National Park, Mato Grosso, Brazil, on April 8, 1983. Report submitted to the National Museum of Natural History, Washington.

Menezes Bastos, Rafael José de. 1984–1985. O payemeramaraka kamayurá: Uma contribuição à etnografia do xamanismo no Alto Xingu. *Revista de Antropologia* 27–28:139–77.

Piedade, Acácio Tadeu. 2004. O canto do Kawoká: música, cosmologia e filosofia entre os Wauja do Alto Xingu. PhD dissertation, Universidade Federal de Santa Catarina.

Pollock, Donald. 1995. Masks and the Semiotics of Identity. *Journal of the Royal Anthropological Institute* 1(1):581–97.

Reichel-Dolmatoff, Gerardo. 1975. *The Shaman and the Jaguar: A Study of Narcotic Drugs among the Indians of Colombia*. Philadelphia: Temple University Press.

Rivière, Peter. 1995. AAE na Amazônia. *Revista de Antropologia* 38(1):191–203.

———. 2001. A predação, a reciprocidade e o caso das Guianas. *Mana* 7(1):31–53.

Stolze Lima, Tânia. 1999. Para uma teoria etnográfica da distinção natureza e cultura na cosmologia juruna. *Revista Brasileira de Ciências Sociais* 14(40):43–52.

Viveiros de Castro, Eduardo. 2002a. Perspectivismo e multinaturalismo na América indígena. In Eduardo Viveiros de Castro, *A inconstância da alma selvagem e outros ensaios de antropologia*, pp. 345–99. São Paulo: Cosac and Naify.

———. 2002b. Esboço de cosmologia yawalapíti. In Eduardo Viveiros de Castro, *A inconstância da alma selvagem e outros ensaios de antropologia*, pp. 25–85. São Paulo: Cosac and Naify.

6

Valuables, Value, and Commodities among the Kayapo of Central Brazil

Terence Turner

At the edge of the open grave, two women fought desperately, each trying to pull the shotgun from the other's grasp. One was the sister of the dead man lying flexed in the round grave pit. Her head was shaved and her scalp was covered with fresh gashes from which blood streamed down over her face. The other woman was the dead man's widow. The shotgun had belonged to her dead husband. Her head was also shorn and gashed. Each woman, in a customary mourning gesture, had cut her hair and then repeatedly tried to chop her head open with a machete until others had wrestled the weapon away from her. Both women's relationships to the dead man had been integral parts of the man's identity while he was alive, like his shotgun and other possessions. The women's cutting of their heads is a standard symbolic gesture for bereaved relatives that serves the same purpose as the breaking of the deceased's belongings: the severance of a connection that the dead man's ghost could follow back to the living, with the purpose of killing them so that they might accompany him in the world of the dead (see fig. 6.1).

The corpse of the widow's husband lying flexed in the grave had been painted and adorned with bunches of arara plumes tied to its arms. A broken hunting knife and other possessions, including a shattered bird-bone whistle, lay beside it in the grave. These objects, like other belongings of the dead man, had been deliberately broken, magically "killed" to make them share in the death of the person of whose life they had been part, and above all to prevent their use by any surviving kin, for the objects would then provide pathways for the dead man's "shade" (*karon*) to follow back to the social world of the living, where he could kill the new possessors of the objects so that they might join him in the place of the dead (Turner 1965:381–403).

Figure 6.1. The sister of a dead man struggles to keep his widow from chopping her head off with a machete as a gesture of grief by his open grave. *Photo*: Joan Bamberger, 1962.

The dead man's sister demanded that the gun also be broken and thrown into the grave. His widow, however, claimed that he had wanted her brother to have it. There had been no such conflict over the bird-bone whistle, but a shotgun is something else again, a high-priced commodity and a symbolic badge of masculine status as an accomplished hunter and warrior. As such, it is an object that might well be worth risking attack by the lonely spirit of a deceased affine. Eventually, the widow, a younger woman, tore the gun from her sister-in-law's hands and walked away. The grieving sister sank down by the grave, sobbing and keening the metrical chant for the dead that calls upon the dead man's ghost to go away and never return to seek its living relatives.

The widow could not return directly to her house, where she had lived with her husband in keeping with the Kayapo practice of matri-uxorilocal post-marital residence. Traditional Kayapo practice calls for the destruction of a house in which someone has died, just as it demands the destruction of the other objects used in life by the dead person. A dead man's hunting weapons, a dead woman's swidden gardens, her calabashes and metal pots and her mats and baskets, as well as a man's or woman's clothing—in short, all personal possessions that participated in the social identity of the deceased—must be destroyed. Any of these possessions, it is believed, if left intact and used by the living, could become channels the original owner's ghost could follow back to the living user.

The destruction of a dwelling house was easily enough accomplished in the days when houses were constructed like the rough lean-to shelters still built in trekking camps. To destroy such a house and build another one is the work of a single day. Contemporary Kayapo houses, however, have come to be built in the regional neo-Brazilian style: permanent, labor-intensive structures with heavy log frames, wattle-and-daub walls, and peaked thatched roofs. They require many days and the work of many men to build or destroy (see fig. 6.2). Fortunately for the widow in question—an inhabitant of the village of Gorotire—her fellow villagers had found a creative way around the inconvenient dictates of traditional mortuary practices concerning houses. The Evangelical missionaries in the village were accustomed to keeping a pine-scented aerosol deodorizer in their privy. The Gorotire had somehow discovered that the pungent chemical, if sprayed around the house of a dead person, would ward off the ghosts of dead housemates as effectively as it did the odors emanating from the missionaries' latrine, thus obviating the need to destroy and rebuild the house. The widow's house had just been treated with the borrowed spray, which, whatever its effects on the souls of the dead, rendered it temporarily uninhabitable by the living. The widow, accordingly, avoided her freshly pine-scented house and walked on across the village plaza toward the house of her brother's wife, bearing the shotgun she had saved for her brother from the grave.

Her passage across the plaza, however, was interrupted by a line of dancing men. They were performing a dance that forms part of the Bemp naming ritual. (For a full description of this ceremony, see Turner 1965:167–246.) The dead man had possessed a Bemp name. The dancing men were themselves bearers of Bemp names, and their dance was an obligation attached to their name-identity. Their ritual gesture asserted the continuity and value of the name-identity they shared with their dead name-mate, even as it symbolically severed the tie that identity gave them with the dead man as an individual and as a ghost. Their dances' combination of meanings was conveyed by a critical difference between their performance of the dance as a mortuary ritual and the form of the dance as performed to bestow Bemp names on a living person. When done to confer the Bemp name-identity on a living person, the dance is performed

Figure 6.2. Brazilian-style houses of the type normally built in contemporary Kayapo villages. In foreground, a group of initiates with palm fronds for the construction of a sleeping shelter. *Photo:* Joan Bamberger, 1963.

by a double file of dancers. The paired dancers comprising the ranks of the double file embody the essence of living sociality, consisting of friends, relations, and, if possible, name-givers and name-receivers dancing side by side (see fig. 6.3). The dance performed for the dead man, in contrast, consisted of a single file only. The social relationship that serves as the basis of the dance formation when performed for a living person is thus suppressed when performed for the dead. This suppression of the social form of the performance for the living expresses the severance of the social connection of the living performers to the dead name-bearer, a connection that his spirit might otherwise have followed back to attack them as they danced. The crude palm-leaf headdresses worn by the dancers were also unlike the complex feather headdresses worn by dancers in the Bemp ceremony as celebrated for the bestowal of names on living boys. These headdresses were made to be discarded and left on the dead man's grave immediately after the dance, so they would not be able to lead the ghost back to those who danced for the dead man.

The bird-bone whistle that had been broken and cast into the grave and the bunches of arara feathers fastened to the arms of the corpse

Figure 6.3. "Funeral March." A dance performance in the Bemp naming ceremony and boys' initiation. Note double file of dancers. The same dance would be performed in single file for a deceased Bemp name bearer. *Photo*: Joan Bamberger/AnthroPhoto, 1962.

belong to a special class of ritually valuable objects—called *nêkrêtch*, or "valuables"—that imply membership in ritual societies and bestow rights to perform distinctive ritual acts (see fig. 6.4).

Objects and Values: Names and Valuables (*Nêkrêtch*)

Nêkrêtch are passed on, like personal names, between certain categories of kin. On the senior end of the relationship, these categories include grandparents, paternal aunts, and maternal uncles; on the junior end, they include grandchildren, sororal nephews, and fraternal nieces. Normally, names—which are gender-marked—are bestowed by each gender on relatives of the same gender (e.g., mother's brother to sister's son or mother's mother to daughter's daughter) but never by mothers or fathers on their own offspring (Turner 1965:129–31, 170–78).

Some idea of the main features of Kayapo kinship and extended family structure is essential for understanding the values attached to these

Figure 6.4. An example of ritual *nêkrêtch* (valuables). A group of initiates in the initiation that forms part of the Bemp naming ceremony wearing distinctive forms of the standard headdress, consisting of a trefoil plume of arara feathers (*àkàpari*) inserted in a beeswax helmet (*kutom*). Note that each àkàpari is differently decorated. These differences are distinctive personal nêkrêtch bestowed by maternal uncles or grandfathers. *Photo:* Joan Bamberger, 1963.

objectified aspects of identity. The Kayapo do not recognize descent (that is, a continuous line of collective identity extending unbroken from generation to generation). The standardized structure of their extended family households is based on a matri-uxorilocal rule of post-marital residence, not on any rule of descent, matrilineal or otherwise. Filiation takes the form of a bilateral kindred, radially organized around a monogamous nuclear family defined as a unit of "natural" relations (in the sense of animal-like, infra-social relations of sexuality and biological reproduction). Nuclear family relations, as such, are conceived as qualitatively discontinuous with the purely social relations between alternate generations or relations between cross-sex parental siblings and their nephews or nieces that constitute the outer periphery of the kindred. Relations of these peripheral categories are considered the only appropriate channels for bestowing the tokens of social identity (names and ritual valuables or nêkrêtch) on children. The continuity of social identity carried by names and nêkrêtch is thus produced by excluding and bypassing the nuclear family and the relations of parents to their children. Fathers and mothers and their parallel-sex siblings are expressly prohibited from passing their own names and nêkrêtch to their own children. The principles of the system are thus the opposite of unilineal descent. Names and nêkrêtch are the properties of the individuals who give and receive them, not of any communal society or household considered as a corporation, contrary to what has been claimed by Vanessa Lea (cf. Lea 1986, 1992, 1995). Kayapo kinship, in sum, must be grasped as a system of processes of producing persons, households, and communities: processes, in a word, of objectification. The objectified forms of these processes become the constituent units of the structure of Kayapo culture—the embodied person, the household unit, the community, and the cosmos (Turner 1997b).

As I have shown elsewhere, the constitutive relations of the extended family household, in the generalized forms of communal rites of passage, serve in turn as the framework of the system of collective institutions (men's houses, men's and women's age sets, and ceremonial organizations) that directly constitute the social community as a totality (Turner 1978, 1979a, 1979b). This is why the relationship between name- and nêkrêtch-giving and name- and nêkrêtch-receiving kin is recognized by the Kayapo as the source of fully social identity. This identity is materially embodied by the personal names and nêkrêtch valuables that these relatives pass on to one another over the heads, as it were, of the biological parents of the name-receiving children. The ritual acts through which they transfer these objectified values are themselves processes of objectification.

Many personal names and valuables are passed directly from individual name-givers to their nieces, nephews, or grandchildren without the need for public ceremony. Such names and nêkrêtch are called by the term *kakrit*, which means "common" in the somewhat pejorative sense this adjective has in British English. Kakrit names are semantically transparent and refer to specific things like parts of the body, actions, animals, and plants. They serve only to denote the specific individual identity of the name receiver and his or her identity with the name-giver, and they involve no wider social involvement such as that represented by the great naming ceremonies, which require the mobilization of most of the community for two or more months.

There is, however, another class of names, called "great" (*ruynh*) or "beautiful" (*mêtch*) names, which can be conferred only after the whole village celebrates a complex ceremony associated with that name. "Beautiful" names are distinguished from "common" names in consisting of semantically untransparent (meaningless) prefixes attached to semantically transparent names of the "common" type. These prefixes, of which there are seven, are also the names of ceremonies held to bestow the names. They serve in effect as general class markers, designating an identity common to all those who bear the same name. Those who share such a "great" name-identity are held to share the essential property of "beauty" common to all "beautiful" names: they are called "beautiful" (mêtch) in contrast to the "commonness" (kakrit) of those who have only "common" names. The essence of this distinction is that "beautiful" names, and hence their bearers, are identified with the whole social community, which must perform the ceremony required to give the name. It is this collective performance that elevates the identity associated with the "beautiful" name to a higher structural level (that of society as a totality) than that of the individual dyadic relation between the giver and recipient of a "common" name (Turner 2002).

As a term of value, "mêtch," which I have translated with the general term "beautiful," and its combining form /mê/ (as in mê-kumren, "really beautiful"), connotes both completeness (meaning that all the parts or aspects of a thing are present in the proper proportions) and perfection of production or performance. The word is associated with the principle of repetition, as when a ceremony becomes more fully and perfectly performed the more times it is rehearsed. As a quality of identity, it is considered to increase with social age, as measured not merely in brute duration but in the successive transformations of status through which a person passes from stage to stage of the family cycle and the age set system. The "beauty" of beautiful names and ritually circulated valuables derives from their association with the social totality (that is, the community as a whole. Common (kakrit) names are identified with the lower-level totality of the extended family, as contrasted with the nuclear family of a name-recipient. (The naming relationship frames the extended family that encompasses the name recipient's natal nuclear family.) The character of the extended family as a "totality" can also be expressed in terms of units of social time. In these terms, its association with the social value of "beauty" is more directly comprehensible. The extended family as a complete structure of interfamily relations requires at least three successive nuclear family cycles to produce; it thus represents more cycles of socially necessary production time than the one or two required to produce nuclear families of orientation and procreation. Three family cycles constitute the span necessary for a person born into his or her natal family to reach the senior status of a grandparent and parent-in-law, and as such the head of an extended family household. The names and valuables that he or she is thereby enabled to bestow on his or her nephews, nieces, and grandchildren endow that quality, the essence of the Kayapo value of "beauty," on the personal identity of their recipients. As socially produced "things," names and valuables thus objectify the latent value of the status of the name donor and extended family in a specific, socially circulable form (Turner 2002).

Certain "valuables" or nêkrêtch are associated with specific "beautiful" names. Bearers of Bemp names, as we have seen, may use a certain kind of bird-bone whistle to accomplish this association. Their nêkrêtch also include certain dietary restrictions of a "totemic" character. They may not eat the flesh of araras, because after death they become araras—their souls are said to assume the forms of araras and perch on the rays of the setting sun. Bearers of Bemp names should, if possible, be buried with bunches of arara plumes fastened to their arms, evocative of the arara wings on which their souls will soar from the grave to their perch on the setting sun. They must also avoid eating the flesh of a certain fish, called the Bemp fish, which has a mouth shaped like an arara's beak. All bearers of "beautiful" names, that is, all "beautiful" people, should avoid eating "common" animals like deer, monkeys, and capybara. In theory—while practice does not always follow theory in this regard—they are obliged to eat only "beautiful" animals, like tapir, tortoises, and peccaries. However, most "valuables" are not linked to "beautiful" names. Some consist of special roles or items of adornment used in communal rituals or to connote membership in ceremonial societies, like the bird society that figures in the Bemp ceremony. Others are of a more "common" character associated only with the dyadic relation between the individual donor and receiver, like rights to claim specific cuts of meat from certain animals (Turner 1965:176–78). These two broad classes of valuables, the "beautiful" or "great" and the "common," are defined, in so far as their relative levels of valuation are concerned, with reference to the objectified identities of the two levels of social organization through which they are conferred and circulated: those of the social totality (the village as a whole) and the individual extended family (the segmentary unit of social organization), respectively (Turner 2002).

Social Objects, Personal Objects, Commodities

Both classes of names and valuables thus have an irreducibly social component, although not to the same extent. Neither class can be reduced to merely individual attributes of their bearers, since they are identified with social relations and categories that involve more than one person. Even in the case of kakrit names and nêkrêtch, the individual name recipient shares the name-identity of the donor, while bearers of "beautiful" names share their name-identities with all those who have received the same "beautiful" name prefix. This is why they are all obliged to perform the single-file mortuary version of the name-giving ceremonial dance for those who share their name prefix upon those peoples' deaths. As social rather than individual elements of personal identity, and as ideal forms, names and nêkrêtch are in principle immortal. The individuals who bear them during their lifetimes die, but the names and nêkrêtch go on to become integrated into the identities of other recipients. This is true not only of names and what might be called "virtual nêkrêtch" (items of knowledge or performance that become "valuables," such as the right to sing a certain song, belong to a certain ritual society, or perform a certain ritual function), but even of nêkretch that take the forms of objects that may be ritually "killed" to share the fate of a dead bearer, like the bird-bone whistle broken and thrown into the grave of the Bemp name-bearer described earlier.

Most objects and material appurtenances of everyday existence lack the normative social quality of names and nêkrêtch that are bestowed in the same way as names. Tools and objects of use, from houses to gardens to hunting weapons to baskets to sleeping platforms, are produced by those who use them or as favors for friends in informal exchanges, as when a man helps another to thatch his house or a woman cooperates with a group of neighbors and relations to make a large earth oven in preparation for a ceremonial feast. These are objects and activities through which a person relates to the natural and social world in quotidian ways. The objects become part of the person's individual identity, but they involve no formal social relationship or sharing of identity with other persons of prescribed categories in the way that ritual names and ritually bestowed "beautiful" nêkrêtch valuables do. The same term, "nêkrêtch," however, is applied to all personal possessions, even the most common or kakrit, and indeed even to Brazilian manufactured goods and commodities. At its broadest level of meaning, the term simply refers to "belongings" that have any kind of use value and through use become part of a person's identity.

Purely personal nêkrêtch such as bows and arrows, sleeping mats, and houses have an objective identity. However, as an integral part of a person's life-activity—his or her personal process of self-objectification—the objects' identities become inseparable from the identity of the person who makes and uses them (see Miller, Santos-Granero, and Walker, this volume, for similar Mamaindê, Yanesha, and Urarina notions). Such objects therefore become anomalous when their owner's individual identity is dissolved by death. Like an unburied part of the dead person's corpse, a personal belonging must, or should, be made to share in the death, and it should be de-objectified (destroyed) so as to join the rest of its owner in the grave.

As I have just mentioned, Brazilian commodities—and money itself—are also considered to be nêkrêtch in the general sense, as individual possessions that are acquired for their use value but entail no ongoing social relation or sharing of identity with the vendor, donor, or producer. As commodities, unlike names or ritual nêkrêtch, Brazilian items are acquired through exchange for an equivalent value of money, which eliminates any kind of continuing debt to, obligation to, or social relation with the vendor. The purchaser is thus left in exclusive individual control, or "ownership," of the commodity-object. It thus becomes as much an exclusive part of his or her individual personal identity as any item of traditional Kayapo material culture he or she may have made for personal use. Like all such objects, it should therefore be broken or ritually "killed" and left at its owner's grave when he or she becomes deceased.

As we have seen, this is not invariably the fate of expensive commodities such as firearms, large items of electronic equipment like radio-tape players, and Brazilian-style houses, which frequently end up being taken over by kin of the deceased. This is a point at which the Kayapo conception of things as integral parts of a person and the market-based regime of commodity value enter into conflict. It is a conflict that remains formally unresolved. At the same time, it is important to recognize that this conflict does not threaten the separate domain of social values conveyed by "beautiful" and "common" names and nêkrêtch valuables. The social values mediated by these objects are distinct and incommensurable with the exchange values and use values of marketed commodities. Names and commodities coexist in parallel but mutually unconvertible spheres

Figure 6.5. A village-owned airplane playfully decorated with ritual feather capes as its own *nêkrêtch*. Village of A'ukre. *Photo*: Barbara Zimmerman, 1990.

of exchange (to employ the terminology of economic anthropology), and derive their values from different sources.

An especially ambiguous category comprises commodities of such enormous exchange value that they become, in effect, communal possessions. A supreme example is the airplanes acquired by a few villages with the proceeds of logging contracts in the 1980s and 1990s. The Kayapo felt that these mega-commodities, identified as they were felt to be with the community as a whole, called for ritual recognition as social objects transcending the common run of personally owned trade commodities. And so the planes have received names (albeit kakrit names, like Kutoynkàre, which means "snakeskin") and nêkrêtch of their very own, at least temporarily, in inspired photo opportunities (see fig. 6.5).

Natural Objects and Social Objects: A Kayapo Perspective on the Difference

Up to this point, I have discussed only the world of social things. The Kayapo also consider that there are many things, objective entities and material properties, that are not social. As I have noted, the Kayapo understand society itself, and individual social persons, to include and depend upon nonsocial biological properties common to humans and animals (the nuclear family as a breeding and primary socializing unit in the case of society and the body and its senses and powers in the case of the individual)(Turner 1980, 1995). There is thus no mutually exclusive distinction between "society" and nonsocial "nature" in the sense of a spatial boundary between village and forest; society is built upon, and thus includes, a "natural" infrastructure. However, while recognizing themselves and their society as hybrid combinations of social and infra-social animal features and powers—in this sense affirming a degree of continuity between themselves and other living things—the Kayapo nevertheless distinguish between themselves as social beings and a nonhuman world of animals, plants, and inanimate objects (Turner 1997b). It is not that they do not attribute some social and cultural properties to animal species: large animals, birds, and fish are all thought to hold their own ceremonies and possess songs and other ritual knowledge that they can communicate to shamans.

According to myth, humans have learned many of these animal ceremonies and bird songs and made them the basis of their own ceremonies. The beautiful names they bestow in naming ceremonies, for example, were originally learned from fish when a Kayapo shaman, having assumed the form of a caiman, eavesdropped on a fish naming ceremony at the bottom of a river.

There nevertheless remains an essential asymmetry between animals and humans as social beings. So far as Kayapo myth and other beliefs are concerned, no animal species has ever learned and imitated a human ceremony. Each animal species possesses its own ritual lore and practices as a fixed aspect of its species being, like its mode of locomotion or the pattern of its skin, scales, or feathers. Humans are the only species that learns and imitates the rituals, songs, and bodily patterns of other species, and thus continually renovates its stock of cultural knowledge, practices, and objects. Kayapo myth, ritual, and everyday practice are replete with instances of such borrowings and imitations. In sum, while humans share with animals a "natural" substratum of species-specific biological attributes of corporality, reproduction, and elementary family relations, the superstructure of imitated and replicated forms comprising the stock of specifically cultural practices, semiotic representations, and traits is unique to the human species. Nature and natural things are thus essential constituents of human culture, but the reverse is not true. The ability to replicate forms through the intermediacy of semiotic representation, and thus to communicate, share, and change them through conscious social activity, is the decisive difference between humans as social beings and animals as natural beings in the perspective of Kayapo myth and cosmology.

Body, Village, and Cosmos as Super Objects

The socialized (painted, coiffured, and ornamented) human body, as the form of the social person, is the site where the animal or "natural" aspects of human existence and the "cultural" aspects of social person- hood associated with gender, generation, kinship, and other social roles converge. The social body is thus itself a synthetic super-object, which is organized according to the same paradigm of space-time dimensions as that ultimate, all-encompassing super-object: the cosmos. The cosmos is culturally modeled at the highest level as a structure and consists of two complementary dimensions of space-time, one a concentric series of zones centered on the village plaza and extending outward to the edge of the world, and the other a linear dimension corresponding to the path of the sun from its rising in the east to its setting in the west. The concentric dimension is also conceived of as a form of reversible movement and thus of cyclical time. The east-west dimension is one of irreversible but infinitely replicable movement and thus also of linear time. The objective structure of the world defined by these overlapping categories of move- ment is thus also the form of the complex temporal process through which it is continually reproduced.

Considered as a material object, in other words, the cosmos consists of a praxis of objectification, in Karl Marx's sense of productive activity as objective (Turner 1997b). As I have shown in detail in other publications, this active materialist paradigm of the fundamental structure of reality is replicated at all levels of social and corporeal structure, from the indi- vidual body through the extended family to the village (considered as the paradigm of human society) to the local setting of the village in its natural environment to the cosmic order of space-time. The notion at work is one of a recursive hierarchy of identical structures of form-giving processes at all levels of the natural and social worlds (Turner 1980, 1995, 1997a).

Objectification and Deobjectification as the Life and Death of Form

To return from the macroscopic structure of the universe as a whole to the microscopic level of particular objects, we have seen that the social world of things consists for the Kayapo of two great classes. One of these consists of utilitarian objects made by the individuals who use them, or Brazilian commodities acquired by purchase or as presents. Objects of this class become associated exclusively with the personal identities of those who acquire and use them. The other major class comprises attributes or objective correlatives of social identity that can be conferred on a person only through specific relations and actions involving others. This latter class is in turn subdivided into sub-categories of "beautiful" and "common" names and valuables (nêkrêtch), thus forming a hierarchy of distinctions of greater and lesser social value. The value distinctions that constitute this hierarchy represent the levels of social organization engaged in their acquisition, possession, and use: the individual person for the first major class, and for the two sub-classes of the second major class, the extended family segment and the community as social totality, respectively. These levels and entities thus represent modalities of social praxis, as elements or levels of the process of objectification through which social persons, relations, and communities are produced as material realities with specific forms.

The process of objectification, however, has as its corollary a complementary process of *deobjectification*, the destruction and dissolution of the forms of the identities and material entities it produces, including individual social bodies and persons. Kayapo graves themselves enact this process of dissolution by deobjectifying themselves. Graves are dug as circular pits, in which the corpse, as we saw earlier, is placed in a flexed position. The pit is then roofed over with logs and mats, after which the earth from the pit is heaped on the mats, creating a rounded tumulus. Many of the deceased's broken possessions, tufts of the shorn hair of mourning relatives—and the leaf headbands used by the performers of the death dance if the deceased possessed "beautiful" names—are fastened to poles stuck in the ground beside the mound or thrown directly onto it. With time, the mats on which the tumulus rests decompose, and the earth from the tumulus filters down between the logs into the grave pit. Eventually, the tumulus vanishes, the logs also rot, and the grave levels

Figure 6.6. Covering the grave chamber with logs and mats. The dirt from the pit will be heaped onto the mats to form a tumulus. As the logs and mats decay, the earth from the tumulus will fall into the pit, filling it up and leveling the grave with the surrounding ground. *Photo*: Joan Bamberger, 1962.

itself with the surrounding earth, objectively sharing its owner's objective dissolution. The grave is the objective aspect of death, the material form of the end and dissolution of personal existence, but it also becomes the process of its own deobjectification. As such, it becomes the instrument through which the personal dissolution of death is turned against death itself (see fig. 6.6).

For the Kayapo, in sum, "the occult life of things" consists of correlated processes of objectification and deobjectification, the dialectical alternation of the production and disintegration of forms as integral aspects not merely of the life but also of the death of things. These opposing tendencies of production and disintegration are reconciled and synthesized at the cosmic level through a combination of different modes of praxis: one cyclical and self-reversing and one linear, with beginnings and ends, but infinitely self-renewing. Through these processes repeated at successive levels of organization, individual actors—as composite natural and social beings—produce themselves and their society as objectified parts of a life-world of activities and relations that are at once subjective, objective, and material. These processes constitute a hierarchy of classes of social value; objects and objective activities belonging to these classes thus assume the form of congealed (objectified) values. The objective existence of the material things and activities comprising this hierarchy is not independently given but contingent on and inseparable from the objective and subjective activities and identities of Kayapo persons and their communities.

References

Lea, Vanessa. 1986. Nomes e nekrets Kayapo: Uma concepção de riqueza. PhD dissertation, Federal University of Rio de Janeiro.

———. 1992. Mebengokre (Kayapo) Onomastics: A Facet of Houses as Total Social Facts in Central Brazil. *Journal of the Royal Anthropological Institute* 27(1):129–53.

———. 1995. The Houses of the Mebengokre (Kayapo) of Central Brazil: A New Door to Their Social Organization. In Janet Carsten and Stephen Hugh-Jones (eds.), *About the House: Lévi-Strauss and Beyond*, pp. 206–25. Cambridge: Cambridge University Press.

Turner, Terence. 1965. Social Structure and Political Organization among the Northern Cayapo. PhD dissertation, Harvard University.

———. 1978. The Kayapo of Central Brazil. In Anne Sutherland (ed.), *Face Values*, pp. 245–77. London: British Broadcasting Company.

———. 1979a. The Gê and Bororo Societies as Dialectical Systems: A General Model. In David Maybury-Lewis (ed.), *Dialectical Societies*, pp. 147–78. Cambridge, MA: Harvard University Press.

———. 1979b. Kinship, Household and Community Structure among the Northern Kayapo. In David Maybury-Lewis (ed.), *Dialectical Societies*, pp. 179–217. Cambridge, MA: Harvard University Press.

———. 1980. The Social Skin. In Jeremy Cherfas and Roger Lewin (eds.), *Not Work Alone*, pp. 111–40. London: Temple Smith.

———. 1995. Social Body and Embodied Subject: The Production of Bodies, Actors and Society among the Kayapo. *Cultural Anthropology* 10(2):143–70.

———. 1997a. Social Complexity and Recursive Hierarchy in Indigenous South American Societies. In Gary Urton (ed.), Structure, Knowledge, and Representation in the Andes: Studies Presented to R.T. Zuidema on the Occasion of His Seventieth Birthday. *Journal of the Steward Anthropological Society* 24(1–2):37–60.

————. 1997b. Il sacro come alienazione della conscienza sociale: Riti e cosmo-logia dei Cayapó. In Lawrence Sullivan (ed.), *Culture e religioni indigine in Americhe, Trattato di Antropologia del Sacro*, vol. 6:253–70. Milan: Editoriale Jaca Book SPA. English version printed in 2000. The Sacred as Alienated Social Consciousness: Ritual and Cosmology among the Kayapo. In Lawrence Sullivan (ed.), *Indigenous Religions and Cultures of Central and South America*, pp. 278–98. New York: Continuum.

————. 2002. Lo bello y lo común: Desigualdades de valor y jerarquía rotativa entre los Kayapo. *Revista de Antropología Social* 11(1):201–18. (Madrid). English version printed in 2003. The Beautiful and the Common: Gender and Social Hierarchy among the Kayapo. *Tipiti: Journal of the Society for the Anthropology of Lowland South America* 1(1):11–26.

III
Materialized Subjectivities

7
Obedient Things
Reflections on the Matis Theory of Materiality

Philippe Erikson

"Kiripi, how did you make those shoes you're wearing?"

When a Matis companion of mine abruptly asked me that, some twenty years ago now, it probably sounded to him like the simplest of questions. But it put me, yet again, in a most embarrassing situation. Fieldwork, especially in its early stages, offers plenty of opportunities for the researcher to experience an extreme feeling of awkwardness. This situation, however, seemed to epitomize it all. Not only was I linguistically incapable of explaining the subtleties of industrial cobbling—how plastic soles are molded and then attached to the upper part of the shoe, how metal eyelets are riveted onto the cloth, etc.—but I even had to admit that I had not made my shoes myself. In fact, I had but a scarce idea of precisely *how* they were made and exactly *who* had made them for me. This only comforted my friend in his idea that I was totally inept as an individual, incapable of fending for myself. He then asked me if the abundance of game in the area was one of the reasons I had come to live in his village, and he ended the conversation by asking me to confirm that back home I didn't hunt and had to rely on other people's meat to feed my family. To make matters worse, we ate meat from *domesticated* animals. This seemed so bizarre to the Matis that I was constantly encouraged to repeat, time and time again, that I was indeed miserable enough to resort to eating my brother's "pets." A few weeks later, my shoes disappeared and when I complained, I was simply told that I didn't really need them since I never seriously went out hunting anyway.

The question about how I made my shoes brought home to me the crucial fact that for the Matis—a small group of Panoan speakers living in the Javari basin in western Brazil—making one's own personal possessions is a basic part of life and probably even a moral imperative. The sole exceptions are foreign goods and those few items that must be obtained from the other sex in accordance with a strict division of labor (on the implications of this, cf. Lorrain 2000). If someone is too young, too clumsy, or too gringo to make her own lean-to shelter, palm leaf basket, fire fan, or mat, another person will help her make it—but never just do it for her. Whoever will be the final owner-user of an object must at least attempt to go through the first stages of manufacturing it, as this seems to be a sine qua non prerequisite to ultimately acquiring legitimate ownership of the implement. This fact is particularly striking when tasks are performed collectively, as we shall see when discussing the making of long houses.

In the following section, another field anecdote will illustrate how strictly the Matis adhere to this principle of personal autonomy and, wherever material goods are concerned, how much emphasis they place on self-sufficiency. Further on, I will also argue that the Matis' insistence on personally being involved in every step of the production of artifacts is closely related to the animistic dimension of their theory of materiality, as well as to the cosmological implications ownership has for them.

Self-Sufficiency as a Moral Imperative

In 1985, when my wife and I first met the Matis, they numbered around one hundred and had only recently been settled by Fundação Nacional do Índio (FUNAI) on the banks of the Itui after decades of interfluvial wandering while in hiding from the neo-Brazilians, who lived in stilted houses close to the larger rivers. In striking contrast with the present-day situation, at that time they could barely swim, preferred to wash in streamlets, and still had absolutely no canoes whatsoever.[1] In order to cross rivers, the Matis relied on crude palm rafts. So when I bought a large dugout from the neighboring Marubo and offered to let anyone interested use it, it was quite an event. The following day, nearly *all* the adult male population was busy carving paddles. The men were all working together, as a close-knit group, and were all basically following the same shape pattern for their paddles. But despite this striking display of social cohesion, the basic principle was "one man, one paddle." Uniformity did not debar individualism. When I attempted to joke about it, wondering why they needed so many paddles when we had only one canoe, the men were more embarrassed than amused. And while the others nodded approvingly, someone answered for the group that they hadn't yet learned how to make canoes themselves and lacked the proper tools to do so anyway.[2]

Working as a group performing uniform tasks, with individuals work-ing side by side—yet with each person retaining total autonomy—is indeed the characteristic Matis way of doing things, whether in the context of producing artifacts, hunting, or gardening. This leads to a very unusual form of egalitarianism, in which differences are kept to a minimum, since everyone is doing more or less the same thing at the same time in the same place, but without any kind of division of tasks, sharing, or even gift-giving involved. Like many native Amazonian peoples (Hugh-Jones, 1992:61), the Matis despise stinginess (expressed by the verb root *kuras-*) more than anything else. But generosity, for them, does not involve goods as much as it does food, sex, and energy; generosity essentially means a willingness to help others perform physical tasks—carrying things back home or chopping trees, for instance. Most artifacts are excluded from the sphere of generosity, although there are a few exceptions, such as necklaces or hammocks, which are made by women and given to men. Yet even these goods, at least until the Matis began to trade them to whites in exchange for neo-Brazilian goods, were handed out only once and never as second-hand objects. They ceased to circulate after having been initially given as new artifacts.

Unlike the Wauja and other Xinguanos described by Aristóteles Bar-celos Neto (this volume), the Matis do not depend on barter and trade to reinforce their social networks. The only exception, which space will not allow me to deal with here, arises when teenagers are being tattooed and all their belongings—such as pots and blowpipes—are destroyed, to be replaced by new ones offered by a wide array of relatives. The very first set of body ornaments worn by a youngster are also given by a kinsperson of a specific kind, as a token of relatedness. Apart from those admittedly rare circumstances, self-sufficiency is the rule, and an adult couple will have personally made each and every item they possess by themselves. The result is that, at least in a traditional setting, the notion of ownership is closely associated with that of craftsmanship. Further, the mere act of making something is tantamount to turning it into a partial extension of one's body—"ensouling" it, in Santos-Granero's words (this volume). For the Matis, just like for the Cashinahua:

> Labor that results immediately in a tangible product invests the worker with individual ownership. Objects are "aspects" of the person, whether this person be the maker of the object or someone who receives it as a present. . . . Things can relate to their owner, then, either as extensions

of self, like a man's bow or a woman's hammock, or, alternatively, as symbols of a person's relationships with specific kin, like a man's hammock, made by his wife, or a woman's carrying basket, made by her husband. (McCallum 2001:93)

Ensouling by Craftmanship

The ensouling potential of physical action was made particularly clear to me when an elderly Matis lady, on the day of my departure from her village, asked me to bite a tree so as to leave something of myself behind to be remembered by. Following a similar line of reasoning, when men gather palm fronds to use as whips, they struggle to force them out of the ground by hand. Cutting them would naturally be much easier, but it is explicitly prohibited because the whips, used in the course of rituals meant to transfer "energy" from whip users to people being whipped, would be deemed useless if their bearers did not sweat while uprooting them.[3] All this goes to show that the physical and mental experience of making something allegedly has an impact on its ultimate properties.

Accordingly, when men prepare the curare they use for blowpipe hunting, each one sits for days on end patiently watching his preparation reduce over a slow fire. A very naïve, very bored, and somewhat provocative anthropologist partaking in this nonaction once suggested that maybe just one or two people could sit there watching while others attempted to do something more exciting. The suggestion was shrugged off with the following explanation: the more still one sits while preparing one's poison, the longer the prospective prey will sit still on the branches. In other words, when a man prepares his curare, he sympathetically instills personal qualities into it. Admittedly, if only because of the somewhat mysterious character of its lethal potential, curare is a rather exceptional product, whose unusually intimate connection with its user has repeatedly been signaled by Amazonianist scholars (Chaumeil 2001; Rival 1996; Scazzocchio 1979). Generally speaking, curare's efficiency is seen as the outcome of its owner's own potency, reflecting his agency. Curare is, to some extent, an extension of its user's self; thus logically, a hunter will never use another man's batch. Indeed, the Matis name for the blue-gray pigmentation found on the sacral area of most newborns (also known as "Mongolian spot") is *pësho kuraste*, "curare stingy-cause-to-be," and this is probably one of the only circumstances in which the Matis acknowledge stinginess without reproof. One must also consider the fact that, just like the aforementioned whips, curare has an essentially transitional nature, having been created with its ultimate recipients in mind. It is therefore meant to reflect a one-to-one relationship between predator and prey. Yet, very similar arguments about an object's ensoulment can be made for nearly all human-made items, which is not surprising considering that nearly everything the Matis make is produced from raw materials originating from a forest itself perceived in an animistic mode. Thus, manufacturing something is tantamount to becoming its new "master," replacing a previous, immaterial one—a point we shall return to in a later section.

The fact that a deceased native Amazonian person's belongings are generally discarded or burned along with his or her corpse, rather than inherited, is usually accounted for by invoking the requirements of genealogical amnesia (Carneiro da Cunha 1978; Taylor 1993). But however convincing this argument may be in general terms, it will not account for the fact that even people like the Matis, who openly refer to their deceased kin, also insist on disposing of the deceased's artifacts along with his or her body. They apparently do this because all artifacts are conceived of as an extension of their maker, and as such, as "inalienable" extensions of their person. The manufacture of any object seems to bestow exclusive rights upon it to he or she who is not only its owner-maker but also, as we shall see, its master. But then, what about commercially manufactured goods?

The Paradoxical Status of Foreign Goods

Since foreign objects were obviously not made by their Matis owners, all the above considerations clearly pose the question of how these recently introduced goods fit into this pattern. The answer is quite straightforward: they don't (unlike the Runa example discussed by Guzmán-Gallegos, this volume). One remarkable feature of foreign goods, *nawan chu*, is that they never really seem to belong to anyone as intrinsically as *matisën chu*, homemade Matis goods.[4] It is unthinkable to use someone else's blowpipe, or to wear someone else's bead necklaces, for instance, but using anybody else's baseball cap to go out fishing is quite acceptable. At least to some extent, as we have seen, the same even goes for shoes. Metal tools, although they do have owners, are also willingly lent. A FUNAI employee once told me that in the first few years after so-called "first-contact"[5] with Brazilian nationals, the Matis would drive them mad by leaving machetes and axes lying around all over the place for anyone to use. This might be because so many machetes were handed over during the initial stages of "pacification" that they might have seemed available in limitless supplies. But I can't help but suspect that among the Matis, whoever "owns" a cap or a machete, having not made it his- or herself, has no intimate relationship with it. He or she has therefore neither right nor reason to be stingy about lending it to others. Let us note, by the way, that the term *kurasek*—which I have hereto translated as "stingy" (as it appears in pësho kuraste, translated as "curare stingy-cause-to-be" for "Mongolian spot")—might just as well be rendered as "having a proximate/intimate relationship with something" (Erikson 2007). Maintaining a relationship of this kind is, of course, more difficult to accomplish when dealing with "foreign" goods.

Very significantly, during the first fifteen or twenty years following initial contact with Brazilians, manufactured items were not only symbolically but also quite physically set apart. No metal tools, cotton clothing, flashlights, or shotguns were ever allowed into a village's long house. Twenty years ago, I was always asked to take off my T-shirt before entering the long house. Special buildings—individual houses on stilts clearly imitating the regional riverine style—were erected for the main purpose of storing axes, machetes, woven hammocks, and other foreign objects, and such houses were aptly called *nawan shobo*, "foreigners' houses." Nowadays, many nuclear families choose to live permanently in their stilted houses, which have grown in size. But for many years, they were mainly used as storage units for nawan chu.

This practice of storing foreign goods separately, of course, can be interpreted as a mere precaution—a consequence of the widespread belief that white manufactured commodities exude invisible fumes, which are thought to be responsible for the epidemics that regularly follow the commodities' acquisition. This theme of lethal, odorless scents has been beautifully illustrated by Bruce Albert (1988) in his analysis of data collected among the Yanomami, whose vision of foreign objects as olfactory threats would probably also ring a bell in the Javari basin: the Matis strongly object to the burning of any foreign substance (such as plastic or cardboard) and not so long ago, most of them believed that matches caused coughing. A group of men once explained to me that the fumes of the dynamite sticks formerly used by riverine Brazilians to fish in the Itui could cause epidemics, as proved by the presence of numerous dead three-toed sloths near the place where one infamous fishing party had taken place. Exotic goods might very well have been set aside in order to fulfill a quarantine of sorts. However, it could alternatively be argued that foreign goods were instead being treated like pets—that is, beings coming in from the outside "ready made," and thus requiring a phase of seclusion on the outskirts of the village before being fully incorporated and gradually allowed to follow their new master wherever he or she may go (Erikson 2000a). The main difference between the treatment of pets and that of foreign goods in Matis society is that what usually takes a few days or a few weeks for a prospective pet took a few dozen years for trade goods.

Be that as it may, the Matis had no qualms about the legitimacy of acquiring manufactured goods, even though they did not master the techniques involved in their making. Foreign goods were, and to a large extent still are, considered a form of compensation offered by the *nawa*, the outsiders, for the massive decimation brought about by post-contact epidemics. Significantly, conversations about the numerous deaths that followed re-contact in the '70s systematically gave way to complaints about nawa stinginess. The general impression was that no matter how many trade goods were offered, they could never fully make up for the cruel loss of kin the Matis had to suffer to gain access to them. And still, in actual practice, because the nawa expect tokens of reciprocity, there is nevertheless a more literal price to pay for these foreign goods that have so strongly disrupted the Matis' relationship to objects. Many of the older people are clearly ambivalent about and even fearful of now having to give away their own goods in exchange for manufactured items, just as they are fearful of what might happen to their souls in the afterlife with so many people taking their pictures. Women at first tried to take back the necklaces their husbands had given to FUNAI employees (Montagner Melatti 1980:89, 99), and men, until quite recently, made sure the curare pots and the masks they sold were either empty or had never been used (see Santos-Granero, this volume, for similar precautions taken among the Yanesha).[6]

The Matis insist that trade should involve only objects that are absolutely new (see fig. 7.1). They seldom accept second-hand clothing, for instance, and are usually reluctant to give away things that have been previously used, despite the gringo's fondness for patina and their own idea that an older blowpipe is more reliable than a newer one (Erikson 2001a). This is because FUNAI employees early on instilled the idea that trading new things was better in order to avoid the introduction of illness and unfair trade in the guise of old T-shirts being exchanged for a massive amount of meat, for instance. Yet I suspect a deeper motivation on the

Figure 7.1. Empty "make-believe" curare pots for the tourist trade. *Photo*: Philippe Erikson, 1985.

side of the Matis lies in their notion that brand-new objects are spiritually more "neutral," less contaminated by their maker's "supernatural" imprint than older objects are. In any case, let us now resume our examination of "traditional" Matis workmanship.

Always Alike, Never Interchangeable: Communitarian Individualism

The impressive homogeneity of Matis material culture has always struck me as exceptionally high. When I measured the men's blowpipes, for instance, the differences in length were minute. A man making an arrow will typically use another one as a measuring stick, so that all the pieces of his new arrow have roughly the same dimensions as those of any other. Pots similarly come in a very limited number of shapes. Potters can name a variety of different types of recipients, and claim they used to have as many different kinds of pots as the neighboring Marubo. Yet women tend to limit their production to just a few basic forms, and if one person decides to revive an ancient form, her example is bound to be followed by most, if not all, of the other potters. The same is true for bead necklaces (*piskare*), which are all made following the very same pattern: three dark palm nut beads alternating with three reddish ones, strung on palm thread (or nowadays sometimes nylon fishing line).

An inventory of the nonimported material possessions of the Matis, even if things have changed a bit since the early '80s, is easily done. Family quarters seem quite unencumbered, as there are very few different types of objects and very few specimens of each. Furthermore, no effort is made to produce stylistic diversity, despite the remarkable complexity of social identity, revealed by the bewildering number of ethnonyms used in contexts of self-presentation. There is no "emblazoning with designs" (see Hill, this volume), as heraldry is clearly not an issue here, allowing Matis craftspeople to prove overall remarkably conservative. Nonetheless—and this is another aspect of their paradoxical relationship with material goods—the Matis put tremendous emphasis on individual ownership. Their artifacts may be all very much alike, stylistically and functionally speaking, but having so much in common does not make them in any way communal. Stools may be but mere half-spheres of balsa wood, but men tend to sit exclusively on their own, and unlike the neighboring Marubo, the Matis have no communal benches. Bead necklaces may all look very much alike to a foreign eye (and even to most Matis men), but whenever one is lost and found again, most Matis women can immediately tell who had made it and who has been careless enough to lose it. Artifacts are designed to be similar to others of their type, but they are certainly not meant to be interchangeable.

As a matter of fact, despite the Matis' spectacularly communal way of life, despite their affection for doing everything in groups, despite their emphasis on sharing food and even sexual partners (Erikson 2002), despite the fact that unlike other Panoan languages, theirs uses the same pronoun for first-person singular and first-person plural, these people are passionately individualist. They are extremely concerned by what at first glance seem to be purely "formal" rights over things. Everything around them has an owner or a master, including such seemingly communal things as forest trails and long houses, long houses being one of the very few kinds of material objects that require a collective effort to be built (the others being canoe-shaped maize mortars and, in former times, hollowed-out tree trunks used as drums).

Long houses, which can lodge several dozen people, are necessarily constructed by team work. Thatching is tedious and time consuming and pillars require several people to be carried back from the forest. Yet people always say the house belongs to so-and-so and his wife, and they insist that it was built by so-and-so and his wife *alone*—the others just helped them out.[7] And indeed, a group of people building a house will immediately rest as soon as the future owner stops working, only to resume the task when he does so himself, no matter how restless any one member of the work party might feel.

In a similar vein, Matis gardens tend to be adjacent to each other and men generally work in them in groups. Yet the precise boundaries of each lot are recognized with extreme precision, and even unmarried teenage bachelors can be considered "owners" of a small plot (unlike neighboring groups such as the Kanamari, among whom only married men can have a garden of their own; Jeremy Deturche, personal communication). Once a garden has grown, women generally go there to gather manioc or plantains in groups, taking turns going to one another's patch. But despite their obvious preference for generalized reciprocity when it comes to gathering vegetables, women always know exactly who each and every manioc plant "belongs" to. While a Matis settlement typically consists of a single house on a hilltop surrounded by a single circle of gardens, nothing is really "communal"; each and every pet, plant, or object in the settlement has what the Matis call its *igbo*.

Of Masters, Owners, and Other Spirits

The concept of *igbo* can be roughly translated in European languages as a term meaning either "owner" or "master," depending on whether igbo applies to an inanimate "object" or to an animate "being." The distinction, of course, is ours, not the Matis', and the very fact that Matis language ignores the animate/inanimate distinction when it comes to defining igbo is of course noteworthy. This will comfort proponents of radical animism, but only to a limited extent, considering that the animate/inanimate distinction does appear at least in a covert form, in the guise of an associated concept, introduced by a specific morpheme, *wiwa* (or *wiw-* in its verbal form): that morpheme applies only to animates. Wiwa describes the state of being subjected to an igbo, but its use seems restricted to living beings, especially pets and plants taken from the forest and replanted in the vicinity of the village (vines, for instance). Complementarily, *chu*, "possessions," is merely used for inanimates (see note 4). Only invisible *maru* spirits, the Matis equivalent of the Curupira—harmful supernatural beings of Brazilian folklore whose backward feet confuse hunters who try to track them—seem to disregard this latent animate/inanimate distinction by literally implementing animate pets. The maru are said to use stingrays (*ihi*) as plates (*ancha*), caimans (*kapët*) as seats (*tsate*), and electric eels (*dendu*) as digging sticks (*mekte*)—and all these animate "objects" are included in the list of their wiwa alongside jaguars, which they perceive as white-lipped peccaries, and collared peccaries, which they perceive as dogs. But then, according to the Matis, the maru always get everything wrong (Erikson 2007), and unlike other Amazonians, who ascribe a pet status to musical instruments, the Matis never use "wiwa" to refer to inanimate things.

The semantics of the term "igbo" (or cognate forms such as *ibo* in Shipibo and *ifo* in Sharanahua) have been largely discussed in the literature devoted to Panoan peoples and give clear insights into the core of these peoples' ontology. One constant is that an igbo always enjoys a dominant status as master over all it relates to, the very idea of having *control* over the other participant in the relationship being one of an igbo's defining characteristics. As previously stated, artifacts, houses, trails, and garden plots all have an igbo, but more interestingly, so do animals, plants, and even spirits.

Humans, who impersonate and/or embody *mariwin* spirits when wearing masks, have been described to me as the spirits' igbo (see fig. 7.2). Among the Matis, I have never heard "igbo" used in reference to one human being acting as the igbo of another, but the case is not unheard of. The Sharanahua, for instance, describe the foster parents of orphaned children as the children's "ifo," and terms derived from "ibo" have been used in other languages such as Chacobo to refer to God as both maker and master of all creatures. Here again, the idea of subordination comes to the foreground, and the concept of igbo has undeniable intersubjective connotations, which might explain why—unlike among the Xinguanos described by Barcelos Neto (this volume), for instance—rituals are not "owned" among the Matis. The idea, among Panoans, has less to do with formal rights than with one-upmanship in a dialogic relationship.

As Pierre Déléage (2005) has recently argued, Panoan animism rests less upon the notion that all things in the universe are endowed with a "spirit" of their own than upon the notion that all things are susceptible to "remote control" and that spirits (*yoshi*) are perceived first and foremost

Figure 7.2. Clay mask, in use, not for sale. *Photo*: Philippe Erikson, 1985.

as masters: ifo. Therefore, when interacting with nonhuman beings or material things, people are not necessarily thought to be interacting with equals in disguise, as radical perspectivists might have it. Rather, they are believed to be interacting with other igbo, sometimes infringing upon the former masters' "rights"—competing with them—and sometimes, on the contrary, asking for their cooperation. In one Matis ritual, during which hunters speak to the cooked heads of recently killed white-lipped peccary, the concluding statement is *eobi min igbo*, roughly: "From now on, I am your master" (Erikson 2000b). Here, the aim is clearly hegemonic. In other cases—among Shipibo herbalists, for instance (Leclerc 2003)—the intention is not to take over and become the new "owner" oneself, but to summon the help of the original "master" (of medicinal plants, in this case).

This "mediative" variant of animism, however, does not foreclose the possibility that objects might be deemed to independently display "subjective" properties of their own. As argued by Santos-Granero (this volume), imputations of agency, when it comes to nonhumans, are above all a matter of degree. Philippe Descola (1994) quite convincingly claims that native Amazonian peoples' notion of "subjectivity" is far too all-encompassing to leave any room whatsoever for a native theory of "objects." The fact that something, or the raw material something is made of, has a master does not bar its being potentially endowed with its own personality, intentionality, volition, and other characteristics of a subjective being.

The Agency of Inanimates

As argued by Eliane Camargo (2006), the lines drawn by the animate-inanimate distinction are often quite different in the Amazon from what our European languages have accustomed us to. The Sikuani language provides a fine example of this by marking gender for animates only, with the sole exception of pots and weapons (Queixalós 1993). Strikingly, the objects Sikuani grammar sets apart by linguistically marking them as "honorary animates" happen to be the very same items that Matis aesthetics sets apart by means of incised decorations. Pots (including clay masks and clay flute resonators), as well as bamboo quivers, are physically marked with parallel crisscrossed lines called *musha* (see fig. 7.3). Blowpipes do not bear such incisions; instead, their dark stems have sets of egg-shell rings, which I have interpreted as attempts to imitate Bactris palm trees—but which I have also recently been told act as the weapons'

Figure 7.3. Ishma, carrying his uncle's dart quiver. *Photo*: Philippe Erikson, 1985.

musha, as well as making them look like striped poisonous snakes (*isan-tawi*). Considering that one of the acceptations of musha is "face tattoo," and considering that *Mushabo*, which means "bearers of face tattoos," is one of the generic names (as opposed to specific ones) the Matis give themselves, it is tempting to consider the Matis' "tattooing" of pots and blowpipe dart quivers as a potent statement about where the objects stand with respect to their igbo—they are literally marked as people. And indeed, the sanctions incurred by a man who might prove thoughtless enough to abandon his "tattooed" quiver in the forest are the same that would be brought upon he who might drink his own blood. In either case, one of his brothers would die, as if to say that one should never mistreat an alter ego. Understandably, Matis hunters are always very careful with their quivers, never put a cut finger to their mouth, and systematically scold the anthropologist who tends to do it without thinking. Whenever a hunter gets unlucky and fails to retrieve meat, he may apply medication either to himself or to his bow or blowgun.

The ritual making of palm-frond figurines, called *darawate*, is another instance in which animate and inanimate beings are sometimes given similar treatment. Darawate are usually made in order to communicate with the spirits of game, asking them to provide the actual bodies of those animals whose skeletons have been represented by the palm fronds. Yet darawate are sometimes also made to represent the anticipated bundles of curare vines or the clay that people set out on expedition to get, once again lumping animates and (for us, at least) inanimates together in a covert category.

Body ornaments are another element of material culture whose status deserves close scrutiny. Matis body ornaments, as I have previously intended to show, are in many ways inalienable possessions, not unlike extra-somatic body parts, that grow along with their bearer and act as potent reminders of the social connections they stand for (Erikson 2003). For a long time, I was therefore puzzled by the fact that body ornaments are systematically classified as chu, "possessions," alongside other objects with which humans seem to have a much less intimate relationship. However, since I have read Joana Miller's paper (this volume) and have recently paid closer attention to the "occult side" of all inanimate forms of being, this ethnographic detail now bothers me much less.

In a similar vein, taking seriously the idea that native Amazonian peoples tend to consider artifacts in an animate mode will lessen the culture shock one might experience while reading Cecilia McCallum's

(2001:16–17) vivid description of how the Cashinahua describe the work involved in making babies, which they do in terms quite reminiscent of those used to describe the production of material crafts. And returning to the Matis, the fact that any newly made item is systematically covered with red annatto, just as people's faces are whenever they go through a phase of renewal or rite of passage, is another clear indication of the native Amazonian tendency to treat inanimates in an anthropomorphic vein.

Conclusions

Twenty-two years ago, just before I began to ponder the mysteries of cobbling, I produced the hypothesis that "familiarization" might be the key metaphor used by Amerindian thought when it came to dealing with "spirits" (Erikson 2000a). Because the major focus of my study was then what Loretta Cormier (2003) has since coined "the predator-pet paradox," I then believed this overwhelming concern with *control* had its roots in pet-keeping and rivalry with the masters of animals. In light of the recent extension of the great animism debate to include considerations about objects as well as considerations about animals (and to a lesser extent, plants), I am now convinced that what Carlos Fausto (1999) has since then aptly labeled "familiarizing predation" is but a specific instance of a much broader phenomenon: the generalized interactive quest for "non-overlapping mastership" that native Amazonian people seem constantly engaged in. The debate started off with a discussion of enemies and pets, but it is now time to extend it to other "things" as well.

From an Amerindian point of view—at least from a perspective rooted in the Javari basin—"things," rather than being conceived as *independent subjects*, seem to be considered as semi-autonomous *subordinates*. In other words, "things" seem to be less perceived as full subjects than as fully subjected. Apart from leading an "occult life" of their own, they are also submitted to an "overt life" of dependency as "obedient things."

Notes

1. Nowadays, the Matis number around 250, many men own outboard "peque peque" motors, and youngsters organize swimming races across the Itui River.

2. A few days later, everyone had a paddle except for the anthropologist—not much of a carpenter—who ended up having the hardest time using his own boat, the other villagers being reluctant to lend him *their* paddles.

3. Indeed, as if to confirm this, during the ritual the masked whip bearers sometimes pass sweat from their bodies onto the fronds.

4. The term *chu* generally refers to one's possessions of the inanimate sort, in contrast with the word *wiwa* (discussed later in this chapter), which is applied to animate beings (including plants) that happen to be under one's control. Another term, *mishnibo*, literally "little things," is also used to refer to one's minor possessions.

5. For reasons exposed in Erikson 2001b, the episode of recent Matis history usually presented as "first contact" would be better described as merely being the latest instance of "re-contact."

6. The idea is that a man's innermost power (*sho*) is ingrained in his curare and it would therefore be dangerous to show it to the outside world. Similarly, masks are said to retain a close relationship with youngsters who have been whipped by the masks' wearers—the youngsters might die if the masks were taken away by a foreigner, carelessly handled, and broken.

7. This is probably quite common in lowland South America. Jean de La Mousse, a seventeenth-century missionary who lived some time with the Galibi, describes the bewilderment of an informant when he told him the mission house belonged to all of the missionaries rather than to anyone in particular (Collomb 2006 :142).

> Il y en eut un qui vint me demander un jour à qui appartenait notre habitation, si elle était à moi, ou au père de Creuilly, ou au frère Lacombe. Je lui répondis qu'elle appartenait à tous; mais ceux qui sont dans notre maison du bourg de Cayenne n'y ont-ils point de part? Tout autant de part que nous, lui dis-je. Il crut que je ne lui parlais pas sincèrement, cette communauté des biens est quelque chose qui le passe.

References

Albert, Bruce. 1988. La fumée du métal: Histoire et représentations du contact chez les Yanomami (Brésil). *L'Homme* 28(2–3):87–119. Portuguese version printed in 1992. A fumaça do metal: Historia e representações do contato entre os Yanomami. *Anuario Antropologico* 89:151–89.

Camargo, Eliane. 2006. Animate/Inanimate in Cashinahua (Huni Kuin) Grammar and Sociability. (unpublished ms.)

Carneiro da Cunha, Manuela. 1978. *Os mortos e os outros: Uma análise do sistema funerário e da noção de pessoa entre os índios Krahó*. São Paulo: Hucitec.

Chaumeil, Jean-Pierre. 2001. The Blowpipe Indians: Variations on the Theme of Blowpipe and Tube among the Yagua Indians of the Peruvian Amazon. In Laura Rival and Neil Whitehead (eds.), *Beyond the Visible and the Material: The Amerindianization of Society in the Work of Peter Rivière*, pp. 81–99. Oxford: Oxford University Press.

Collomb, Gérard. 2006. *Les Indiens de la Sinnamary: Journal du père Jean de la Mousse en Guyane (1684–1691)*. Paris: Chandeigne.

Cormier, Loretta. 2003. Animism, Cannibalism, and Pet-Keeping among the Guajá of Eastern Amazonia. *Tipiti: Journal of the Society for the Anthropology of Lowland South America* 1(1):81–98.

Déléage, Pierre. 2005. Le chamanisme sharanahua: Enquête sur l'apprentissage et l'épistémologie d'un rituel. Doctoral thesis, Ecole des Hautes Etudes en Sciences Sociales.

Descola, Philippe. 1994. Pourquoi les indiens d'Amazonie n'ont-ils pas domestiqué le pécari? In Bruno Latour and Pierre Lemonnier (eds.), *De la préhistoire aux missiles balistiques: L'intelligence sociale des techniques*, pp. 329–44. Paris: La Découverte.

Erikson, Philippe. 2000a. The Social Significance of Pet-Keeping among Amazonian Indians. In Paul Podberseck and James Serpell (eds.), *Companion Animals and Us*, pp. 7–26. Cambridge: Cambridge University Press. (Originally published in 1987 as De l'apprivoisement à l'approvisionnement: chasse, alliance et familiarisation en Amazonie indigène. *Techniques et Culture* 9:105–40.)

———. 2000b. "ɪ," "ᴜᴜᴜ," "sʜʜʜ": Gritos, sexos e metamorfoses entre os Matis (Amazônia Brasileira). *Mana* 6(2):37–64.

———. 2001a. Myth and Material Culture: Matis Blowguns, Palm Trees, and Ancestor Spirits. In Laura Rival and Neil Whitehead (eds.), *Beyond the Visible and the Material: The Amerindianization of Society in the Work of Peter Rivière*, pp. 101–21. Oxford: Oxford University Press.

———. 2001b. Korubo: O último contato? In Carlos Alberto Ricardo (ed.), *Povos indígenas no Brasil 1996/2000*, pp. 431–33. São Paulo: Instituto Socioambiental.

———. 2002. Several Fathers in One's Cap: Polyandrous Conception among the Panoan Matis (Amazonas, Brazil). In Stephen Beckermann and Paul Valentine (eds.), *Cultures of Multiple Fathers: The Theory and Practice of Partible Paternity in South America*, pp. 123–36. Gainesville: University Press of Florida.

———. 2003. "Comme à toi jadis on l'a fait, fais-le moi à présent . . ." Cycle de vie et ornementation corporelle chez les Matis (Amazonas, Brésil). *L'Homme* 167–168:129–52.

———. 2007. Faces from the Past: Just how "Ancestral" Are Matis "Ancestor Spirit" Masks? In Carlos Fausto and Michael Heckenberger (eds.), *Time and Memory in Indigenous Amazonia: Anthropological Perspectives*, pp. 219–42. Gainesville: Florida University Press.

Fausto, Carlos. 1999. Of Enemies and Pets: Warfare and Shamanism in Amazonia. *American Ethnologist* 26:933–56.

Hugh-Jones, Stephen. 1992. Yesterday's Luxuries, Tomorrow's Necessities: Business and Barter in Northwest Amazonia. In Caroline Humphrey and Stephen Hugh-Jones (eds.), *Barter, Exchange, and Value: An Anthropological Approach*, pp. 42–74. Cambridge University Press.

Leclerc, Frédérique Rama. 2003. Des modes de socialisation par les plantes chez les Shipibo-Conibo d'Amazonie péruvienne: Une étude des relations entre humains dans la construction sociale. Doctoral thesis, Université Paris X-Nanterre.

Lorrain, Claire. 2000. Cosmic Reproduction, Economics and Politics among the Kulina of Southwest Amazonia. *Journal of the Royal Anthropological Institute* 6(2):293–310.

McCallum, Cecilia. 2001. *Gender and Sociality in Amazonia: How Real People Are Made*. Oxford and New York: Berg.

Montagner Melatti, Delvair. 1980. Proposta de criação do Parque Indígena do Vale do Javari. Process Funai / BSB: 1074/80. (unpublished ms.)

Queixalós, Francisco. 1993. Les mythes et les mots de l'identité sikuani. In Aurore Monod-Becquelin and Antoinette Molinié (eds.), *Mémoire de la tradition*, pp. 71–106. Paris: Société d'Ethnologie.

Rival, Laura. 1996. Blowpipes and Spears: The Social Significance of Huaorani Technological Choices. In Philippe Descola and Gísli Pálsson (eds.), *Nature and Society: Anthropological Perspectives*, pp. 145–64. London: Routledge.

Scazzocchio, Françoise. 1979. Curare Kills, Cures and Binds: Change and Persistence of Indian Trade in Response to the Contact Situation in Northwestern Montaña. *Cambridge Anthropology* 4(3):30–57.

Taylor, Anne-Christine. 1993. Remembering to Forget: Identity, Mourning, and Memory among the Jivaro. *Journal of the Royal Anthropological Institute* 28(4):653–78.

8

The Crystallized Memory of Artifacts

A Reflection on Agency and Alterity in Cashinahua Image-Making

Els Lagrou

The Importance of the Invisible

Two strands of thought converge in my material on Cashinahua "image-making": the themes of alterity and agency. In this chapter, I concentrate primarily on the Cashinahua conception of the agency of images.[1] In the conclusion, I show how the Cashinahua theory of image-making leads to a theory of the agency and the making of objects: artifacts are embodied images, images that have acquired a fixed body through the hands of their producers. Some germinal ideas developed by Alfred Gell in *Art and Agency* (1998)—a work that has become a new canon for those who want to give the study of art a second chance in anthropology—receive a specific inflection when seen from the vantage point of the importance of alterity for native Amazonian thought. Shortly stated, what makes Gell so attractive when studying both Melanesian and Amazonian ethnology is the fact that he calls for an approach to objects, artifacts, and art "as if they were persons," emphasizing their agential qualities. Applying this approach in the context of Amazonianist theoretical preoccupations, we could join Peter Gow (1988, 1999) in asking: What is the relation between the body and image-making in Amerindian thought? And add yet another question: What is the relation between the body and artifacts in certain native Amazonian societies—specifically, in the case of this chapter, the Cashinahua?

Since in native Amazonian thought nonhuman beings, especially animals, are granted the status of persons or subjects, the question about what to do with artifacts (made by humans out of plants and animals) posits itself. But the question can also be applied to images triggered by the combined agency of plants, memory, songs, and other entities. Can these images also be considered as "persons," that is, as "social agents"? My material on the Cashinahua suggests that some artifacts and images can be indeed considered as such. But although from a Cashinahua viewpoint, objects and designs are endowed with agency, the relationship between artifacts and persons is different in Melanesia and Amazonia. I have chosen to talk about *images* (both verbal, visual, and virtual), as well as of *artifacts*, because I am as concerned with nonmaterial, hidden images and experiences hinted at—but essentially kept secret—as I am with objects interacting with each other in a readily observable world. Other authors have recently shown the same interest. For example, George Mentore speaks of "the glorious tyranny of silence" (2004:132–56), and Anne-Christine Taylor (2003:223–48) speaks of the secrecy surrounding the encounter with an *arutam*, where the interiorization of the relation established with an ancestor is made visible in body painting but the content of the encounter is never revealed. In *Mimesis and Alterity* (1993), Michael Taussig also points at the importance of thinking about what escapes "objectification." Thus, when speaking about the verbal imagery used by Florencio, a Colombian ayahuasca drinker, Taussig (1993:62) states: "It seems to me vital to understand that this power can be captured only by means of an *image*, and better still by entering into that image. The image is more powerful than what it is an image of." Taussig's words hint at a theme that has been recurrent in recent writings on the anthropology of images (see Severi 2003; Freedberg 1989), namely, the *power* of images to *affect* people emotionally.

When speaking of *image-making*, I include those images made in the mind and often expressed by very indirect means, as well as images hinted at in songs but never representationally depicted anywhere. What does it mean *not* to depict, paint, or otherwise make visible or materialize visions that one has actively searched for in perilous vision quests? The following description by the young Cashinahua cineaste Siã Osair, explaining the way in which a shaman is initiated by the spirits, well illustrates my point:

Pajé [the shaman] can give life and take it away. To become a shaman, you go alone into the forest and tie up your body with bark and palm leaves. You lie down on a crossroads with arms and legs spread out. First come the nightly butterflies, called *husu*, covering your whole body. Then come the *yuxin* eating the husu until they touch your head. You embrace them with all your force. The yuxin transform into a *murmuru* palm tree, full of thorns. If you are strong enough and do not let go, the palm tree will transform into a snake that coils itself around your body. You hold on; it transforms into a jaguar. You go on holding it in your grip and thus it goes until you are holding nothing. You have succeeded in the test and go on to explain to him [the yuxin] that you want to receive *muka*. He will give it to you.

Power is related to the capacity to transform, a capacity that can be endowed by spirit beings called *yuxin* or *yuxibu*. These spirit beings are able to produce animated images in the minds or "perceptual bodies" of people. "Yuxibu" is the superlative of "yuxin," which means "spirit" or "soul"—maybe "agency" or "energy" would be a better translation. These yuxibu beings are unrestricted by form and are therefore capable of transforming both their own bodily form and the form of the world around them. They also have the capacity to travel very quickly with the wind, although they are brought back from far away by the rain.

Cashinahua phenomenology turns around the tense relation between the fabrication of solid form—where the soundly embodied and rooted person is the prime artifact of Cashinahua collective labor—and the power of free-floating images. These images make themselves manifest in three different kinds of forms: in the form of spirits or their owners (yuxin and yuxibu); in the form of transformations in images and visions (called *dami*, "their lies"); and in the form of paths drawn by design (*kene*), which are called "the language of yuxin" and can be produced only by women. The drawing of these designs is called *kene kuin*, "the art of writing the real thing," while writing language with the alphabet is called *nawan kene*, "the writing of strangers" (see fig. 8.1). All these images, those that are drawn or woven in order to be contemplated and those that are invoked only in song, actively influence the forms life takes in the Cashinahua world.

Alterity

The concept of "alterity" has been crucial in Amazonianist ethnology ever since the writings of Claude Lévi-Strauss, Pierre Clastres, Joanna Overing, and Manuela Carneiro da Cunha, and its importance continues today with the writings of Philippe Descola, Eduardo Viveiros de Castro, and a whole new generation of ethnologists.[2] According to these ethnologists' views, the vast majority of native Amazonian peoples understand the human condition and sociality as a carefully controlled process of predation. Predation needs to be controlled carefully, for it is conceived

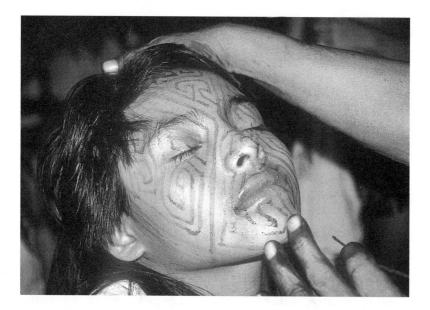

Figure 8.1. Young girl painted by her mother with genipapo on a thin layer of achiote. *Note:* This facial painting combines the *pua kene* ("crossed design") and *nawan kene* ("design of the enemy" or "writing of strangers") designs. *Photo:* Els Lagrou, 1995.

of as being constitutive of the production of life in general, and of social life in particular (Overing 1986). The collapse of the precarious "tranquil life" is within the scope of Amerindian discourse on illness, death, and misfortune.

The importance of alterity for the constitution of the self receives a special inflection among Pano-speaking peoples such as the Cashinahua. Panoans are so explicit with respect to the notion that the self is constituted by the other that they are considered to be especially interesting to think about when studying the native Amazonian way of relating to otherness. Put briefly, this Amerindian way of relating to otherness implies that one becomes self through partially becoming other, and that the subjectivity of self is significantly enhanced by intimate contact with—and even incorporation of—the other, be it an enemy, spirit being, animal, or plant. This incorporation can take various forms. The most spectacular ones, well known from the literature, are: eating the enemy, taking enemies' heads as trophies, incorporating their souls or songs, adopting their children, and stealing and marrying their women.

Although in their most objectified form these practices have become increasingly rare, the same logic that governs them continues to apply to relationships established with animals, plants, and other beings. This has consequences for the meaning of artifacts. All of these practices are more or less related to a specific *predatory* model, in which the other, even when killed or captured, is never totally annihilated but is somehow kept alive inside the killer himself—as is the case with Araweté killer-singers (Viveiros de Castro 1986)—or incorporated into the community of those who abducted it as an equal member. The Cashinahua always recognize the other as somehow being part of self in both a temporal and constitutive sense. Thus, everything that is proper is made out of other. This logic also holds for "all things made." All selves are on their way to becoming other.

Among the Cashinahua, the production of society consists, in a certain sense, of the *domestication* of otherness. The problem with this term is that it generally refers to the domestication of animals, a practice that Amerindians explicitly have chosen not to follow (Descola 2001; Hugh-Jones 2001). Philippe Erikson (1984) and Carlos Fausto (1999) use the term *familiarize* to refer to the Amerindian process of turning wild animals into pets. The term is equivalent to the Portuguese term *acostumar*, which the Cashinahua use to translate the vernacular term *yudawa*, the process of making the body anew or making the body become accustomed to a new situation, a new food, a new environment, or another novelty. The literal translation of "yudawa" is "to make the body." This refers to the idea that a new body is produced through the slow process of getting used both emotionally and bodily; if a person's body is not used in this way, it is thought that he or she might fall ill and die.[3]

This complex process of "getting hold" of otherness knows several strategies, ranging from mimesis and transformation to predation, trapping, and, last but not least, seduction. In the last case, a self gets hold of the other not by taming the wild forces of otherness, but by carefully diminishing the distance between self and other in spatial, cognitive, and bodily terms. The fact that the other is credited with an existence of his/her own, resisting reduction to stereotypical counter-images, is made evident in the ambiguity of the category of other (*nawa*) in Cashinahua thought. One can be neither predator nor victim, but both; neither stingy nor generous, but both; neither beautiful nor ugly, but both. The Cashinahua self's qualities always depend on the context in which it exists, on the relational quality conquered by that self and not on any essentialist reifying. The Cashinahua use the same notion of acostumar—to familiarize pets or enemies—to describe the adaptation of anthropologists to the Cashinahua society, since anthropologists allow their bodies—which is tantamount to saying their selves—to get used to Cashinahua ways and thus partially become Cashinahua.

The Agency of Art: Relating Different Worlds

It was in the middle of such a process of making my body—which the Cashinahua would call "mindful body"—adapt to Cashinahua ways that I was invited to participate, as a neophyte, in the rite of passage of some young boys and girls. This event was the starting point that allowed me to give form to Cashinahua phenomenology, that is, to understand their description of how life and body acquire their specific Cashinahua shape and style, their specific perceptual and meaningful form. It was also during this ritual that the meaning of designs and artifacts, as well as their relation to body- and image-making, became clear to me. Until then, it seems I had been asking "the wrong questions," such as, paraphrasing Gow (1999:230): "Who made it, what is it called, what does it look like, and what does it mean?"

The answers to these questions had been disappointing—short and confusing, especially since I was trying to confirm a supposed relation between the division of society in moieties and marriage sections and the use of certain motifs and design patterns in body painting and weaving. Other specialists had stated a priori that such a relation should exist among the Cashinahua without ever going further to demonstrate their hypothesis. This is an example of the problems that may arise when priority is given to taking a taxonomic or language-oriented approach to design, an approach criticized by both Gell (1998) and Gow (1988, 1999).

It should be said that the motifs painted with achiote during increase rituals are indeed related to the skin of animals associated with the moieties. In such cases, to be discussed below, achiote is used in the context of masking. This kind of painting is called *dami*, "masking" or "transformation," and not *kene*, "design" or "graphic pattern." Here, I am interested in the use of motifs within the kene design system.

The operating meaning of "kene" is found neither in the specific names given to different motifs nor in the differences between categories of designs, although those certainly exist; instead, it emerges in the unifying pattern found in the way in which the unique Cashinahua style is generated. By observing the use of designs in rites of passage, I could once and for all discard both the notion that the main function of Cashinahua body art is to reflect social organization and the idea that its iconographic function is the *representation* of entities. Names of motifs refer to beings and/or parts of their bodies (such as boas, parrots, specific plants, etc.), as well as to relations and paths. The translation of songs related to designs reveals the cosmic maps present in Cashinahua graphic style (Lagrou 1991, 1996, 1998, 2007). The names of motifs do not "represent" their owners, but rather lead to them. Being the language of the yuxibu, designs function as paths leading to their owners. In female initiation songs, women address the yuxibu that own the different weaving patterns, asking them to give them an eye for the design patterns they own. The agential aspect of the connection between the yuxibu and their designs is revealed by the fact that designs link different worlds of perception. Rather than functioning as a means for sociocognitive classification, they open up pathways for perceptive transformation.

Design among the Cashinahua is about "relatedness." It hints at relations, linking different worlds, as well as pointing to the interdependence of different kinds of people. It is in the quality of being a "vehicle pointing toward relatedness" that lies a design's capacity to act upon the world—upon the bodies to which designs adhere as a second skin, as well as upon the minds of those who travel in imaginary worlds during dreams or visions, where the visualization of design functions as a map, allowing men's and women's *bedu yuxin*, or "eye souls," to find the dwelling places of the yuxibu without getting lost.

The use and agency of designs in rites of passage became clear to me when I saw the difference between the facial designs used by adults and those used by the children undergoing the ritual intervention. The *nixpupima* designs (see fig. 8.2) do not differ in pattern or form from true kene kuin designs (see fig. 8.1), but they do differ in the way they are applied, as well as in the width of their painted lines. The designs painted on neophytes are called "broad designs" (*huku kene*), or "badly done designs" (*tube kene*). They are made with a maize cob or with the fingers. In contrast, the genipapo designs painted on the faces of adults are executed with a fine pencil made of a splinter from the roof. The point is wrapped in cotton so as not to scratch the skin while painting. The reason for the "broad web"—*malha grande*, as Edivaldo, head of the village

Figure 8.2. Boy with *nixpupima* facial design. *Photo*: Els Lagrou, 1995.

Moema (Alto Purus), calls it—of designs painted on the neophytes is to be found in their ritual efficacy. These designs are painted with broad lines so that propitiatory songs can enter into the bodies of the neophytes. After these songs have entered into their bodies, the neophytes will think about them and the songs will guide their thoughts. As Edivaldo explained: "The songs that are sung over his or her body, these prayers go into the body. From there they pass into the head. The child will be a great worker, a great thinker. That is why he or she is not painted black. The design is made to make the songs enter and stick."

The bodies of adults are also painted, but while the designs painted on their bodies are always larger than those painted on their faces and can equally be executed with maize cobs, these designs do not have the same intention as those painted on the initiates. According to Edivaldo, the designs painted on adults are only for adornment: "The parents are painted because of their children." Body designs work as a filter. The difference in distance between the lines has to do with the agency of designs, songs, and the medicinal baths that have to penetrate the skin. Designs emphasize the permeability of the skin to outside influences. The body can incorporate substances through its orifices, but also through its skin.

The Cashinahua, as well as the Shipibo-Conibo (Gebhart-Sayer 1984; Illius 1987) and the Piro (Gow 1988, 1999), attribute great importance to designs in visionary experiences as well as in daily life. In all of these societies, there is a gendered specialization related to designs, according to which the consumption of ayahuasca (a drug known for its potent vision-inducing effects) is considered to be a male activity, whereas the painting of designs is considered to be a female specialization (although in all three societies, exceptions are possible). Among the Cashinahua, designs are both woven in cotton textiles and basketry and painted on the body and on pottery.

Elsewhere (Lagrou, 1998, 2007), I have extensively explored the topic of how weaving designs—and, to a lesser extent, drawing designs—seems to be the Cashinahua core metaphor for thinking about how identity is made out of alterity. Like other native Amazonian peoples, the Cashinahua conceive of forming life as weaving strands together. They have elaborated a weaving technique through which the interwoveness of contrasting qualities is expressed through the use of two different colors to produce figures and counter-figures of equal visual force, producing a dynamic effect whereby the eyes cannot decide where to focus to distinguish figure from ground. Thus, figure and ground are reversible, conferring Cashinahua designs their special kinetic effect.

One could elaborate on the many resonances between this formal characteristic of style and a particular way of thinking, as suggested by Peter Roe (1982) for the Shipibo and by David Guss (1989) for the Yekuana. These authors have stressed the interplay between the visible and the invisible or, as we would say today, the transformational nature of reality found in the cosmologies of these two Amerindian peoples. The resonances between style and lived world can be extended to the way in which society is built up, according to the Cashinahua, from the combined productive capacities of women and men and of people belonging to the *inu* and *dua* moieties. Inferences from the correlations between style and society explained "in terms of synchronic ideological and cultural forces," as Gell suggests (1998), are still, however, very uncertain and ephemeral. We are immediately reminded of Franz Boas who, already at the end of the nineteenth century, was very suspicious of the correlations between form and content put forward by anthropologists eager to find meaning everywhere in remote places of the world, for they supposedly had not lost their density of meanings yet.

The correlations between style and society might be nothing but conjectures or speculations on silent forms if the people who make these forms had nothing to say on the topic. Here, we are faced once more with the importance of silence. When I spoke with Cashinahua women about the meaning of designs, they were very quiet—yet they had said much in what at the time seemed to me a very indirect way of conveying sense. Several women explained to me that designs are *habiaski*—"They are all the same! It is all one big design!" After I posed too many questions to old Maria, my protector and a woman who knew what she was talking about (since she knew the yuxin and had been treated to stop seeing them), she finished her explanations with the following comment: *Keneki yuxinin hantxaki*, "Designs are the language of yuxin."

At this point, it is interesting to remember that yuxin, and their amplification in yuxibu, are beings in search of form, always transforming into something else. They are powerful, floating images, powerful because they can cause bodies to change form and even adopt other bodies, as demonstrated in some cases of illness, getting lost in the forest, and especially death. The transformation of bodies is also at the core of Cashinahua rites of passage, in which bodies are painted, modeled, and hardened—that is, in which the future shape and strength of the initiates' bodies is being worked on. Rites of passage are concerned with the fabrication of bodies, whereas the ritual ingestion of ayahuasca has to do with temporal metamorphoses, what ritual song describes as "putting on the clothes"—that is, the bodies—of other beings, animals, and other kinds of people. Designs play an important role in both ritual contexts, a role that is different from that played by designs among the Piro in similar contexts of fabrication and metamorphosis of the bodies. Among the Piro, designs seem to either complete or announce a visual or corporeal transformation, as at the end of the ritual seclusion of pubescent girls or as a prelude in visionary experiences (Gow 1988, 1999). In contrast, among the Cashinahua, designs play a crucial and active role in the process of visual and corporeal transformation.

To understand the origin of design, it would be necessary to discuss several myths and explore several possible lines of interpretation, something that is beyond the scope of this work. Here, I will discuss only the myths of origin of design and of Boa, the owner of design. Designs were taught to a Cashinahua woman by Sidika, the spirit boa, who took the form of an old lady and taught the woman her designs through weaving.

The primordial technique said to be taught by the spirit boa was the basis for the specific stylistic characteristics of painted designs. Following the Boasian lead, Alice Dawson (1975) and Peter Gow (1988) did not allow this technical detail, namely the difference between weaving and painting as design originating techniques, to escape their attention. The labyrinthine motifs of Grecian frets and lozenges found in much Amazonian basketry are also found in Cashinahua body and facial painting. But the Cashinahua are unique for weaving these patterns into cotton textiles (see fig. 8.3).

Another version of the myth of origin of design depicts another learning setting, one marked by the intention of seduction. A young girl goes at every sunset into the forest to meet her boa lover, Yube, who appears to her in the form of a handsome young man. After making love to her, Yube transforms himself again into a boa. In such a shape, he encircles her body and teaches her, with his tongue close to her face, all the secrets about design.

This version of the myth of design's origin closely resembles the myth of male initiation into the world of images. In the latter myth, the spirit boa appears to a hunter in the form of a beautifully painted young woman. The man wants to make love to her and is taken to the water-world, where he learns to prepare and drink ayahuasca, called *dunu himi* or *dunuan isun*—that is, boa's blood or urine. When the hunter dies, out of the buried man's body grows both the ayahuasca vine and the *Psychotria viridis* bush, which provides the leaves used to prepare the ayahuasca brew. Briefly put, the spirit of the boa gave men the knowledge of preparing the hallucinogenic brew, that is, the knowledge to produce visions, while he gave women the knowledge to produce and generate design. All possible designs are said to exist virtually on the snake's skin, where one design can be transformed into another following certain rules of composition.

Mythical parallelism is corroborated by ritual parallelism: female initiation in the production of designs is equivalent to male initiation in hunting and visionary experience. Both men and women can ritually kill boas to communicate with their spirits. This ritual killing often involves consuming parts of the spirit boa: women eat the snake's eyes, whereas men eat its heart. This consubstantiation makes them similar to the boa. Severe dieting and reclusion are required for achieving success in this controlled act of predation. The killing of the snake implies the acquisition of control over the flow of blood—in hunting, in the case of men, or in menstruation, in the case of women—as well as over the flow

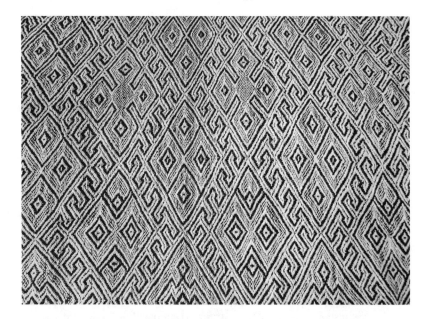

Figure 8.3. Handwoven textile. *Note*: The overall design in this piece is the *dunu kate kene* ("design of back of the boa"); its central motif is the *inu tae kene* ("jaguar's claw design"), surrounded by the *kape hina kene* ("cayman's tail"). Notice the subtle transformation of the jaguar's feet motif into a *hua kene*, a flower motif. *Photo*: Els Lagrou, 2000.

of images. An intimate relation therefore exists between these two kinds of flows: the flow of images and the flow of blood. Gow (1999) noted a similar relation among the Piro between the flow of liquids associated with the domain of female agency (menstrual blood, milk, beer) and the flow of painted design. Among the Cashinahua, the logic relating different domains and bodies is not limited to one of the genders but encompasses both. Thus, the Cashinahua revisit, in an original way, a theme that is classical in Amerindian literature—to wit, the relation between the blood of the warrior and menstrual blood.[4]

The ritual killing of the boa is both powerful and dangerous. It is surrounded with great secrecy, since what is said to the spirit boa gains a virtual existence of its own. If revealed to others, it can be turned against the one who communicated with the boa. Women negotiate with the boa to obtain an "eye for design," but certain aspects of fertility can also be controlled by means of an encounter with the boa. Thus, when applied to a prepubescent girl, the blood of a boa can prevent her from menstruating.

Men can become lucky in hunting through a pact with the spirit of the boa achieved through the boa-killing ritual. They can also, however, express their wish to cause the death of enemies. Luck in hunting is as much associated with vision as the female art of design is. The spirit boa localizes its victim, drawing it closer through its hypnotic gaze. Luck in hunting is also related to caution on the part of the hunter, who does not walk away from the forest trails. These paths, *bai*, compose the kene (design patterns). Instead of pursuing game animals, hunters must attract them, seducing them to make them come closer.[5] The power of vision acquired by women can also be used as love magic, hypnotizing men, just as the designs of the boa attracted the solitary hunter.[6]

After a Cashinahua man or woman engages in the ritual killing of a boa, sometimes *reminders* of their encounter with the spirit boa—headdresses made of snake skin, in the case of men, or a piece of the boa's skin, in the case of women—are brought back home and kept hidden or hung under the roof. These tokens, which are indexes of a past but lasting encounter that enhances the owner's subjectivity, have to remain hidden in order not to cause the anger of their original owner, the spirit boa. The headdresses kept by men are displayed during *katxanawa* fertility rituals, but the snake skins of women are always kept hidden.

The treatment of the snake skins and headdresses attest to the fact that the boa continues to live in these objects—which are relational objects. They enhance the charisma and productive capacities of those who underwent the boa-killing ritual by keeping the memory of the encounter alive while, at the same time, keeping the content of the event hidden from everybody else. Artifacts such as these hint at a person's capacity to act upon the world through productive knowledge, much in the same way that the decorated chest bands of Yanesha women refer to the accumulated life experience of their owners (see Santos-Granero, this volume), or that the amount of necklaces of the Piaroa *ruwang* makes visible his tapping of productive knowledge from sources outside the human social world (Overing 1988, 1989). A similar logic seems to be at work among the Nambikwara, who never take off their necklaces and bracelets because of the risk of soul loss (see Miller, this volume).

The relationships between artifacts and humans resemble those between humans and animals, one set of relations being the consequence of the other. In the case of the ritual killing of the boa in a forest, the intention is to talk to and later on dream with the boa's yuxin, or else to ingest parts of the boa's body to become "like the boa"—a process of consubstantiation. The snake is killed, but it does not take revenge. On the contrary, it enters the body of its killer and stays with him or her. Agosto, my old "adoptive" Cashinahua father, revealingly mentioned an alternative to the killing of the boa: "You can also keep a small one as a pet in a bottle," he said. The same basic rule holds in relationships between humans and their enemies in general. Thus the relationship between male or female human hunters and the boa is revealing.

The agency of the spirit boa manifests itself through an increase in vision. The boa passes on to humans its capacity to generate designs. In turn, design provides the framework and condition for the generation of any kind of form. This phenomenon was explained to me by Edivaldo in the following terms: "The design of the boa contains the world in itself. The spots on its skin can open themselves and show a door to enter into new forms. There are twenty-five spots on Yube's skin; they are the twenty-five designs that exist."

But is the boa really a good representative of otherness for the Cashinahua? One possible answer can be found in the myth of the great flood, which says that most human beings vanished or were transformed into something else during a devastating mythical flood. (This myth is very important in the context of our reflection on the agency of artifacts, since not only humans but also their artifacts were transformed into animals.) According to this myth, two people making love in a patterned hammock at the time of the flood were transformed into a single boa. This is also the myth of origin of humanity, for it says that only one human, Nete, survived the flood—a woman who gave birth to humanity through parthenogenesis after spitting in her own womb. Thus, the consubstantiality of humans and the great snake is already alluded to in mythic narratives. The boa was not only human, but it came into being through the combination of a man and a woman who were making love in a hammock when they were overcome by the flood. Thus, the spirit boa combines both male and female agency. However, since humanity in its actual form was produced only *after* the flood, boas and humans are really very different kinds of beings. Interaction between them entails the dangers inherent to alterity, dangers that are thought of in terms of predation—and that is why the boa is killed in the boa-killing ritual.

Duality is inherent to the figure of the spirit of the boa in Cashinahua thought. This is expressed in the boa's capacity to live both on land and in the water, to have two tongues and two penises (both the tongue and penis of the boa represent a bifurcation), and to engender twins. This duality is also present in the designs taught by the boa, as well as in their agency. Here I will concentrate on only one aspect of the agency of designs: that of seduction. It is with knowledge of the preceding myth of the couple making love in their hammock that the following statement begins to make sense: "Look!" a young Cashinahua man told me. "Do you see that all the lines have to meet? Every good design has to join the lines; there should be no loose ends. That is so because these lines mean 'making love.' They have to touch each other, like the joint of the knee."

The same themes of lines and making love are present in a love song, a song about making love on the beach, in which the movements of the couple are described in terms of "the design of the snake"—their design being their movements, as well as the traces they leave in the sand:

Nabaka debukii ee	The headwaters of the *nabaka* river
Nabaka debukii ee	The headwaters of the nabaka river
Txanabaka debuki	The headwaters of the *txanabaka* river
Badiwaka debuki	The headwaters of the *badiwaka* river
Atsa debu nakaxun	Chewing the headwaters of the sweet manioc
Mitxu mitxu xinayê	Thinking of the spitting, spitting
Nawa tete peiwen	With a feather of the harpy eagle
Aku tadun tadunma	Drumming. Tun! Tun! Tun!
Aku tadun tadunma	Drumming. Tun! Tun! Tun!
Maxi kene dunu	In the sand, patterns of the snake
Bai kene dunu	Patterns of the movements of the snake
Hawen bake buyabi	Making her child
Hawen bake buyabi	Making her child

The traces left by the couple in the sand are compared to those left by a gliding snake.

Another instance in which lines are seen as depicting movements is when the lines of a design are described as "rivers" (*duni*) or "paths" (bai). This meaning of designs is present not only in ayahuasca-induced visions, in which songs are said to paint paths in front of the neophyte's closed eyes, but also in visions altered by illness. It is for this reason that sick people should not sleep in a decorated hammock, for his or her eye soul could get lost in the labyrinth of its designs while dreaming, and could thus be taken to the other side and die (Keifenheim 1996).

Conclusions

In this chapter, I have explored the question of the agency of images, designs, and forms, whether or not they have a material expression. I have discussed the power of images in their relation to imagination—a perceptive imagination that actively constructs a possible world from percepts informed by the specific way in which the Cashinahua live their world. For the Cashinahua, however, designs and images are not the only things conceived of as possessing agency. Artifacts are also candidates for an agential status, since the materialization of images can be as much a source of power and agency as their dematerialization.

Thus it is not surprising that glass beads, associated with both the mythical Inka and white men, have a central place in initiation rituals. These beads are used to weave bracelets profusely decorated with designs. Elsewhere, I have analyzed the relation between the beads, the origin of design, and the complex interweaving of relationships inside and outside the community that these bead bracelets stand for (Lagrou 1998, 2007). These artifacts partake of the qualities that Fernando Santos-Granero (this volume) classifies as "objects originating through mimesis" insofar as they incorporate and transform the agency of materials obtained from abroad.

The logic of agency, alterity, and relatedness can also be seen at work in the fabrication of the ritual stools used by children to rest during the initiation ritual. These are sculpted, cut out of the tubular roots of a lupuna tree that is not cut down for this purpose, but rather carefully addressed in song so that it passes on to the initiates its qualities and knowledge of how to live a tranquil life. Lupuna trees, however, are as predatory as the boa and the mythical Inka. They are feared for their capacity to cause dizziness and fainting and are considered to be the home of powerful yuxin and yuxibu. The stools made out of lupuna timber will become ritually identified with the initiates through ritual bathing, which infuses each stool with a voice and, thus, with a "soul" (Lagrou 2002).

This evidence should suffice to tie the strings of my argument together. What I set out to demonstrate in this chapter is a lesson learned from Gregory Bateson (1972), namely, that art (that is, image-making in its broadest sense) is a metalinguistic or nonlinguistic statement about relatedness, about the relations between human beings and between human and nonhuman beings—the latter of whom can be seen as human if we adopt a certain perspective, such as that of native Amazonians.

In contrast to the Melanesian context, in native Amazonia, artifacts do not stand for, or substitute for, persons and relations. They are beings of their own, with agency of their own. This, however, does not negate the extremely intimate relation between persons and their personal possessions, which are destroyed in almost all native Amazonian societies after the owner's death. The process of ensoulment of objects either during the process of fabrication (see Erikson, this volume) or as the result of becoming "subjectivized through direct contact with a subject's soul" (see Santos-Granero, this volume), also holds for Cashinahua artifacts. Among the Cashinahua, however, artifacts also refer to the invisible net tying individuals to other entities, who live in or with them by means of the crystallized memory of the objects that surround them.

As suggested by Descola (2001), the priority in native Amazonian thought is not the elaboration of complex systems of exchange based on the possibility of *heterosubstitution*, as is the case in Melanesia, where pigs or bracelets can be exchanged for humans—although complex systems of exchange do exist and have certainly existed in more elaborated form before contact in lowland South America (see Barcelos Neto and Hugh-Jones, this volume). Amerindian thought systems seem to value bodily and subjective accumulation in the form of embodied knowledge—the knowledge of establishing relations—over the accumulation of relationships mediated by artifacts. This "bodily knowledge" establishes relationships anchored in a subjectivity that is constructed on the basis of being (and knowing to be) related to others (Kensinger 1995; McCallum 1996; Lagrou, 2000).

More important than the things themselves is the knowledge of how to make things. In the Cashinahua case, this is illustrated by the fact that designs are frequently interrupted in the middle of a pattern, suggesting their continuation beyond the support. Emphasis is placed upon the capacity to invoke the image in the mind. Designs are there to suggest their existence in the world, not to exhaust their being in their visualization in painted or woven designs. This attitude can be compared to that of the Pirahã, who are capable of describing all sorts of objects they know how to make—without ever materializing them (Gonçalves 2001).

Not only are artifacts individuated because they participate in the agency of their makers, they also gain an existence of their own that goes beyond the kind of individuality generated by *synecdoche*, where a part partakes in the characteristics of the whole, as proposed by Gell (1998:161–62). Ritual stools, as well as certain garden products, such as peanuts and corn, represent a new synthesis, a new being capable of acting on the world. It is in this sense that they "are like persons." Ritual stools receive the same treatment as recently harvested maize or peanuts. They are seated at the poles that sustain the house. While maize and peanuts are addressed in song as if they were persons, with their proper names, the stools have a life cycle of creation and destruction that parallels that of a person and is similar to that described by Lucia Van Velthem (2003) for the Wayana-Apalai.

In native Amazonia, object makers have a parent-child relationship with the products of their thoughts (Overing 1988). This means that they give origin to entities that have goals and destinies of their own. Children are only partly a replication of their parents' identity. They always share in other identities and thus become *unique*. It is in this sense that children are like artifacts and artifacts are like children. The songs sung to the ritual stools turn them into beings. They infuse them with a voice, with agency, and with the capacity to act and to collaborate in the production of a new being, who will be the synthesis of all combined efforts: a child who has undergone the initiation ritual and already has "thoughts of his/ her own."

This Amerindian mode of relatedness places emphasis on *incorporation*, intimately related to a lack of *accumulation* of goods (but see Erikson, Hugh-Jones, and Santos-Granero, this volume, for a distinction between exchangeable and nonexchangeable objects). Everything points toward a theory of power related to knowledge; the knowledge of how to make persons and artifacts and of how to bring strangers close enough to persuade them to collaborate. Thus, Cashinahua rituals can be regarded as an aesthetic process to bring enemies close, that is, to make predatory enemies happy enough (*benimai*) to generously give away during the ritual encounter the kind of knowledge they have notoriously refused to share in myth. This style of dealing with the enemy does not reduce subjects to predators and prey to objects. Rather, among the Cashinahua, subjects treat prey—whether animal or supernatural beings—as subjects in order to *seduce* them into collaborating with them.

Notes

1. See Els Lagrou (1998, 2007) for a more extended discussion of the role of alterity in Cashinahua image-making and the attribution of meaning to different kinds of objects.

2. For the mentioned authors, see the bibliography.

3. Eliane Camargo (2006) shows how, among the Cashinahua, pets receive a diffent morphological treatment than wild animals do, and are thus assimilated to the category of "humans."

4. For examples of this, see Bruce Albert (1985), Beth Conklin (2001), and an extensive comparative study of this theme among native Amazonian peoples by Luisa E. Belaunde (2005). For a discussion of the theme outside the Amerindian context, see Françoise Héritier (1996).

5. For hunting techniques, see Patrick Deshayes (1992) and Kenneth Kensinger (1995).

6. Among their Culina neighbors, the Cashinahua are famous for their love magic, which is capable of killing someone if the victim is not properly healed by a Pano specialist. Ayahuasca specialists are considered to be responsible both for the love magic and its cure (Pollock 2004:210).

References

Albert, Bruce. 1985. Temps du sang, temps des cendres (Yanomami). Doctoral thesis, Université de Paris X-Nanterre.

Bateson, Gregory. 1972. *Steps to an Ecology of Mind*. New York: Ballantine Books.

Belaunde, Luisa E. 2005. *El recuerdo de Luna: Género, sangre y memoria entre los pueblos amazónicos*. Lima: Centro Amazónico de Antropología y Aplicación Práctica.

Camargo, Eliane. 2006. Animate/Inanimate in Cashinahua (Huni Kuin) Grammar and Sociability. (unpublished ms.)

Carneiro da Cunha, Manuela. 1978. *Os mortos e os outros*. São Paulo: Hucitec.

Clastres, Pierre. 1974. *La société contre l'État*. Paris: Les Éditions de Minuit.

Conklin, Beth. 2001. Women's Blood, Warrior's Blood, and the Conquest of Vitality in Amazonia. In Thomas Gregor and Donald Tuzin (eds.), *Gender in Amazonia and Melanesia: An Exploration of the Comparative Method*, pp. 141–74. Berkeley: University of California Press.

Dawson, Alice. 1975. Graphic Art and Design of the Cashinahua. In Jane P. Dwyer (ed.), *The Cashinahua of Eastern Peru*, pp. 131–49. Philadelphia: Haffenreffer Museum of Anthropology.

Descola, Philippe. 2001. The Genres of Gender: Local Models and Global Paradigms in the Comparison of Amazonia and Melanesia. In Thomas Gregor and

Donald Tuzin (eds.), *Gender in Melanesia and Amazonia: An Exploration of the Comparative Method*, pp. 91–114. Berkeley: University of California Press.

Deshayes, Patrick. 1992. Paroles chassées: Chamanisme et chefferie chez les Kashinawa. *Journal de la Société des Américanistes* 78(2): 95–106.

Erikson, Philippe. 1984. De l'apprivoisement à l'approvisionnement: Chasse, alliance et familiarisation en Amazonie amérindienne. *Techniques et Cultures* 9:105–40.

Fausto, Carlos. 1999. Of Enemies and Pets: Warfare and Shamanism in Amazonia. *American Ethnologist* 26(4): 933–56.

Freedberg, David. 1989. *The Power of Images*. Chicago and London: Chicago University Press.

Gebhart-Sayer, Angelika. 1984. *The Cosmos Encoiled: Indian Art of the Peruvian Amazon*. New York: Center for Inter-American Relations.

Gell, Alfred. 1998. *Art and Agency: An Anthropological Theory*. Oxford: Clarendon Press.

Gonçalves, Marco Antonio. 2001. *O mundo inacabado: Ação e criação em uma cosmologia amazônica*. Rio de Janeiro: Editora Universidade Federal do Rio de Janeiro.

Gow, Peter. 1988. Visual Compulsion: Design and Image in Western Amazonian Art. *Revindi* 2:19–32. (Budapest)

———. 1999. Piro Designs: Painting as Meaningful Action in an Amazonian Lived World. *Journal of the Royal Anthropological Institute* 5:229–46.

Guss, David. 1989. *To Weave and Sing: Art, Symbol, and Narrative in the South American Rain Forest*. Berkeley: University of California Press.

Héritier, Françoise. 1996. *Masculin/Féminin*. Paris: Éditions Odile Jacob.

Hugh-Jones, Stephen. 2001. The Gender of Some Amazonian Gifts. In Thomas Gregor and Donald Tuzin (eds.), *Gender in Amazonia and Melanesia: An Exploration of the Comparative Method*, pp. 245–78. Berkeley: University of California Press.

Illius, Bruno. 1987. Ani Shinan: Schamanismus bei den Shipibo-Conibo (Ost-Peru). Doctoral thesis, Tübingen: Verlag S and F.

Keifenheim, Barbara. 1996. Snake Spirit and Pattern Art: Ornamental Visual Experience among the Cashinahua Indians of Eastern Peru. (unpublished ms.)

Kensinger, Kenneth. 1995. *How Real People Ought to Live: The Cashinahua of Eastern Peru*. Prospect Heights, IL: Waveland Press.

Lagrou, Els M. 1991. *Uma etnografia da cultura Kaxinawá: Entre a cobra e o Inca*. Master's thesis, Universidade Federal de Santa Catarina.

———. 1996. Xamanismo e representação entre os Kaxinawá. In E. Jean Langdon (ed.), *Xamanismo no Brasil*, pp. 197–231. Florianópolis: Editora Universidade Federal de Santa Catarina.

———. 1998. Cashinahua Cosmovision: A Perspectival Approach to Identity and Alterity. PhD dissertation, University of St. Andrews.

———. 2000. Homesickness and the Cashinahua Self: A Reflection on the Embodied Condition of Relatedness. In Joanna Overing and Alan Passes (eds.), *The Anthropology of Love and Anger: The Aesthetics of Conviviality in Native Amazonia*, pp. 152–69. London: Routledge.

———. 2002. Kenan, the Ritual Stool: A Reduced Model of the Cashinahua Person during the Nixpupima Rite of Passage. In Thomas Myers and M. S. Cipolletti (eds), Artifacts and Society in Amazonia. *Bonner Amerikanische Studien* 36:95–113.

———. 2007. *A fluidez da forma: Arte, alteridade e agência em uma sociedade amazônica (Kaxinawa, Acre)*. Rio de Janeiro: Topbooks.

Lévi-Strauss, Claude. 1991. *Histoire de Lynx*. Paris: Plon.

McCallum, Cecilia. 1996. The Body that Knows: From Cashinahua Epistemology to a Medical Anthropology of Lowland South America. *Medical Anthropology Quarterly* 10(3): 347–72.

———. 2002. *Gender and Sociality in Amazonia: How Real People Are Made*. Oxford and New York: Berg.

Mentore, George. 2004. The Glorious Tyranny of Silence and the Resonance of Shamanic Breath. In Neil Whitehead and Robin Wright (eds.), *In Darkness and Secrecy: The Anthropology of Assault Sorcery and Witchcraft in Amazonia*, pp. 132–56. Durham: Duke University Press.

Overing, Joanna. 1986. Images of Cannibalism, Death and Domination in a "Non-Violent" Society. *Journal de la Société des Américanistes* 72:133–56.

———. 1988. Personal Autonomy and the Domestication of Self in Piaroa Society. In Gustav Jahoda and Ioan M. Lewis (eds.), *Acquiring Cultures: Cross-Cultural Studies in Child Development*, pp. 169–92. London: Croom Helm.

———. 1989. The Aesthetics of Production: The Sense of Community among the Cubeo and Piaroa. *Dialectical Anthropology* 14:159–75. Portuguese version printed in 1991. A estética da produção: O senso da comunidade entre os Cubeo e os Piaroa. *Revista de Antropologia* 34:7–33.

Pollock, Donald. 2004. Siblings and Sorcerers: The Paradox of Kinship among the Kulina. In Neil Whitehead and Robin Wright (eds.), *In Darkness and Secrecy: The Anthropology of Assault Sorcery and Witchcraft in Amazonia*, pp. 202–14. Durham: Duke University Press.

Roe, Peter G. 1982. *The Cosmic Zygote: Cosmology in the Amazon Basin*. Rutgers: State University of New Jersey Press.

Severi, Carlo. 2003. Warburg anthropologue ou le déchiffrement d'une utopie. *L'Homme* 165:77–128.

Taussig, Michael. 1993. *Mimesis and Alterity: A Particular History of the Senses*. New York: Routledge.

Taylor, Anne-Christine. 2003. Les masques de la mémoire. Essai sur la fonction des peintures corporelles jivaro. *L'Homme* 165:223–48.

Van Velthem, Lucia. 2003. *O belo é a fera: A estética da produção e da predação entre os Wayana*. Lisboa: Assírio and Alvim / Museu Nacional de Etnologia.

Viveiros de Castro, Eduardo. 1986. *Os Araweté, os deuses canibais*. Rio de Janeiro: Zahar and Anpocs.

———. 2004. Exchanging Perspectives: The Transformation of Objects into Subjects in Amerindian Ontologies. *Common Knowledge* 10(3): 463–84.

9

Identity Cards, Abducted Footprints, and the Book of San Gonzalo

The Power of Textual Objects in Runa Worldview

María A. Guzmán-Gallegos

This chapter discusses the role particular textual objects play in the constitution and de-constitution of persons and bodies among the Amazonian
Runa of Ecuador.[1] Runa people consider that certain textual objects central
to their experience with the white-mestizo world, such as identification
and identity cards, are capable of affecting their bodies, as well as their subjectivity and agency. My analysis relates to two theoretical approaches. The
first deals with native Amazonian ideas of the body. Recent ethnographical
contributions have suggested that native Amazonians conceive of the body
as the locus of sociality. This notion derives from the Amerindian idea that
the human body is not naturally given, but is rather the result of kinship
relations and particular acts of caring (Belaunde 1992; De Mattos Viegas
2003; Guzmán-Gallegos 1997; McCallum 2001). Perspectivist authors connect these Amerindian ideas about the body to notions of subjectivity,
intentionality, and agency that, they suggest, relate mainly to the possession
of a soul (Vilaça 2002, 2005; Viveiros de Castro 1998). Furthermore, they
connect native perceptions of the soul with ideas of otherness, perceptions
about nonhuman beings (especially animals and spirits), and notions of
affinity (Viveiros de Castro 2001; Rival 2005). Thus, though in different
ways, these authors' works focus on the significance of consanguineal and
affinal relations in Amazonian understandings and constructions of the
body and subjectivity. By analyzing modes of conceiving the deconstitution
of the body among the Amazonian Runa, I attempt to widen this focus to
account for the importance the Amazonian Runa attribute to other types of
social relations, which they do not conceptualize either in terms of consanguinity or in terms of affinity. Here, I am concerned with the Amazonian

Runa's relations to both shamans and non-Indians. I seek also to broaden the discussion of native Amazonian notions of subjectivity and agency by highlighting the connections Amazonian Runa establish between human subjectivity and their theories of materiality, which conceive of objects as having varying degrees of subjectivity and agency.

The second theoretical approach to which this chapter relates focuses on local understandings of textual objects. As Peter Gow (1990) has rightly observed, this approach has been largely absent in the ethnography of native Amazonian societies, despite the importance of texts in missionary and governmental practices. The lack of interest in this approach might be related, as Stephen Hugh-Jones (this volume) has pointed out, to the inbuilt tendency to downplay the importance that manmade objects have for native Amazonians in theoretical interpretations of Amerindian notions about the body. This tendency—which Hugh-Jones attributes to the prominence that the notion of "nature" has in Euro-American constructions of Amazonia and its inhabitants—results, I would add, in many ethnographers ascribing less significance than they might have to asymmetrical relations and other configurations of power associated with the state and the Catholic Church.

Scholars studying textual objects in other Amerindian contexts have proposed that texts are often understood as potent, performative objects, and also as repositories of power that in and of themselves can produce reality and shape the outcome of social processes (see e.g., Gordillo 2006). They propose that these understandings are the result of colonial experiences in which texts in general have been related to violence and marginalization (Gordillo 2006; Lienhard 1991; Rappaport 1990, 1994; Wogan 1994, 2004).

The objects this chapter focuses on are identification cards and identity cards. In Ecuador, identification cards are issued by the Ministry of Social Welfare. They certify that a particular person is a member of a legal, recognized association. These cards display the person's name, surnames, and document number. In contrast, identity cards are issued to all Ecuadorian citizens—at least in principle—by the Civil Registry. These cards also display the person's name, surnames, and document number. In addition, they include a photograph. Both identification and identity cards are codified, written texts. Here, I will argue that the importance the Runa attribute to these cards is informed by the experiences they have had with the local administration, the haciendas, and the Catholic Church, as well as with various registration and documentation practices. In this regard, these cards are closely associated with particular constellations of power.

I suggest, however, that Runa understandings of these identity documents are also mediated by specific belief configurations and ontological assumptions. These configurations and assumptions relate to notions of the body and human subjectivity as being in a permanent process of construction. They relate, as well, to the idea that objects have different degrees and types of subjectivity and agency. As Fernando Santos-Granero and Harry Walker (this volume) point out for the Yanesha and the Urarina respectively, the Amazonian Runa consider that not all objects are endowed with subjectivity and not all subjectivized objects possess the same degree or type of animacy and agency. Moreover, in the Runa context, subjectivity does not necessarily suppose the presence of a soul, while not all agency presupposes will and intentionality. Inspired by Gow's (1990, 2003) analysis of Piro perceptions of European writing, I explore how identity and identification cards relate to notions of subjectivity and agency that are manifested in Runa shamanistic paradigms. Central to these paradigms are the transformations that allow shamans to see realities and beings that are otherwise occult. This capacity for "seeing" presupposes and reveals various and distinct corporeal transformations. Some of them occur within the body of the person affected by shamanic attacks that can result in the deconstitution of a person's body and of his/ her subjectivity. In these transformations, to paraphrase Santos-Granero's observations (this volume), objects can initiate a process that can affect the physical condition or the location of another entity.

Situating the Amazonian Runa

The Amazonian Runa, or Amazonian Kichwa as they also call themselves, number more than sixty thousand persons. Although Amazonian Runa communities share important cultural and social features that allow for their characterization as both Amazonian and Runa, there are, and have always been, important differences among them. One of the most significant differences is their varied experiences with the mestizo population and, more particularly, with the haciendas and the debt peonage system. In later times, they have also had different exposure to the process of colonization of Ecuadorian Amazonia. From my point of view, the linkages between identification cards, identity cards, and shamanism must be seen in relation to these experiences.

Figure 9.1. Mariano and Carmelina telling about the history of their place and of the villages around San Miguel. *Photo*: Maria A. Guzmán-Gallegos, 2003.

The Runa whose stories about identity documents and stolen footprints I discuss in this chapter live in a community that I shall call San Miguel.[2] A small village of about 350 people, San Miguel is situated on the borderlands between the Pastaza and Napo provinces. Since the 1960s, it has been surrounded by colonies (*colonias*) inhabited by white-mestizo and highland Kichwa peasants, many of whom are originally from Tungurahua and Chimborazo, two central Andean provinces. The people from San Miguel, as well as the Amazonian Runa that live in other communities close by, identify themselves as Napo Runa and trace their origins to Archidona and Tena, two of the first towns founded in the region by the Spanish conquistadores in the sixteenth century (see fig. 9.1).

According to oral histories, San Miguel was founded by two families who migrated from Archidona and Tena while fleeing from an epidemic that struck the region, as well as from white-mestizo patrons to whom they were indebted. Moving in search of unoccupied lands and goods provided by the owners of local haciendas, the immigrant Runa families settled on the outskirts of these haciendas. Shortly after, they incurred new debts with the local hacienda owners with whom they exchanged gold and pita for highly appreciated goods such as machetes and gunpowder. Around

1938, this area was affected by another epidemic and many of the indebted Runa ran away again. In 1955, the Catholic order of the Redentoristas acquired two haciendas in which the returning Runa worked. They were paid in a variety of goods (Alvarado 2001).

Fleeing from debts and asymmetrical relations with white-mestizo patrons as well as entering into new debt relations were common events in the past lives of the inhabitants of San Miguel. Although working for the hacienda owners allowed the Runa to obtain valued goods, being in debt (*diwuiyashca*) was regarded as being highly constrained. Debt limited their ability to move about freely whenever they liked to. But getting rid of debts was considered to be something almost impossible. Furthermore, the Amazonian Runa thought that the payments they were obliged to make in order to cancel their debts were unfairly high. Hence, to pay them was seen as an unfavorable exchange, resulting in a profoundly unjust appropriation of what the Runa had produced through their own efforts. Indebtedness, which required Runa people to work constantly for others, also limited their capacity to produce for their own kin.

Experiences of indebtedness and debt peonage were always mediated and materialized by certain artifacts, namely the books in which the names and surnames of debtors, as well as the amounts they owed, were registered. These books were part of an even wider experience with texts and writing. The Runa of San Miguel, as well as the Napo Runa in general, have for a long time been aware of the crucial importance of textual objects in the regional system of interethnic power relations. They share this experience with other Latin American indigenous peoples (see Gordillo 2006; Rappaport 1990, 1994). The appropriation of Runa labor and time has been historically enacted through a variety of written devices such as registration books, orders issued by local authorities, written demands from hacienda owners, and national laws.

In the case of the Napo Runa of Archidona and Tena, familiarity with literacy has also been related to the acquisition of writing and reading abilities since the turn of the nineteenth century, when Jesuit missionaries established boarding schools for indigenous children as part of the missionaries' "civilizing" project. In the following decades, various missions opened and ran schools for boys and girls. The attitude of Runa people toward literacy has been ambivalent. On one hand, they were suspicious of the possible disempowerment entailed by the acquisition of literacy. They feared that learning to read and write would hinder children from learning Runa ways of life. Furthermore, they were afraid that the ability to read and write would pave the way for children to become servants of local patrons and for young men to be recruited by the military and sent to war (see also Muratorio 1987). On the other hand, Runa people considered acquiring writing and reading abilities extremely important—and they still do. Indeed, in the past thirty years, the Runa and the indigenous organizations they support have constantly demanded from the Ecuadorian state the building and financing of schools in their villages. Like other indigenous peoples, the Runa believe that through learning to read and write, they will be able to defend themselves and resist exploitation (Gow 1990, Rubinstein 2007, Veber 1998). Runa people believe as well that by knowing how to read and write, they will gain access to central devices of power such as textual objects, through which they can demand recognition of their ways of life, power, and knowledge configurations. In so doing, they seek to reverse the asymmetries that often characterize their relations with white-mestizo persons and institutions.

The ambiguity attached to literacy as both disempowering and empowering constitutes, in my view, an important background for the role that identification and identity cards have for Runa people. Although both types of identity documents are relatively new in San Miguel as registration devices, the Runa consider their possession and appropriation important. For them, as for other indigenous peoples in Ecuador, the issuing of identification cards by the Ministry of Welfare to shamans who are members of a legal association is evidence of state recognition of indigenous knowledge, as well as of the role shamans have both in practicing this knowledge and in the lives of Runa people. The Runa of San Miguel consider such recognition to be the result of the demands and struggles of their organizations.

In contrast to identification cards, which are issued only to some persons, identity cards are obligatory registration devices that all Ecuadorian citizens must obtain after reaching the age of eighteen. An important indigenous demand regarding identity cards has been that the Civil Registry allow the registration of indigenous names, something that was not possible until the 1980s. Although elderly Runa persons living in distant communities often do not have identity cards, nowadays the vast majority of Runa do possess them. Identity cards indeed are widely used and are important in many ways in the daily life of Runa people. They are necessary in order to register a newborn child in the Civil Registry, to enroll a child in school, to get any job paid by the local administration or in the oil companies, and to receive a state poverty bonus. As the Amazonian provinces are under special security regulations, all persons traveling throughout the region must have an identity card (or a passport), which they are required to show at every military post. Identity cards also enable Runa people to obtain small credits from local shopkeepers, who may register Runa people's debts by noting their identity card numbers.

In this chapter, I suggest that the multiple connections between literacy and textual objects—as registration devices on the one hand, and as used for the exercise of power in interethnic relations on the other hand—also inform the role played in shamanistic attacks through the manipulation of identification and identity cards. I propose, moreover, that Runa notions and practices of power and particular interethnic power configurations are expressed and confronted through these documents. As we shall see, shamanistic power, which has bodily effects, is constituted and exercised through significant objects to which Runa people attribute various degrees of subjectivity and agency. This is the case with identity documents, as becomes clear from Manuel's story about his mother's illness, which I discuss below. Considered to possess a certain degree of subjectivity and agency, identity documents are often related to the inhibition of a person's bodily capacities, which the Runa conceive of as being closely linked to a person's subjectivity and his or her capacity to comply with the obligations of significant social relations, such as those that people have with respect to their kin.

The integration of identification and identity cards in shamanistic attacks is in itself a subversive act that places and reinterprets state and church constellations of power within shamanistic paradigms. In this sense, the significance of identity documents shows, as Norman E. Whitten Jr. (1985) suggests, a duality of power patterning through which the Runa appropriate and transform power emanating from outside through local systems of meaning. At the same time, the use of these cards confirms the involvement of the Runa in asymmetrical interethnic power relations. The Runa of San Miguel experience this asymmetry as problematic. They believe that to counteract it, they must obtain control over certain domains associated with white-mestizo institutions—a task that is both desirable and difficult.

Manuel's Story: The Abducted Footprint

I first heard about abducted footprints, shamans' identification cards, and the registration of a person's identity card in San Gonzalo's book in the house of my Runa friend Beatriz. One day, at dawn, Beatriz, her daughter

Elvira, her nephew Manuel, and I were sitting in silence drinking guayusa tea and listening to the radio. The radio channel was broadcasting from Tena greetings, local news, and ads about different doctors, magicians, and a saint called San Gonzalo. Beatriz broke our silence and started complaining about one of San Miguel's three shamans. He was considered a *millai yachac*, or "mean shaman," who spent his time harming people. Elvira replied that someone should take away his shamanic stone to put an end to his evil acts. During our conversation, Manuel started telling us about his mother's illness. She had been sick for almost three years and was seriously weak. She had a constant fever and her legs and feet hurt so much that she was unable to walk. She could not take care of her garden and could not even benefit from the two community development projects that provided people with fish and a little cash. Thus, she and her husband did not have enough food to eat or enough manioc beer to drink. When people visited them, they could not receive their visitors properly. It was as if all of Manuel's mother's force and will had vanished.

Manuel asserted that she, her husband, and her children had visited several shamans over the years in search of a cure. Finally, he said, they visited a shaman who was a member of the Tena Association of Shamans. To find out what was making her ill, the shaman drank ayahuasca (*Banisteriopsis caapi*). In his visions, he saw that someone had taken away (*japishca*) Manuel's mother's footprint and left it in the house of San Gonzalo, in the outskirts of Ambato, the capital of the Andean province of Tungurahua. The shaman could not say who had bewitched his mother, but Manuel assumed that the culprits were members of the community who out of envy of his family had paid another shaman to harm her.

Manuel arranged to travel to Ambato with the consulted shaman in order to retrieve his mother's footprint. According to Manuel, it was very hard to find San Gonzalo's house. They walked for many hours along unfamiliar streets. When they finally arrived at the saint's house, the place turned out to be a large, imposing building with a shining façade. The lady who opened the door was very beautiful. She was dressed in striking clothes and was nicely made up. She was San Gonzalo's owner (*paipak duiñu*). When the owner saw them, she asked which one of them was the shaman. The shaman said: "I am. I am the one who saw. Here is my card. I am the owner of the card. I am part of the ministerial agreement." When he showed his identification card, on which his name and card number were written, she let them in and led them to a waiting room where she invited them to sit down. From there, they could see two other rooms. In one, there was a bookshelf containing thick and heavy books; in the other, the walls were painted black, and there were hundreds of lit candles.

While sitting in the waiting room, Manuel explained to the owner of San Gonzalo that his family was poor. He said that his mother was not even old, and he begged the woman to help cure her. The lady listened to him carefully. Then she went to the room containing the bookshelf. She came back with an old, thick book that she handed over to them. The book had lined sheets similar to those belonging to the Civil Registry. On each line, there were the names, surnames, and identity card numbers of both Napo Runa and Andean people. In a column on the right-hand side, different amounts of money were listed. According to Manuel, it was then that he understood that San Gonzalo and his owner had taken the identity cards of the people who appeared in the book. Parts of the lines on the pages had been torn and taken away. Sometimes, the missing bit of a page had included a digit of a person's identity card number; sometimes, it had included a letter of the person's name. After reading many pages, Manuel finally found his mother's name. Next to her name and identity card number he read the sum of 1,200 USD.

The shaman asked the owner of San Gonzalo what they could do in order to retrieve his mother's footprint. She replied that they had to pay the sum indicated in the book. Then she invited them to enter the room lit by candles. On each candle was written the name of one of the persons registered in the book. Two days a week, a mass was performed in order to make each person become weaker and weaker until she or he died. Manuel said, desperately, that he had only 100 USD. The owner of San Gonzalo said that such a small amount of money would only be enough to stop performing the masses. Manuel answered, quite upset, that this was a ripoff. Since he did not have the required amount of money to liberate his mother, he simply left.

Bodies and Objects

Manuel's story caught my attention because, as other similar stories did, it seemed to condense Runa notions of corporality and subjectivity, as well as common ideas about processes of bodily deconstitution. Shamans play an important role in such processes due to the powers they derive from their relationship with a host of spiritual beings. In Manuel's story, however, a Catholic saint, and certain textual objects—the shaman's identification card and the victim's identity card, all of which are associated with the mestizo world—also play a particularly important role.

Manuel's description of his mother's illness follows a familiar pattern. When a person is the victim of a shamanic attack, her body, called *aicha* in Kichwa, is reported to deteriorate gradually. The person's vital force disappears, inhibiting her capacity to walk, work, and reproduce, as well as her ability to act in socially appropriate ways. For the Runa, as for other native Amazonians, the body, a product of arduous work and loving care, contains the *samai*. "Samai" can be translated as "breath," "vital force," and/or "will." A person's body and her samai should be strengthened in the course of her life (Whitten 1976; Guzmán-Gallegos 1997; Uzendoski 2004).

People may receive samai from their parents, other kin, or a shaman. Through receiving another person's vital force, one's own samai becomes stronger. The strength of a person is related to the strength of both her aicha and her samai in close interaction. A strong person—a *sinzhi* woman or man—is capable of caring for his or her people, and thus maintaining a proper home. A person's body, vital force, and will are the result of various relations and are thus gradually constructed. This view implies, however, that a person is a fragile, unstable being who can be deprived of her life, subjectivity, and agency. Indeed, in the same way in which a person's body and samai are carefully built up, they can also disintegrate. This happens when a person's samai is weakened, as when a shaman either shoots the victim with darts or abducts her footprints, causing her to become ill. In either case, the victim becomes gradually weaker, losing her will and her capacity to care for others. This marks the beginning of the transformation of the person's body, subjectivity, and agency, culminating in her social and physical death. The shaman has the power to bring about such a transformation thanks to his capacity to enter into the world of powerful spiritual beings; it is a capacity that, as we shall see later, also implies the possibility of self-transformation.

This capacity is derived from the relationships that shamans establish with particular spirits, *supay*, either as owner (*duiñu* or *amu*, which come from the Spanish words *dueño* and *amo*, respectively) or as acquaintance, ally, or spouse. The establishment of these relationships, which entails the acquisition of certain extraordinary powers, takes place during the process of shamanic apprenticeship. Among the San Miguel Runa, as among other Amazonian Runa (Muratorio 1987; Whitten 1976, 1985), songs (*taquina*), darts (*birutis*), and stones (*rumi*) are the most frequently mentioned manifestations of shamanic power. The taquina are unique to each shaman; they are said to carry with them the shaman's samai. They also constitute an expression of the strength of his samai.

When the shaman initiates a journey to the worlds of powerful spiritual beings after drinking ayahuasca, songs become extremely important. While he travels through the forest and along rivers, his vision is transformed. He sings as well as sees and talks to powerful beings such as the owners of certain places, including lakes and mountains. He sees them as human beings with whom he can establish close relations. He can enter into exchange relations with them by paying them with spiritual money—*supay kullki*—or by marrying a *supai huarmi*, usually an anaconda that appears as a beautiful woman with long black hair, her face decorated with delicate black designs. The establishment of such relations implies that the shaman is transformed, and he begins seeing the world as these powerful beings do. The worlds they inhabit are usually described as places of wealth and abundance, either as cities with beautiful houses and cars or as forests teeming with animals (see also Kohn 2002).

The birutis are described as sharp, pointed objects, such as blowgun darts, jackknives, or injection needles. When asked about the birutis, people in San Miguel relate them to a person's envy and anger, which sets off a wish to harm. The person in question can be either the shaman himself, whose power is manifested in the birutis, or another person who has paid the shaman to attack the victim. As Gow (2003:149) has aptly suggested in his interpretation of Piro shamanism, the birutis are thwarted desires most often transformed through a shaman's will into harmful objects. Once inside the victim's body, they cause it to decay.

Rumi are powerful stones that a person—generally a shamanic apprentice—finds along a forest trail or a river.[3] It is said that shamans always carry their shamanic stones with them when performing a curing session or when inflicting illness and death. For this reason, shamanic stones are of great concern to the people of San Miguel. In the literature about the Amazonian Runa, shamanic stones have been described as containing spirits or souls that are both liberated and commanded by a shaman. They have also been depicted as soldiers who protect the shaman (Muratorio 1987; Whitten 1976, 1985). In San Miguel, shamanic stones are commonly described as crucial helpers and powerful agents. People argue that these stones have agency and that, in curing or bewitching, it is not the shaman but his stone that acts. Indeed, according to this view, shamanic stones not only have their own agency but also make possible a person's shamanic agency. When a shaman is punished for abusing his power, he is deprived of his shamanic stones. Such millai yachac, "angry/ aggressive/mad shamans," can be whipped publicly or have their eyes rubbed with red pepper; their stones can be boiled in hot water for many hours, causing them to die. These acts diminish a mad shaman's powers considerably, until the powers finally fade away. Shamanic stones are such an important element of a Runa shaman's paraphernalia that the people in San Miguel, and in the whole Tena-Archidona zone, have asked the public local authorities to confiscate and destroy the stones of shamans believed to be sorcerers (see Muratorio 1987).

In order to grasp the role that identity documents play in Manuel's story, I will focus specially on Runa understandings of shamanic darts (biruti) and stones (rumi). I suggest that the Runa of San Miguel ascribe to these objects different types of subjectivity and degrees of agency, attributes that are closely related to their status as particularly power- ful transformational objects and, as Santos-Granero points out in the introduction to this volume, to their varying communicational skills. Birutis, which materialize harmful feelings and desires, can be seen as an inversion of another transformative process through which desirable qualities ascribed to an object, such as the chonta palm, are transmitted and become part of the strength and skills of a person's body.

The objects that transmit desirable qualities and capacities and strengthen a person's body and subjectivity—as well as those that are transformations of bad or thwarted feelings, such as shamanic darts—are not conceived of by the Runa of San Miguel as possessing a soul, vitality, or self-will. They are, however, considered to be subjectivized or personal- ized objects in the sense that they relate in different ways to a person's vitality, breath, and will. Borrowing Alfred Gell's (1998) words, I suggest that we can view subjectivized objects as "secondary agents" in the sense that they contribute to the constitution of a person's identity, either as a strong woman or as a shaman.[4]

In contrast, Runa people assert that shamanic stones are endowed with subjectivity and agency of their own. They are considered to be alive and able to communicate with the shamans that posses them. Ownership of such stones does not imply the possibility of either controlling the stones' acts or of taming them, as seems to be the case with the Urarina *egaando* discussed by Walker (this volume). Rather, being the owner (duiñu or amu) of a stone entails the establishment of a collaborative relation, a relation of companionship or friendship, as it were, between the stone and its owner. The relationship between the shaman and the stone is one of mutual dependency. When a shamanic apprentice finds a stone, its supay is liberated and the shaman can command it. At the same time, the Runa consider that the stone's supay can act of its own free will. The stone does not only protect and help the shaman, it can also inflict harm. In such cases, the stone's subjectivity and agency replace those of its owner and the relation of companionship and collaboration is transformed into one of possession, through which the shaman's subjectivity as a common human being—as a Runa—becomes blurred.

How, then, does the shaman's spirit connections and possession of powerful objects relate to the illness of Manuel's mother, her identity card, and the curing shaman's identification card? These cards are, as we shall see, related to a person's vitality and agency, as well as to the shaman's capacity to act as such. In this sense, they are similar to shamanic darts and stones. They communicate the capacities of those who possess them. In addition, they are textual objects produced within the white-mestizo realm that insert Runa people into power constellations that have been marked by lasting ethnic asymmetries. Let me now take a closer look at San Gonzalo, his white-mestizo duiñu, and the journey that Manuel and the shaman undertook to visit the saint.

Footprints, Textual Objects, and Saints

San Gonzalo is a famous saint who is known not only in Tena, San Miguel, and the neighboring Runa communities, but also in the Salasaca indigenous communities and among the poor white-mestizo farmers of the province of Tungurahua. Peter Wogan (2004:27–29), who has worked among the Salasaca, describes San Gonzalo as the patron saint of the Church of the Holy Medal in Ambato, where he is represented in a life-size statue. Unlike other saints, he has a frightening appearance, his statue showing a sword stabbed into the back of his neck and blood dripping from his ears and nose. To gain access to San Gonzalo's power, those who want to inflict harm on somebody—or those who have been affected by the saint—visit the house of a white-mestizo family who is not associated with the church. According to Wogan, this family owns a smaller replica of the church's statue of the saint, as well as registration books in which the names of those affected by San Gonzalo's harmful actions are written.

San Gonzalo, the mestizo intermediaries, and their books constitute a significant and widely acknowledged power configuration in the region. In the stories commonly told in San Miguel and in the surrounding communities, this configuration is, however, redefined according to Runa shamanic notions of power. Little attention is given in these narratives to the saint himself or to the church in which his image is kept. These are hardly mentioned. The focus is mostly upon the person who is known to be the saint's duiñu or owner, as well as that person's house. It was this house that Manuel and the curing shaman were searching for when they began their journey. As my earlier descriptions have shown, Manuel portrayed the house as a lavish building with shining outer walls, access to which was extremely difficult, and he depicted the saint's owner as an extremely beautiful woman. This description presents a stark contrast to Wogan's (2004) depiction; Wogan asserts that the saint's image is kept in a little shop in a working-class neighborhood and is taken care of by two middle-aged women—not by one beautiful woman, as in Manuel's description.

Manuel's emphasis on the wealth of the saint's house and the beauty of its owner is reminiscent of the descriptions of the wealth of the spiritual worlds that shamans and other Runa describe visiting after drinking ayahuasca, as well as the beauty of the spirit women who inhabit these worlds. In addition, the relationship of ownership between the beautiful lady and the saint recalls the relationship between shamans and their supay. It is as the saint's owner that the beautiful lady opened the door of her house and invited Manuel and the shaman to come in, thus making San Gonzalo's world accessible to them. San Gonzalo, however, is strikingly absent in Manuel's story; he does not mention seeing a statue of the saint. Instead, his attention is focused on the saint's beautiful owner. I suggest that this is so because, in Manuel's eyes, it is the owner of the saint who concentrates the saint's power. In line with Runa understandings of the relationship between shamans and supay, Manuel seems to consider the beautiful owner of San Gonzalo as personifying or manifesting the relation with the saint. This is, as it were, a state of identification in the sense that the owner acts as San Gonzalo, killing or not killing the victim at whim.

In order to have access to San Gonzalo's world, one has to comply with some requirements. According to Manuel's story, the lady asked the shaman who accompanied him to identify himself. Using the same expressions employed by shamans when taking ayahuasca and both seeing the spirits and seeing *as* spirits, the shaman answers to San Gonzalo's duiñu that he is the one "who has seen" the abduction of the footprints. He immediately associates his capacity to see as a Runa shaman with his position as the owner of an identification card. The origin of the card is clearly stated, as well: it is the product of a "ministerial agreement." As Manuel explained to me later, without this card, they would not have been able to enter San Gonzalo's house. It was because of the card that the saint's owner invited them in.

The importance attributed to the identification card is suggestive. The card becomes a potent textual object whose possession is necessary both for the acknowledgment of the shaman's role and for the revelation of San Gonzalo's world to the shaman and Manuel. The efficacy of the identification card is explicitly credited to the agreement, via the Ministry of Social Welfare, between the Tena Association of Shamans and the state. In his analysis of identity documents in the Chaco region, Gastón Gordillo (2006) conceptualizes the potency and power ascribed to these documents in terms of fetishism. He suggests that the power attributed to identity papers in Chaco is conceived of as a quality granted by the state that, when incorporated into the object, acquires a force and value of its own (Gordillo 2006:164). Thus, he claims, the social relations that create the value of the object are absorbed into its materiality, becoming thereby blurred. As a result, it is the object rather than the social relations that is considered to be able to influence the outcome of a process or sequence of actions.

In the case of identification cards among the San Miguel Runa, I would contend that something else is at play. In this context, identification cards are seen as an explicit materialization of specific social relations: first, those among shamans belonging to the Tena Association of Shamans, and, second, those between members of the association and the state. It is because of these relations that it is possible to view identification cards as possessing agency in at least two senses (Gell 1998). To start with, in Manuel's view, it is the shaman's identification card that made the saint's owner act in a certain way, that is, made her open the door and invite them in. In other words, the card is seen as influencing the acts of others even though no will, vitality, or intention is ascribed to it. There is, however, a second aspect manifesting the agency attributed to this type of textual object. Although the shaman accompanying Miguel mentions that he is the owner of the card, this does not necessarily imply a relation of collaboration or mutual dependence between him and the card, as is the case with shamanic stones, which are considered to contain a spirit and, thus, to have their own vitality and will. Nevertheless, identification cards are conceived of as a crucial component of a shaman's identity and agency in specific contexts, such as the spiritual world of San Gonzalo. In this world, shamans cannot exist and act as such without an identification card. It is the identification card that makes the shaman what he is—that is, a person endowed with the capacity to enter into and see particular spiritual worlds, such as that of San Gonzalo.

Identification cards are not the only textual objects that acquire significance in Manuel's story. In it, Manuel traces important connections between his mother's footprint, specific written information about her, and her identity card. He says that when his mother fell ill, they took her to a shaman belonging to the Tena Association of Shamans, who told them that his mother's footprint had been abducted. The abduction of a person's footprints leads to a weakening of her body and affects essential bodily capacities, such as walking. It also affects her samai—her vital force and will—thus impeding basic activities such as taking care of her garden and kin. Despite the importance of the abduction of footprints in the explanation of the illness of Manuel's mother, there is no mention of this event once Manuel arrives in San Gonzalo's house. While in the saint's house, neither Manuel nor the shaman saw her abducted footprint or a graphic representation of it. Instead, they saw a written, codified text about Manuel's mother containing her name, surnames, and identity card number. Manuel identifies this codified, written information about his mother—which also existed for other victims—as her "identity card." Indeed, in his story, he portrays himself as saying, astonished: "They have taken their identity cards." The codified information that, according to Manuel, appeared in the book of San Gonzalo certainly mimics that which appears in identity cards. In this context, an identity card becomes a *prinda*, or pawn, which in shamanic idiom refers both to one of a person's qualities and to one of her or his personal objects.

In my view, there are several significant transformations that take place through the sorcerous activities involving identity cards. Through the actions of a shaman, the thwarted feelings of other persons—their envy, for instance—lead to the removal (not to the insertion, as it happens with the birutis) of something closely related to the victim's body, originally her footprint. The footprint is then given to San Gonzalo, in whose spiritual domain it is transformed into a codified textual object controlled by the owner of the saint. The captivity of the codified object destroys the victim's bodily capacities and skills, her will and vitality. In this sense, it can be contended that both the footprint and the identity card are considered to be constitutive parts of a person, together comprising a manifestation of her subjectivity and agency. Rescuing the abducted footprint/identity card is indispensable in order to restore the person's health and her capacity to act adequately.

When compared with other objects such as shamanic stones and darts, however, identity documents, I suggest, perform and thereby assert profound *limitations* on a Runa person's agency *in* a particular spiritual domain. This domain, through the house's aesthetic and the saint's owner's registration devices, is associated with white-mestizo institutions such as the state and the Catholic Church. As mentioned above, the identification card both stated the position of the shaman accompanying Manuel and allowed him to enter and see the world of San Gonzalo, thereby constituting him as a shaman in this particular spiritual world. In contrast with shamanic stones, however, there is no relation of collaboration between the identification card and the shaman. Nor does the identification card facilitate identification between the shaman and the owner of San Gonzalo. In the spiritual world of San Gonzalo, seeing does not imply adopting the point of view of the spirits or becoming like them. In my view, this is due to the fact that in the spiritual world of San Gonzalo, the shaman does not acquire the saint's potent objects or the powers of its mestizo owner—namely, the registration books, the lit candles inscribed with the names of the victims, and the masses in which the victims' names are read aloud. This severely limits the shaman's agency. In this context, he can only diagnose. He can see the victim's abducted footprint/identity card, but he cannot heal the victim. When curing a patient who has fallen ill through the shooting of birutis, the shaman can suck them out. He cannot, however, tear the codified texts containing the victims' information out of the registration books. Once the abducted footprints have become textual objects, the owner of San Gonzalo is the only person who can facilitate or prevent the death of the victim.

As I have suggested, in Manuel's story—as in other similar stories—identity cards are considered to be crucial constitutive components of a person's subjectivity and agency insofar as they are related to her vitality and will. Their relevance is particularly clear in the spiritual context in which San Gonzalo and his owner show themselves as powerful actors. It is in the spiritual world of San Gonzalo that a person can be bewitched through her identity card. In my view, the relevance of identity cards, precisely in this context, reveals the Runa people's awareness that, as registration devices, these textual objects relate to and are part of asymmetrical interethnic power relations. This could explain why shamans can extract birutis from a patient's body but are unable to rescue abducted footprints-turned-identity-cards. First, their repossession requires entering into a relationship of exchange that is considered profoundly unjust, insofar as it traps the Runa in asymmetrical relations and creates a debt that is impossible to repay. Second, the conditions of repossession highlight the maintenance of a particular configuration of power that, in the experience of the Runa people, is not easily transformed or taken away.

Conclusion

In this chapter, I have argued that the importance that Amazonian Runa ascribe to identification and identity cards is closely related to their notions about the body and the subjectivity and agency of both humans and objects. Runa people consider the body to be the product of relations and loving acts of caring. This view of a continuous and relational bodily constitution implies, however, the possibility and danger of bodily deconstitution. Bodily deconstitution entails the weakening of a person's subjectivity and capacity to act. The Runa understand such a process as a result of shamanic action.

The significance of different objects is related to the degree of subjectivity and agency that Runa people ascribe to them. "Subjectivized" objects carry with them something closely associated with a person, either a person's thwarted feelings, a shaman's will (in the case of the birutis), or the victim's capacities (as in the case of the footprint/identity card). Moreover, the Runa consider that some of these objects possess a certain degree of agency. Objects such as the biruti and the shaman's identification card "act" in the sense that it is through them that the shaman is able to act as a shaman. In this sense, both the biruti and the identification card are constitutive of his identity and the manifestation of his power. "Subjective" objects, on the contrary, are ascribed with agency of their own. Runa people believe that objects such as shamanic stones can act by themselves; in certain cases, their agency can even overshadow or blur the subjectivity and agency of their human companion/associate, the shaman. In cases of healing or bewitching, Runa people consider that it is the object that is acting, not the shaman.

I contend that, in accordance with their understanding of human bodies, subjectivities, and agency, Runa people conceive of "subjectivized" and "subjective" objects as the product or manifestation of particular relations. Thus, I suggest that to interpret Runa understandings of potent and performative objects—such as birutis, shamanic stones, and identity documents—as a form of "fetishism" is erroneous. A shaman's acquisition of these objects presupposes close and collaborative relations both with older shamans who guide the process of shamanic apprenticeship and with a host of spirits. The Runa always acknowledge these relations. Equally, they consider subjectivized objects, such as identity documents, to be part of a system of interethnic asymmetrical relations. According to Runa perceptions and experiences, these relations have imposed, and continue to impose, severe limitations on their people's subjectivity and agency precisely through the use of textual registration devices.

In my view, the Runa approach to identity documents highlights the asymmetrical character of the system of interethnic power relations in which they are immersed, their efforts to overcome it, and the limitations inherent to the system. As subjectivized objects, identification cards—the product of a ministerial agreement—allow Runa shamans to enter into and see the spiritual realm of San Gonzalo. The capacity to act conferred by identification cards is, however, limited. In the realm of San Gonzalo, Runa shamans neither communicate with nor enter into exchange relations with powerful subjective objects that enable them to heal, that is, to rescue the identity card—a subjectivized textual object—of the bewitched person. The limited capacity to act that identification cards confer on shamans underlines, I suggest, the Amazonian Runa people's awareness that certain powerful textual objects are still generated in the restricted realm of white-mestizo dominance.

Acknowledgments

I am particularly grateful to Fernando Santos-Granero for his incisive and constructive comments and suggestions on earlier drafts of this chapter. I would also like to thank Randi Kaarhus, Esben Leifsen, Sarah Lund, Bente Nicolaisen, Michell Tidsel Flikke, and Astrid Stensrud, as well as the two reviewers who offered remarks and suggestions and helped me to clarify my arguments.

Notes

1. I use the term "Amazonian Runa" to refer to the Napo and Pastaza Runa, also known in the literature as Quijos and Canelos Kichwa respectively.

2. All names in this chapter are fictitious.

3. Women who are considered to be extraordinary healers usually possess this kind of stone, although they are not considered shamans.

4. Discussing alternative ways to conceptualize agency, Gell (1998:17–21) proposes to distinguish between "self-sufficient agents" and "secondary agents." Self-sufficient agents have intentionality and consciousness, while secondary agents can act only in conjunction with certain human associates, whose identities these agents constitute.

References

Alvarado, Juan. 2001. *Valores culturales de las etnías Kichwas del Cantón Santa Clara*. Santa Clara: Unidad Educativa Mons. Alberto Zambrano Palacios.

Belaunde, Luisa E. 1992. Gender, Commensality and Community among the Airo-Pai of West Amazonia (Secoya, Western-Tukanoan Speaking). PhD dissertation, London School of Economics and Political Science.

De Matos Viegas, Susana. 2003. Eating with Your Favourite Mother: Time and Sociality in an Amerindian Brazilian Community. *Journal of the Royal Anthropological Institute* 9(1): 21–37.

Gell, Alfred. 1998. *Art and Agency: An Anthropological Theory*. Oxford: Clarendon Press.

Gordillo, Gastón. 2006. The Crucible of Citizenship: ID-Paper Fetishism in the Argentinean Chaco. *American Ethnologist* 33(2): 162–76

Gow, Peter. 1990. Could Sangama Read? The Origin of Writing among the Piro of Eastern Perú. *History and Anthropology* 5(1): 87–103

———. 2003. *An Amazonian Myth and Its History*. Oxford: Oxford University Press.

Guzmán-Gallegos, María A. 1997. *Para que la yuca beba nuestra sangre: Trabajo, género y parentesco en una comunidad quichua de la Amazonia Ecuatoriana*. Quito: Editorial Abya Yala.

Kohn, Eduardo. 2002. Natural Engagements and Ecological Aesthetics among the Ávila Runa of Amazonian Ecuador. PhD dissertation, University of Wisconsin.

Lienhard, Martin. 1991. *La voz y su huella: Escritura y conflicto étnico-social en América Latina 1492–1988*. Hannover: Ediciones del Norte.

McCallum, Cecilia. 2001. *Gender and Sociality in Amazonia: How Real People Are Made*. Oxford: Berg.

Muratorio, Blanca. 1987. *Rucuyaya Alonso y la historia social y económica del Alto Napo, 1850–1950*. Quito: Editorial Abya Yala.

Rappaport, Joanne. 1990. History, Law, and Ethnicity in Andean Colombia. *Latin American Anthropology Review* 2(1): 13–19.

———. 1994. *Cumbe Reborn: An Andean Ethnography of History*. Chicago and London: University of Chicago Press.

Rival, Laura. 2005. The Attachment of the Soul to the Body among the Huoarani of Amazonian Ecuador. *Ethnos* 70(3): 285–310.

Rubenstein, Steven. 2007. Circulation, Accumulation, and the Power of Shuar Shrunken Heads. *Cultural Anthropology* 22(3): 357–99.

Uzendoski, Michael. 2004. Manioc Beer and Meat: Value, Reproduction and Cosmic Substance among the Napo Runa of the Ecuadorian Amazon. *Journal of the Royal Anthropological Institute* 10(4): 883–902.

Veber, Hanne. 1998. The Salt of the Montaña: Interpreting Indigenous Activism in the Rain Forest. *Cultural Anthropology* 13(3): 382–413.

Vilaça, Aparecida. 2002. Making Kin out of Others in Amazonia. *Journal of the Royal Anthropological Institute* 8(2): 347–65.

———. 2005 Chronically Unstable Bodies: Reflections on Amazonian Corporalities. *Journal of the Royal Anthropological Institute* 11(3): 445–46.

Viveiros de Castro, Eduardo. 1998. Cosmological Deixis and Amerindian Perspectivism. *Journal of the Royal Anthropological Institute* 4(3): 469–88.

———. 2001. GUT Feelings about Amazonia: Potential Affinity and the Construction of Sociality. In Laura Rival and Neil L. Whitehead (eds.), *Beyond the Visible and the Material: The Amerindianization of Society in the Work of Peter Rivière*, pp. 19–44. Oxford: Oxford University Press.

Whitten Jr., Norman E. 1976. *Sacha Runa: Ethnicity and Adaptation of Ecuadorian Jungle Quichua*. Urbana: University of Illinois Press.

———. 1985. *Sicuanga Runa: The Other Side of Development in Amazonian Ecuador*. Urbana: University of Illinois Press.

Wogan, Peter. 1994. Perceptions of European Literacy in Early Contact Situations. *Ethnohistory* 41(3): 407–29.

———. 2004. *Magical Writing in Salasaca: Literacy and Power in Highland Ecuador*. Colorado and Oxford: Westview Press.

10
Materializing the Occult

An Approach to Understanding the Nature of
Materiality in Wakuénai Ontology

Jonathan D. Hill

This chapter explores questions about the relations between humans, natural species, and material objects among the Arawak-speaking Wakuénai of Venezuela. I will begin by addressing questions about what, how, and why material things become subjectivized through an analysis of grammatical categories, or numeral classifiers, that are used in everyday verbal expressions of quantity. Analysis of these grammatical features will show how language and speech partake simultaneously in two complementary and mutually interdependent ways of producing meaning. On one level, numeral classification is an explicitly taxonomic process of putting kinds of persons, animals, and things into their proper places. As a taxonomic process, nominal classifiers serve as a parsimonious way of condensing and organizing a myriad world of sensuous objects into a finite number of semantic sets. By arranging the "mesocosm"—the world as experienced on the scale of human sense perception (Delbrück 1986)—into shared categories of meaning based on common interactional processes, numeral classifiers provide a set of cognitive "handles" on reality. At the same time, these explicit taxonomic tools are the basis for linguistically marking species and objects that are especially powerful. Thus, numeral classifiers provide a way of creatively reformulating the representation of objects through experientially based categories into implicit subsets of more dynamic, powerful species and objects. Analysis of these grammatical markings requires knowledge of mythic narratives that explain how the world came into being and how the transformative processes of creating a culturally differentiated world of distinct peoples, places, species, and objects from the undifferentiated world of primordial animal-humans are episodically reenacted in shamanic singing, chanting, blowing tobacco smoke, and other ritual activities. Both the taxonomic and shamanic dimensions of numeral classification provide insight into how the experiential world of objects and species is subjectivized, or animated.

After exploring that subject, I will turn to a consideration of the complementary process of how subjectivities become "thing-like" or materialized by exploring the indigenous concept of *línupanáa* ("ritual power," "danger," or "harmfulness") as embodied in musical dimensions of chanted and sung speeches performed in rites of passage and shamanic curing rituals. I will also draw upon two important mythic narratives that shed light on the role of musical sounds, or musicalized word-sounds, as key operators in the materialization of subjectivities. Following Ellen Basso's pathbreaking work (1985) on levels of animacy in Kalapalo narratives and ritual performances, I will argue that musicalized speech genres, such as shamanic singing (*malirríkairi*) and chanting (*malikái*), provide ways of making subjectivities into "thing-like" materials.[1] Exploring the complementary processes of subjectivation and objectivation will lead to a consideration of how the Wakuénai concept of "ownership" is grounded in indigenous ideas on the nature of materiality.

Subjectivizing the Material

Nominal classifiers provide a rich and largely untapped source of insight into how speakers of indigenous languages construct categories of things (species, substances, places, persons, and artifacts), thereby imbuing the physical world with a culturally specific worldview. From a linguistic perspective, systems of nominal classification are important demonstrations of the integration of cultural knowledge into semantic and syntactic dimensions of everyday speech. Yet despite the fact that nominal classifiers result in linguistic forms that are culturally specific and historically unique, the cross-linguistic study of nominal classifiers has demonstrated that they are based on a limited pool of underlying classificatory processes (Dixon 1983; Lakoff 1982, 1987; Greenberg 1972; Craig 1982). Moreover, cross-linguistically, nominal classifiers are used for organizing the same basic range of things: those that people make, eat, handle, use, or in some way bodily interact with in the course of their everyday lives and during ritual or ceremonial events. From a more sociocultural perspective, nominal classifiers provide a way of studying semantic taxonomies in naturally occurring speech acts and exploring how these semantic sets are situated within (and co-constructed with) broader structural and semiotic relations of meaning and power.[2]

Numeral classifiers in all five dialects of Wáku are concerned with arranging the "mesocosm" (Delbrück 1986) into shared categories of meaning based on common interactional properties: edibility, utility, gender, and place. The ordering of numeral classifier sets in table 10.1 was elicited from native speakers of the Curricarro dialect (Dzáwinai phratry) along the lower Guainía River in Venezuela during fieldwork in 1980–1981. At first glance, the list of noun sets in table 10.1 presents a bewildering mosaic of semantic contents, rather like the northern Australian (Dyirbal) noun classes studied by Robert Dixon (1983). However, both the overall pattern of numeral classifier sets in Wáku and the majority of the sets' internal contents begin to make sense when the numeral classifier system is examined in relation to the generic classifiers, or "spirit-names," used in ritually powerful chanted and sung speech (malikái) and to materials and species that are considered to be especially powerful due to their significance in mythic narratives or ritual and ceremonial performances.

My approach to numeral classifiers in Wáku follows Dixon's "semantics prior" approach (1983) by identifying basic concepts associated with the semantically defined sets of nouns and then exploring "the way several different sets (or parts of sets) may be mapped onto the same grammatical class" (Dixon 1983:179). Dixon (1983:179) found four basic concepts associated with each of the four noun classes in Dyirbal: (1) animateness/ (human) masculinity, (2) (human) femininity/water/fire/fighting, (3) nonflesh food, and (4) everything else. Other semantic sets, or parts of sets, are then superimposed on this basic, four-fold taxonomy through two rules.

1. If some noun has characteristic X (on the basis of which its class membership would be expected to be decided) but is, through belief or myth, connected with characteristic Y, then it will generally belong to the class corresponding to Y and not that corresponding to X.

2. If a subset of nouns has some particular important property that the rest of the set does not have, then the members of the subset may be assigned to a different class from the rest of the set to "mark" this property; the important property is most often "harmfulness." (Dixon 1983:179)

These two rules have great potential for aiding in the understanding of how noun class and classifier systems become complex, polythetic clusters of nouns with many overlapping semantic sets (and partial sets) rather than simple monothetic classes based only upon the interactional

Table 10.1.   Numeral Classifiers

I.	1	*páda*	child(-ren); also, turtle species; caribe,
	2	*dzamáda*	anchoa, palometta, and bagre (small
	3	*mádalída*	catfish); peccary and agouti species; stones;
	Big	*makádali(-pe)*	pineapples and manioc tubers; grasses;
	Little	*tsúdali(-pe)*	bees; motors
II.	1	*apʰéepa*	adult men; also, groups of objects counted
	2	*dzamʰéepa*	in sets of five ("hands") or twenty ("persons")
	3	*mádaʰlípa*	
	Big	*makádali(-pe)*	
	Little	*túpʰe(-pe)*	
III.	1	*apáma*	adult women
	2	*dzamáma*	
	3	*mádalíma*	
	Big	*makádaru(-pe)*	
	Little	*tsúdaru(-pe)*	
IV.	1	*apáka*	large catfish species; also, all species of vine;
	2	*dzamáka*	machete fish (*úʰwi*); anaconda (*umáwari*) and
	3	*mádalíka*	all species of snake; fishing lines
	Big	*makákai(-pe)*	
	Little	*tsúkai(-pe)*	
V.	1	*apaíta*	all fish except those listed in sets I and IV
	2	*dzamaíta*	above
	3	*mándalíta*	
	Big	*makaáita(-pe)*	
	Little	*tsuíte(-pe)*	
VI.	1	*apápa*	all bird species; also, bananas and most
	2	*dzamápa*	species of cultivated fruit trees
	3	*mádalíápa*	
	Big	*makápali(-pe)*	
	Little	*tsuápali(-pe)*	
VII.	1	*apána*	jaguars; also, tapir, deer, and squirrels; dogs
	2	*dzamána*	and cats; wild fruit species (*yúku, yurí,* and
	3	*mádalína*	*awíya*)
	Big	*makáni(-pe)*	
	Little	*tsúni(-pe)*	

Table 10.1. Numeral Classifiers (continued)

VIII.	1	*ap^{h}éwi*	tobacco; also, arrows, awls, hooks, and darts
	2	*dza^{h}méwi*	
	3	*máda^{h}líwi*	
	Big	*makéwi(-pe)*	
	Little	*tsuíwi(-pe)*	
IX.	1	*apáma*	flutes that come in male-female pairs; also,
	2	*dzamáma*	pairs of any objects
	3	*mádalína*	
	Big	*makámali*	
	Little	*tsúmali*	
X.	1	*ap^{h}éku*	pairs of flutes taken singly; also, any single
	2	*dza^{h}méku*	thing that comes in pairs (e.g., "one chicken"
	3	*máda^{h}líku*	= *ap^{h}éku kwáami ínasríku*)
	Big	*makhéki(-pe)*	
	Little	*tsuíki(-pe)*	
XI.	1	*apána*	groups of people (*naíki*), or phratries
	2	*dzamánai*	
	3	*mádaliána*	
	No terms for "big" or "little"		
XII.	1	*ápapúku*	small bunches of fruits; also, bunches of
	2	*dzámapúku*	fish (captured); fish traps; bushes (or plants)
	3	*mádalipúku*	of cultivated fruits or vegetables, except
	Big	*mákapúki(-pe)*	manioc
	Little	*tsúpuki(-pe)*	
XIII.	1	*áape*	large bunches of fruits; also, large bunches
	2	*dzáame*	of any objects
	3	*madáli*	
	Big	*makérri(-pe)*	
	Little	*tsuiérri(-pe)*	
XIV.	1	*apápi*	manioc gardens; also, trees (i.e., thickness of
	2	*dzamápi*	trunk); blowguns and shotguns; bowls
	3	*mádalíni*	
	Big	*makáapi(-pe)*	
	Little	*tsuáapi(-pe)*	

Table 10.1.   Numeral Classifiers (continued)

XV.	1	*áapa*	canoes; also, cups and gourds (as quantities
	2	*dzáama*	of liquid)
	3	*madála*	
	Big	*makáli(-pe)*	
	Little	*tsuiáli(-pe)*	
XVI.	1	*apádapána*	houses
	2	*dzamádapána*	
	3	*madaliápana*	
	Big	*mákadápana(-pe)*	
	Little	*tsúdapána(-pe)*	
XVII.	1	*apákwa*	manioc ovens; also, village-places (*dzákare*)
	2	*dzamákwa*	
	3	*mádalikwa*	
	Big	*makáwi(-pe)*	
	Little	*tsúkwe(-pe)*	
XVIII.	1	*apáp^{h}e*	leaves or fronds
	2	*dzamáp^{h}e*	
	3	*madáp^{h}e*	
	Big	*makáp^{h}e*	
	Little	*tsúpai*	
XIX.	1	*ápawéni*	man-made fire
	2	*dzámawéni*	
	3	*mádaliwéni*	
	Big	*mákawéni(-pe)*	
	Little	*tsuwéni(-pe)*	

properties of objects. Historical drift may account for some of the apparently anomalous members of noun classes or classifier sets. The override principle of linguistically marking objects to which are attributed the quality of "harmfulness" in mythic narratives and ritual performances may account in large part for the complexity of noun class and classifier systems, at least in societies where ritual speech varieties are the dominant form of truly specialized discourse. Dixon's semantic methodology and formal rules are significant because they mean that nouns making up noun classes or classifier sets are verbal clues as to how the speakers of a given language perceive the most "harmful," or powerful, objects in the local environment. To the field ethnographer, nominal classifier systems can indicate the social processes of attributing meaning and value to highly selective portions of natural and social worlds.

Perhaps the most noticeable feature of numeral classifiers in Wáku is the prevalence of gender and age as basic concepts. Sets II and III (see table 10.1) specify "adult human masculinity" and "adult human femininity" respectively. "Children," the first noun in set I, are classified together with "all turtles" and a variety of other objects and species. This tripartite arrangement makes sense in terms of the sacred mythic narratives about Iñápirríkuli, Ámaru, and Kuwái, the prototypic father, mother, and child, since it is the differentiation of adult male from adult female, expressed as a mythic battle of the sexes, that sets in motion the birth of Kuwái, the "opening-up" of the world into its present size, and the creation of living species through musical naming power. The mythic importance of gender and age in defining human, cultural separateness in both myth and ritual is concretely and parsimoniously embodied in the numeral classifier sets I, II, and III.

The override, or "mythic," principle of linguistically marking "harmful," or powerful, species and objects is most clearly evident in sets IV and VIII of the numeral classifiers. The first named members of set IV are "large catfish," a partial set of fishes that is split off from the majority of edible fishes in set V. Large catfish species are uniformly regarded as having great "strength" (línupanáa) and are the last fishes to be eaten by persons after recovering from a serious illness or having gone through a major rite of passage. Kulírri, a large catfish species with black stripes along each side, is the namesake of an important ceremonial trumpet called the *kulirrína* that—although it is not one of the sacred instruments of Kuwái, the prototypical child of myth—has certain ritual powers due to its peculiar construction. In the trumpets' manufacture, their resonators—conical-shaped baskets made from strips of palm bark—are woven around a balsa-wood frame and then covered with a thick, airtight layer of resin (*maíni*). Short mouthpieces of hollow palm wood are inserted into the "heads" of the catfish-resonators by lashing them to a circular rim of vine, which fits snugly along the inner walls of the resonators. The heads of the resonators are then tied shut and covered with maíni resin. Women of childbearing age are strictly forbidden to see the closing of the kulirrína trumpets' heads because it is believed that this activity could make their unborn children become "stuck" inside their wombs, endangering both

242   Jonathan D. Hill

the mothers' and the infants' lives (Hill 1987). The wheel of vine used to connect the mouthpieces of kulirrína trumpets to the resonators is made of *dzámakuápi* (literally "two snakes"), a species that is highly charged with ritual and mythic power. In myth, dzámakuápi is one of the plant materials that grows out of the ashes of Kuwái after his fiery "death" and which becomes part of the sacred flutes and trumpets stolen by Ámaru, Kuwái's mother, and the women. In sacred ritual, dzámakuápi is the species of vine used to make the most powerful whips (*kadápu*), used only for marking time during the malikái songs and chants for sacred food (*káridzámai*) and for striking initiates across their backs at the end of male and female initiation rituals.

Far from forming an arbitrary set of nouns, the grouping of "large catfish, vines, and snakes" in set IV is highly motivated by the ceremonial, ritual, and mythic significance of these seemingly disparate semantic subsets. Other connections include the mythic description of vines as part of the body of Kuwái and the ritual classification of vines as a member of the classifier set of "water animal-spirits" (*umáwarinái*). The machete fish (*úhwi*) belongs in set IV because in myth, this species is an enemy of the trickster-creator (Iñápirríkuli), who punishes the úhwi by shoving a sharp stick up its anus until the stick exits beneath its mouth. Classifier set IV is thus a subset of fishes with strongly feminine connotations that is split off from the majority of edible fish species in set V. Classifier set IV also demonstrates how a new loan word can enter an existing category through "chaining" or the continuation of an existing, motivated semantic relation (see Lakoff 1982:87 on classifiers in Japanese). Nylon fishing line is placed into set IV because it resembles the "long-thin-smoothness" of vines, anacondas, large catfish, and the úhwi (an eel-like species). Nylon fishing lines also belong with "water animal-spirits" by virtue of shared habitat. In set IV, the nouns all specify "long-thin-smooth" objects associated with water and femininity, thereby indirectly creating a "shape" classifier out of a numeral classifier. The cultural importance of this shape is obvious to anyone familiar with malikái chanting and singing for childbirth and initiation rituals: the "long-thin-smooth-watery" relation specifies the umbilical cord believed to connect newborn infants with their fathers' work activities and the celestial umbilical cord (*hliépulékwa dzákare*) invoked in initiation rituals as the pathway connecting the world of powerful, mythic beings to the world of living human beings.

A similar combination of taxonomic and mythic principles forms an implicit "shape" category in classifier set VIII, or "tobacco, arrows, awls, hooks, and darts." In this case, the power of tobacco in myth and ritual, as well as in everyday social contexts, is all pervasive. Every major and minor ritual requires tobacco for its performance, and in mythic narratives, tobacco is described as a supernatural "switch" that enables powerful beings to travel in and out of dreams and other altered states of consciousness. Tobacco is thus a culturally marked object par excellence. In classifier set VIII, tobacco is allocated to the same category as sharp, pointed tools. This allocation makes sense in light of the ritual uses of the term "tobacco" in malikái chanting and singing, in which it is often invoked as a sharp tool for cutting up, killing, or otherwise operating upon the spirit-names of edible animal species and other potentially harmful, disease-causing agents. Set VIII creates a category of "long-thin" objects that are "stiff, hard, penetrating, and pointed," whereas set IV creates a category of "long-thin" objects that are "soft, smooth, flexible, and watery." Both masculine and feminine varieties of "long-thinness" imply an equal potential for causing harm, the masculine through delivering a piercing blow to the body and the feminine through tying up and strangling life, like the anaconda killing its prey.

Numeral classifiers in Wáku establish meaningful relations in the world of objects as they enter into basic human interactions, as well as the multiple ways in which the objects' interactive properties bring them into a shared universe of cultural meanings and "powerfulness." The scale of powerfulness connects objects in ways that often contradict their basic interactive properties. The classifier sets draw upon concrete—often eso- teric and singular—power relations as building blocks for constructing broader, more condensed and polythetic sets of powerful meanings, or for constructing the triad of human masculinity, human femininity, and the proto-human animacy of children.[3]

Given the prominence of gender as a taxonomic principle in the numeral classifiers, the low overall number of classifier sets (nineteen), the existence of four "sets" consisting of only one noun each, the pre- ponderance of marked linguistic expressions of power relations, and the obligatory usage of numeral classifiers, it makes sense to explore the numeral classifier system as a "quasi-" noun class system which rests upon four basic properties: (1) human masculinity, (2) human femininity, (3) presexual animacy, and (4) quantity. Following Dixon's "semantics prior" analysis of nominal classifiers (1983), it becomes possible to arrange all nineteen numeral classifier sets into four basic semantic "classes," onto which a number of additional semantic sets, or parts of sets, have been mapped in accordance with the mythic principle of marking unusually powerful objects and species.

As indicated in table 10.2, numeral classifier set I is an incipient noun class. Set I is strikingly similar to Dyirbal noun classes (Dixon 1983) insofar as it organizes a diversity of semantic sets and partial sets by packing them all into a single "supercategory." Most of the subsets it contains allude to mythic and ritual power. Motors are power sources, like the mythic child, Kuwái, whose energy "drives" the expansion of the cosmos and the creation of living species. According to Wakuénai belief, each person has such a child-like "motor" within their body, and shamans seek to restore its power by blowing tobacco smoke over their patients' heads. Stones are shamanic tools for manipulating lightning, wind, and spirits. Also, stones were the major sources of blade tools and microliths for cutting and grating prior to the advent of steel tools in the upper Río Negro region in the eighteenth century. Bees are the source of honey, the primal curing substance, and they are allocated to classifier set I because in myth, bee-spirits are said to appear as little old men who have the bodies of children.

The fish species allocated to classifier set I are the two most powerful and the two least powerful. The *caribe* fish (piranha) is strictly taboo to children and women of childbearing age because of its extremely sharp teeth and bones. The freshwater *anchoa* is strictly taboo to all members of the highly ranked patrisibs of the Dzáwinai phratry, since it is one of their sacred totems. On the other hand, the *palometa* (*Mylossoma duriventris*) and *bagre* (various species of small catfish) are the fish species believed to have the least strength (línupanáa) and are the first animal-flesh foods eaten by very young children or individuals who are recovering from serious illness or who have recently gone through a rite of passage. The use of the mythic principle here is unique, since nowhere else does it result in a double splitting of semantic sets into most and least powerful subsets. For the Wakuénai, children are ambiguous, precultural, and presexual creatures. They are the most powerful and the least powerful members of the human community, since they embody the potential to create anew the search for the mythic ancestors but they remain as yet without the powerful names and sexuality of adult men and women.

The quantifiers are listed as a separate "quasi-" noun class in table 10.2 because they do not specify objects per se but pairs or other quantities of objects (e.g., "cups of water," "bunches of fruit," and "groups of people"). Quantities, mass nouns, and numerals have their own unique properties

Table 10.2.   A "semiotics prior" analysis of numeral classifiers in
Wáku (Curricarro dialect)

1.	2.	3.	4.
Human masculinity	Human femininity	Protohuman presexual animacy	Quantity
Human houses	Human fires	Human children	Things that come in male-female pairs
Human villages	Manioc ovens		
Most fishes	Some fishes	Some fishes	Bunches of fruits
Most forest animals		Some forest animals	Rations of fruits
All birds	All snakes and vines	All turtles and bees	Cups of water
Most garden fruits	Manioc gardens	Manioc tubers	Groups of people
Tobacco and most tools and weapons	Some weapons	Some tools (stones and motors)	
Some quantities (boxes)			
Human hands and "persons" as counters of objects			

and play on basic intuitive feelings that people have in relation to objects.
Most of the quantities specified by numeral classifiers in Wáku are mass
nouns: "pairs," "bunches," "rations," "groups," and "measures." These quantities are not made up of countable individuals or integrated wholes. However, the Wakuénai have developed ways of counting individual, whole
objects, based on human digits as units of five, ten, fifteen, and twenty
(and multiples thereof). These expressions are made from the classifier
set II, or "adult (human)masculinity," together with the words for "hand"
(*káapi*, or five) and "human being" (*naíki*, or twenty—ten fingers plus ten
toes). "Ten fish," for example, is rendered as *kúpje dzajméepa káapi* ("fish-
two hands"), and "twenty fish" as *kúpje apjéepa káapi* ("fish-one person").
The mythic principle is at work in shifting these counting expressions to
the (human) masculine classifier set. In *kwépani* (the "Kuwái-dance," a

246 Jonathan D. Hill

sacred ceremonial exchange of wild palm fruits) and initiation rituals, adult men dance with flutes that come in pairs and triplets, and these sacred instruments are said to represent the thumb and index finger plus the outer three fingers of the hand of Kuwái. Expressions of counting in Wáku are thus derived from ritual quintets (or "hands") of adult male flute players. In large ceremonies and rituals, several quintets, or "hands of Kuwái," perform simultaneously to represent the entire "person" (or ten fingers and ten toes) of Kuwái.

Numeral classifiers in Wáku implicitly define masculine and feminine powerfulness, as well as the proto-agency embodied in children, and map these gender- and age-based concepts of agency onto the objects and species that people make, eat, use, or interact with in bodily ways in the course of everyday activities or in ritual and ceremonial events. The classifier sets also establish hierarchical levels of animacy in which some objects or species are marked as more powerful through being shifted into different classifier sets or through elaboration of especially complex groupings of things (e.g., set I). Numeral classifiers speak to basic questions raised in this volume, such as what material things become subjectivized, how they do it, and why. Things that are most likely to become subjectivized are those that come into bodily contact with a person through eating, using, or touching; things that come in pairs or that are otherwise involved in quantitative expressions; and things that are believed to have exceptional power to cause harm in ritual and myth.

Shamanic Singing as Materialization of Subjectivities

Shamanic singing (malirríkairi) is a musical and choreographic process of journeying from the world of living people to the houses of the dead, located in a dark netherworld, and retrieving the lost soul of a sick or dying person. This process of journeying away from the living and returning with the patient's soul is enacted in a number of ways. Movement, which represents breaking through to the houses of the dead, is performed with music through the use of sacred rattles made with powerful quartz stones. The accelerating and decelerating percussive sounds of a shaman's rattle serve as sensible markers charting the course of his spiritual travel. In their singing, shamans repeat each verse in a soft—almost ventriloquistic—echoing that musically effects a return to the world of the living. In addition, the shamanic activity of bringing back the patient's lost soul is acted out in dramatic movements between songs, which are always performed while the shaman is seated on a low bench and facing the eastern horizon. The shaman then stands up, takes several steps away from his bench, and begins pulling spirits into his rattle by sucking in air and tobacco smoke. He returns to the patient and his or her family, blows tobacco smoke over their heads, sucks on the patient's body, and vomits up splinters or other disease-causing agents. Shamanic ritual mobilizes a combination of musical sounds and bodily actions to transform subjective relations—fear of death, illness and misfortune, conflict and anger—into sensuous, audible, visible, tangible materialities. In short, shamanic singing "materializes the occult."

The fact that shamanic rituals—especially the singing, percussive sounds, and tobacco smoke they feature—are understood as a way of effecting changes in the material world was brought home to me during my fieldwork with Wakuénai shamans living along the upper Rio Negro (Guainía) in Venezuela in the early 1980s. During the early months of my doctoral fieldwork, I had talked with shamans (malírri) and nonspecialists about their ritual activities and had elicited important mythic narratives that explain the origins of shamanic healing powers. But it was not until I began recording and documenting actual healing rituals that I began to really "get it." Shamanic rituals create a kind of physical energy that affects anyone who is in close proximity and that is not entirely explicable in terms of rationalist or other intellectualist orientations. When I first recorded shamanic singing in a healing ritual, I felt a surge of physical energy that blocked out or overrode all the usual physical discomforts of working under the midday equatorial sun on an increasingly empty stomach.[4] From that time forward, I no longer had to ask people for information about ritual singing and chanting but was told about them, often in advance, and asked to bring my tape recorder, camera, and notebooks to document the ritual activities.

Over the following months, I listened to recordings of shamanic singing with a local ritual specialist, or "chant owner" (malikái limínali), named Horacio Lopez Pequeira, who helped me transcribe and translate the songs and provided me with wonderfully detailed commentaries and exegeses on them. Upon learning that the leitmotif of shamanic singing is the bringing back of patients' lost souls from the world of the dead, I asked Horacio why shamans blew tobacco smoke over the heads not only of their patients but also of their patients' family members, as well as everyone else present (including the resident anthropologist and his tape recorder) at ritual gatherings. Horacio answered me with an interesting analogy by explaining that each person's body-soul is like the compression inside a motor. Shamans seek to gather up the collective force of everyone present by blowing tobacco smoke over their heads, thereby linking their body-souls together into a collective force that helps the shamans attract their patients' body-souls back from the netherworld of the dead to the world of the living.

Horacio then expanded his analogy by commenting that shamanic curing power works very much like my tape recorder and note taking. Just as the shamans' singing and smoke blowing are ways of pulling in their patients' body-souls, so also were my tape recorder and note taking ways of pulling in the sounds, words, and sensations of the curing ritual. He also explained that the shamans were initially afraid that their songs would destroy my tape recorder but later decided that my work was both good for me and helpful to them in their attempts to gather up "compression" to bring back their patients' souls. It was in the course of that conversation with Horacio in 1981 that I began to understand why I had felt such an unusual burst of physical energy while recording shamanic singing, why people began to seek me out in advance of their rituals, and why shamanic rituals are much more than esoteric "expressions" about spirit-beings and their travels through the cosmos. What I learned was that shamanic sing-ing is not a performance *about* moving or traveling around the cosmos; rather, it *is* a set of journeys away from death and back to life, a harnessing of the collective physical energies of the living that transforms subjectivi-ties into materialities—a materializing of the occult.

Materializing Subjectivities

The complementary process of materializing subjectivities is most evi-dent in sacred ritual contexts, such as the shamanic singing described in the previous section of this chapter. The principles of classification and linguistic marking that operate in an implicit way in the numeral classifiers of everyday speech become topics of explicit, conscious dis-course in the principles of spirit-naming that prevail in sacred singing and chanting (malikái) performed in rites of passage and healing rituals. In these contexts, spirit-naming serves to verbally specify the same range of things based on their functional, interactive properties as the numeral classifiers of everyday speech. However, these spirit-names (which take the form of generic classifiers) are all "hyperanimate" (Basso 1985) and "musicalized" (Hill 1993). All things, species, and places that are specified in spirit-naming are ritually powerful or "dangerous" (línupanáa). Some spirit-names are more powerful than others, especially those that "have stories"—spirit-names that convey an esoteric, intertextual meaning that shifts a species or object into a different or special category.[5]

Just as language and verbal categories provide the key way of understanding how material things become subjectivities, it is musical sounds and closely related ritual actions and objects that are the most crucial features for approaching the complementary process of making subjectivities become sensible and material. In ritual performances of malikái singing and chanting, musical and other nonverbal dimensions of ritual action become direct, sensual instantiations of mythic meanings that are verbally constructed in narrative discourses or in the esoteric, secret "language" of spirit-naming (see Hill 1993). In these sacred contexts, the organization of musical sounds, tempo, and rhythm acts as a materialization of subjective relations. Shamanic singing, rattling, and tobacco smoking gives audible, visible, tangible, and olfactory substance to the fear and anger of sorcery victims whose body-souls have been taken away and to the shaman's efforts to restore their patients' health by bringing their spirits back to the world of the living.

Perhaps the most dramatic expression of the musical "materialization" of subjectivities is the moment when a young woman is initiated into adulthood through a series of malikái songs and chants over the sacred food (káridzámai) that marks the end of her period of ritual fasting. Female initiation rituals are called wakáitaka iénpiti, which means, "We speak to our child," referring to the elders' ritual advice given after the six hours of singing and chanting that begins at noon and continues almost until sundown. On the morning of the girl initiate's coming-of-age ritual, her mother prepares a pot of hot-peppered, boiled fish or game meat in a large bowl and presents it to a chant owner (malikái limínali). The food is covered with yagrumo leaves, but small holes are left in the covering to allow the chant owner to blow tobacco smoke over the food during intervals between periods of singing and chanting (see fig. 10.1). The chant owner places a large woven basket upside down over the pot of sacred food and, together with a shaman or other assistant, begins tapping out a loud, rapid rhythm on the basket with ritual whips (kapéti). In the opening song for female initiation, the chant owner uses four distinct pitches and invokes the primordial human mother (Ámaru) and child (Kuwái) of myth living in the sky-world (éenu). After singing the spirit-names of these powerful mythic beings, the chant owner sings the name

Figure 10.1. Chant owner blowing tobacco smoke over an initiate's food.
Photo: Jonathan D. Hill, 1981.

of the celestial umbilical cord (*hliépule-kwa dzákare*) that connects the
sky-world of mythic, ancestral beings to the navel of the world at Hípana,
the place of mythic emergence. The singing and rapid, percussive tapping
of whips continues for several minutes before transforming without inter-
ruption into a slower chanting of place names along the Aiarí and Isana
rivers. In a series of twenty-one chants lasting for nearly six hours, the
chant owner names all the places along the Isana, Negro, Cuyarí, Guainía,
and Casiquiare rivers that form the ancestral territories of the various
Wakuénai phratries. In the final chant, ritual specialists name the mythic
home of Ámaru at Mutsípani ("palm grub-dance"), a site along a curved
stream near the place of emergence at Hípana. Before performing a final
blessing and blowing tobacco smoke over the sacred food for the last
time, the chant owner sings into being the celestial umbilical cord that
connects the sky-world of mythic ancestors to the world of the living at
Hípana. The food and the girl initiate are then both taken outside, where
they become the objects of the elders' collective ritual advice, which brings
the ritual to an end.

Malikái singing and chanting for female initiation rituals invokes a bewildering variety of spirit-names and makes extensive use of a spirit-naming process called *wadzúhiakáw nakúna* ("going in search of the names"). All these names and this naming process are densely interwoven with processes of mythic creation that are described in narratives about the primordial human mother and child, Ámaru and Kuwái. According to myth, after Kuwái had completed the first creation of the world through musically naming into being the various species and objects of nature, an enormous tree sprouted from the ashes of the fire where he had been burned alive. The trickster-creator (Iñápirríkuli), who was also the father of Kuwái, created sacred flutes and trumpets from this tree. The world opened up for a second time as Ámaru and her female companions stole the sacred flutes and trumpets of Kuwái from Iñápirríkuli and played them in various places. Finally, with the help of an army of male companions who took the form of small frogs (*molítu*), the trickster-creator regained control of these sacred instruments and returned to the sky-world.

In mythic narratives, the movements of Iñápirríkuli across the world in pursuit of Ámaru and the women is not described as a mere journey or movement between pre-existing places. Rather, it is characterized as the dynamic "opening-up," or creation and expansion, of a world of culturally distinct peoples and geographically separate places (rivers, villages, landmarks, etc.).[6] This opening-up of geographic space does not unfold in a vacuum but is bracketed by powerful images of the connections between vertically distinct regions of the cosmos: the sky-world of mythic ancestors and primordial human beings and the terrestrial world of living human descendants. Much like the mythical tree that grows from the ashes of Kuwái before being made into sacred flutes and trumpets, the opening song of female initiation is a verbal and musical instantiation of the connection between sky-world and terrestrial world, ancestors and descendants. The use of four distinct pitches in the opening song directly embodies or "materializes" the chant owner's movements up to the sky-world of mythic ancestors, as well as the connection of this powerful realm to the world of living people via the celestial umbilical cord. Loud, rapid drumming of whips on the overturned basket covering the girl initiate's sacred food also makes the connection between sky-world and terrestrial world audible and material. When the chant owner begins a more slowly paced series of twenty-one chants naming places along the rivers criss-crossing the Isana-Guainía drainage area, he materializes the mythic process of creating an expanding world of places through the women's playing of sacred flutes and trumpets in various regions. This dynamic expansion of the world is musically conveyed in the series of chants through the use of different starting pitches, acceleration and deceleration of tempo, microtonal rising, and contrasts between loud and soft. Finally, to reiterate the fact that this geographic movement across the world is not just some aimless meandering or wandering around, the closing málikai song of female initiation returns to exactly the same four sung pitches featured in the opening song and to the loud, rapid percussive tapping of whips over the upside-down basket.

Thus, malikái singing and chanting in female initiation rituals is a material enactment of the second mythic creation of the world. Through the singing and chanting and closely associated blowing of tobacco smoke, the mythic history of the Wakuénai phratries is materially brought into the present and inscribed into the girl initiate's body via the sacred food that forms the focal object of ritual performance. After a morsel of the food is lifted on the end of kapéti whips to the girl's mouth, the chant owner strikes her three times with a kapéti whip across her back. In effect, the mythic ancestors' geographical and historical opening-up of the world has been internalized by the girl's body through her eating of the sacred food, and her body itself becomes the percussive instrument that sounds the connection between this historical opening-up of the world and the sky-world of mythic ancestral power.

Both in mythic narratives about Ámaru and Kuwái and in the malikái singing and chanting for female initiation rituals, a chiasmatic structure is invoked, beginning with a focus on the construction of a vertical axis mundi at the center of the world and returning to the same place of origin at the end.[7] This return to the point of departure is given material expression in the opening and closing malikái songs of female initiation rituals primarily through the use of the same style of percussive whipping and exactly the same four pitches at each ritual's beginning and end.

The importance of musical and other sounds as a bridge between subjective experience and sensory perception of the material world is explored in narratives about the mythic past of Iñápirríkuli, Ámaru, and Kuwái. Most directly, the primordial human being (Kuwái) is said to have used a combination of speaking and sound making to create the species and objects of nature.

Kuwái arrived in the village and began to show himself to the boys. *Kamena liúkakawa dzakalérikojle. Kamena likapéetaka jna iénpetipe.*

He began to "speak" the word-sounds that could be heard in the entire world. The world was still very small.

Kamena kákukani jnéemakaru liaku pjiume jekuápiriko. Tsúukatua jekuapi.

He began to speak. "Heee," he said. The sound of his voice ran away and opened up the world.

Kamena kákukani. "Jeeee," pidaliaku. Limáliatsa pida jiekuita lijméetawa jekuapi.

In this first creation of the world, the voice of Kuwái—his "speaking" (*kákukani*)—is a musical naming power, the power to name-into-being the species and objects of nature through singing and chanting. The world-creating voice of Kuwái in myth becomes the prototype for ritual performances of malikái singing and chanting and the episodic re-enchantment of the material world into a hyperanimate realm of powerful things that can cause harm or even death if not appropriately (i.e., musically) named in rituals. The musical naming power of Kuwái becomes transformed in the second creation of the world into the material objects that allow groups of men to reconstitute the mythic body of Kuwái, or the sacred flutes and trumpets. The fiery mythic death of Kuwái and his rebirth as a set of musical instruments is the prototypic act of materialization. Through this mythic action, the life-creating power of Kuwái as an autonomous being whose voice created the world through musical naming power transforms itself into a set of material objects—plant materials that have been *made* into musical instruments and that are *heard* only when groups of women and men *play* them in different places. The materialization of musical naming power into musical instruments also corresponds to the moment when geographic space becomes differentiated into distinct places and when the social world is divided according to gender, descent, and age.

The cycle of narratives about Kuwái establishes the centrality of musical sounds, bound together by the naming power of language, as a creative force. A narrative about the origins of evil omens (*hínimái*) explores the role of sound as a way of reconnecting subjective experiences to the material world in situations in which creative, life-giving powers have been put to the service of death and destruction. The narrative about evil omens forms the last part of a cycle of stories about the trickster-creator (Iñápir-ríkuli) and his ongoing, violent struggles against a group of animal-affines. As usual, animal-affines—the trickster-creator's brothers-in-law—are eager to kill him, but this time they are especially angry because Iñápir-ríkuli has finally succeeded in killing their father, Kunáhwerrim, who is the trickster's arch-enemy. The brothers send their sister with Iñápirríkuli into the forest with instructions to seduce him at night so that they can come and kill him by throwing poison down from the treetops. When they reach the place where they will make camp for the night, the woman asks Iñápirríkuli for his cartridge of poisoned darts in order to *count* them, but he has already hidden two darts inside the chamber of his blowgun. After resisting the woman's sexual advances, Iñápirríkuli puts her into a deep sleep by blowing tobacco smoke over her. The woman's brothers arrive late at night in the form of *cuchicuchi* monkeys:

> They arrived above him and took out their poison. "Here comes blood, Iñapirríkuli," they said. He jumped to one side. They began to throw poison again. "Here comes blood, Iñapirríkuli," they said. He leapt to one side. Iñapirríkuli looked and saw dark shapes against the moon. "For you the blood is coming," he said. Iñapirríkuli shot one of them with a dart, *tsa!* Again he loaded a dart, *tsa!* He shot the other one with a dart. And he went back.
>
> He returned and lit a cigar. He blew smoke over the woman to wake her up. Then Iñapirríkuli jumped and lay down next to the fire. He blew over the fire, and white ashes fell on top of him. His wife woke up. Her two brothers fell from the trees to the ground. She heard: "*Ti!*," then the other one, "*Ti!*" She tried to wake up Iñapirríkuli:
>
> "Ñapirrikú! Ñapirrikú!" He was sound asleep, snoring.
>
> "Ñapirrikú! Ñapirrikú!"
>
> "Je, jee," said Iñapirríkuli. "What happened to you?"
>
> "I was frightened by what I heard," she said.
>
> "Paa," said Iñapirríkuli. "I was sleeping like a man dying of old age. Just now I woke up because you woke me. What did you hear?"
>
> "What I heard was frightening. Right here I heard something fall close to us. What I heard falling was heavy. *Ti!*" (Hill 2009)[8]

Iñápirríkuli blows tobacco smoke over the woman, who again falls into a deep sleep. After cutting off the heads of the two slain monkey-brothers, he stomps on each of the severed heads, which sprout into *dzapura* fruit trees.

In the morning, Iñápirríkuli tells the woman that he had a terrible dream during the night that might portend illness for someone in her family. The woman decides to return to her village,[9] with Iñápirríkuli following close behind. Iñápirríkuli then proceeds to make a series of evil omens that provoke increasing fear in the woman: a foul smell from picking his teeth, a blowgun placed in her way that trips her, and little white birds that fly in front of her. Finally, Iñápirríkuli tricks the woman into believing that he is injured and cannot continue on the journey back to her brothers' village. She runs ahead in terror, only to learn from her family that her brothers had fallen ill and died during the night.

This narrative about the origin of evil omens reads like a blueprint for how materiality is experienced and encountered in the process of reversing an evil plot of seduction and betrayal that was intended to result in witchcraft, sorcery, and the death of the trickster-creator. The first indication that the intended evil is to be reversed or thwarted comes when the woman *counts* the trickster-creator's darts. As I have demonstrated in the section on numeral classifiers above, the activity of counting and expressions of quantity are anything but neutral or value free for the Wakuénai. The first direct clue that signals to the woman that something has gone wrong with her brothers' plan comes through *hearing* the *sounds* (*Ti! Ti!*) of two large objects falling on the ground nearby. The second clue comes from the trickster-creator's *dream* and his interpretation of the dream, which frightens the woman into turning back to her family's village. Other clues proceed through the senses of *smell*, *touch*, and *vision*, each time increasing the woman's level of fear and causing her to run faster along the path back to her village. Like the cycle of narratives about the primordial human being (Kuwái), the narrative about evil omens also establishes the fundamental importance of sound and hearing as the mediators between subjective states of emotion and the exterior world of material things. The *sound* of the two monkey-brothers' dead bodies falling to the forest floor sets in motion a reawakening of the senses in which the woman's fear is reattached to the physical, material world.[10]

Materialization and the Concept of "Owners"

Focusing on Wakuénai concepts of the material world as a two-way process of subjectivizing materialities and materializing subjectivities leads ultimately to the indigenous concept of male and female "owners" (*-limínali, -límnarru*). Becoming an "owner" is fundamentally about materializing subjectivities through exercising control over the hyperanimate, musical process of awakening, evoking, and implementing the ritual power, or danger, inherent in all things with which people interact in bodily, physical ways (by handling, eating, or making them, for instance). Artifacts and other objects or places that people make, such as gardens, houses, and villages, are thus always imbricated in this two-way process of subjectivizing materiality and materializing subjectivity, especially when a person makes an artifact with the intention of giving it to a specific individual or group. During my fieldwork in 1981, for example, a young man named Samuel was locally known as the most skillful maker of decorative baskets using natural brown and dyed-black strips of palm bark from *pwáapwa* palm strips (*tirita* in Spanish). I was delighted when he asked me if I would like him to make a pair of these baskets for me in return for a modest cash payment. On one of the two baskets, Samuel wove the letters "JONATHAN HILL" in black against a light tan background. This naming of the basket gave it a personal identity that still gives material expression to our friendship as it sits on a shelf in my university office in 2008. Pwáapwa palm strips are one of the most important and widely used plant materials, and in malikái singing and chanting, pwáapwa is called *límutukéku éenu*, or "the ripping-sound sky-spirit," because of the tearing *sound* that results when men separate the long, thin strips of bark from the wood.

The ultimate prototypical "owner" is the primordial human being of myth, Kuwái, one of whose names is Wamínali ("our owner") in *kapetiá-pani* songs (collective men's songs performed in kwépani and male initiation rituals). In male initiation rituals and kwépani ceremonies, the relationship between groups of men and Kuwái is materialized in two different ways. First, the men wear crowns of palm fronds and hang bundles of palm fruits down their backs, transforming their bodies into palm trees that bear edible fruits. Just as the fiery mythic "death" of Kuwái transformed his body into palm trees, so too must men become trees during sacred rituals and ceremonies. The second way in which the relationship between groups of men and Kuwái is materialized in these rituals and ceremonies is through playing sacred flutes and trumpets that are each said to represent a different part of the body of Kuwái. Thus, the orchestra of male flute and trumpet players collectively embodies the primordial human being of myth. Kuwái's power of materializing the subjective is the prototype of human "ownership" and is the paramount example of this type of action. All Wakuénai people participate in this universe of ritual power and the materializing of the occult, but the most agentive individuals are senior men who have gained recognition as powerful chant owners (malikái limínali), whose powers are modeled after those of Dzuli, the first chant owner of myth. In this case, the specialized ritual powers of chant owners is based on the rote memorization of all spirit-names, the ability to perform spirit-naming in rites of passage, and the knowledge of esoteric meanings of especially powerful spirit-names.

Other expressions of "ownership" derive from these prototypes. *Pudalímnali* and *pudalímnarru* are male and female "owners" of *pudáli* exchange ceremonies, which always involve pairs of male- and female-owned offerings of food. Pudáli is fundamentally concerned with musicalizing relations between human communities and nonhuman activities of fish, amphibians, birds, insects, and plants. Through the use of musical sounds and collective dance movements as the key means of transforming the ritual power inherent in natural fertility and regeneration—fish spawning runs and game animal migratory patterns—into materials— offerings of smoked fish and game meat and kulirrína trumpets—pudáli ceremonies are a collective dramatization of materializing the subjective relations between men and women who are members of different descent groups. Kulirrína trumpets, which as I have explained are named after a species of large, striped catfish (kulírri in Wáku; *surubí* in Yeral), are the only musical instruments exchanged during pudáli ceremonies. At the end of the night-long session of drinking songs and other musical dances in male-owned ceremonies, the guest men give their kulirrína trumpets, emblazoned with designs announcing their makers' phratries, to the host men as reminders of the latter's obligation to sponsor a reciprocal, female-owned ceremony a few weeks later.[11]

The terms for male and female "owners" are also frequently used in reference to village headmen (*pantímnali*, or "male house-owner") and their wives (*pantímnarru*, or "female house-owner"). Semantic collapsing of villages into houses reflects the fact that the Wakuénai lived in large round-house communities until the mid-twentieth century (see fig. 10.2). These magnificent house structures are described in firsthand written accounts from the late nineteenth century (Matos Arvelo 1912) and are still in use among Arawak-speaking Yukuna and Tanimuka living along the Mirití-Paraná River (a tributary of the Caquetá) in Colombia. In Wakué-nai social organization, political leadership exercised by "house-owners," or headmen, and their wives overlaps considerably with their abilities to play leading roles in organizing ritual and ceremonial activities at local and intercommunal levels. Although communal round houses have been entirely replaced by smaller, single-family houses made by slapping clay onto wooden frames, the houses of village headmen and other ritually

Figure 10.2. *Tanimuka* communal round house in southeast Colombia. *Photo*: Jonathan D. Hill, 1989.

powerful individuals continue to be located immediately adjacent to the main port at the entrance to public communal spaces that serve as the "stages" for collective rituals and ceremonies. Headmen's houses are subjectivized as animate things in female initiation rituals and pudáli ceremonies through collective singing that refers to the door of the house as "house-mouth" (*pánanumá*). Communal round houses have powerful social effects as architectural structures that materialize the boundary between insiders and outsiders, and it is these socio-religious relations that were the central target of missionary campaigns to destroy the round houses.

Conclusion

In this chapter, I have shown that the nature of materiality in an indigenous Amazonian society is as much about transforming subjective relations of thought and emotion into materials, or at least "thing-like" entities, as it is about bestowing animateness or "subject-like" properties on material things and beings. For the Wakuénai, these complementary processes of objectification and subjectivization are most directly embodied in activities of sound production, such as singing, chanting, speaking, exhaling, playing musical instruments, drumming, rattling, and making objects.

Materializing the occult is a process of awakening the senses through auditory stimulation that then becomes visible through bodily activities, such as dancing or blowing tobacco smoke, which in turn double or reinforce the auditory creation of political, ritual, historical, generational, developmental, and gender-inflected social spaces. Olfactory and tactile sensations also play important roles in connecting the auditory and the visual. The central importance of blowing tobacco smoke in rituals makes sense in terms of this sensuous, auditory, olfactory, tactile, and visual process of materializing the occult. In a single action of blowing tobacco smoke over a patient's head or an initiate's food, shamans and chant owners make the *sound* of exhaling ("h-m-m-m-p-f") visible as a cloud of smoke that can also be smelled and touched.[12] Perhaps that is the reason why chant owners (malikái limínali) are referred to as "blowers" (*sopladores* in local Spanish) and describe their singing and chanting as "blowing tobacco smoke" (*ínyapakáati dzéema*).

Notes

1. The concept of materialization developed in this chapter builds upon Ellen Basso's insight (1985) that musical performances in Kalapalo rituals and ceremonies are better understood as a process of singing-, playing-, and dancing-into-being the powerful spirits of myth than as mere activities of representing or singing *to* these mythic beings. There are also strong parallels between my analysis of Wakuénai shamanic rituals in this chapter and Laura Graham's work on Shavante dream recitations (1995) inasmuch as we are both concerned with demonstrating how subjective relations of thought and emotion are transformed into materials.

2. One of the downfalls of ethnoscience as a theoretical approach was an over-reliance on formal elicitation and frame analysis as a method and the assumption that the classical notion of category was universal (see Lakoff 1982).

3. For a more complete documentation and analysis of numeral classifiers in Wáku, see Jonathan Hill (1988).

4. "The heat was horrible, but I scarcely even felt it. My hand wrote page after page of notes, but it didn't hurt at all, it just flowed along without effort. My little chair was hard and uncomfortable, but I felt comfortable nevertheless. I had eaten only two arepas with coffee at nine, but I felt no hunger at all. And so it went" (Hill field diary, August 6, 1981:278–79).

5. Hill (1993) on spirit-naming processes.

6. See Fernando Santos-Granero (1998) for a discussion of similar toponymic naming processes among the Yanesha, an Arawak-speaking people of eastern Peru.

7. Elsewhere (Hill and Staats 2002) I have written about the importance of chiasmatic structures in shamanic and other sacred verbal art among indigenous peoples of lowland South America.

8. Readers can listen to sound files of the narratives and ritual performances of singing and chanting discussed in this essay on the Web by locating the Curripaco collection (KPC001, KPC002, and KPC003) at the Archives of Indigenous Languages of Latin America (AILLA) at www.ailla.utexas.org.

9. Once again, the mythic narrative exhibits a chiasmatic structure.

10. Shamanic curing rituals, and especially those in which a person's death is revealed to be the result of evil omens, can be understood as a process of re-awakening the senses (Hill 1992). The shaman's use of hallucinogenic snuff and tobacco, musical dynamics, and dramatic physical activities constitutes a controlled overloading of the senses designed to effect an energy-consuming, or "ergotrophic," shamanic state of consciousness, or "SSC" (Noll 1983; d'Aquili, Laughlin, and McManus 1979).

11. Kulirrína trumpets are known as *surubí* ("catfish") in *lingua geral*. In 1927, Kurt Nimuendajú traveled through the northwest Amazon and concluded that these "catfish" trumpets were the most distinctive material artifacts produced by the Arawak-speaking "Baniwa" of the Isana River (Nimuendajú 1950).

12. The importance of exhalation and breathing made audible, visible, and otherwise sensible is explored in Jean-Michel Beaudet's recent study (1997) of Wayapí musical performances and instruments.

References

Basso, Ellen. 1985. *A Musical View of the Universe: Kalapalo Narrative and Ritual Performances*. Philadelphia: University of Pennsylvania Press.

Beaudet, Jean-Michel. 1997. *Souffles d'Amazonie: Les orchestres "tule" des Wayãpí*. Collection de la Société Française d'Ethnomusicologie, III. Nanterre: Société d'Ethnologie.

Craig, Collette. 1982. Jacaltec: Field Work in Guatemala. In Timothy Sharpen (ed.), *Languages and Their Speakers*, pp. 3–57. Cambridge, MA: Winthrop Publishers.

d'Aquili, Eugene, Charles Laughlin, and John McManus. 1979. *The Spectrum of Ritual: A Biogenetic Structural Analysis*. New York: Columbia University Press.

Delbrück, Max. 1986. *Mind from Matter: An Essay in Evolutionary Epistemology.* Palo Alto: Blackwell Scientific Publications.

Dixon, Robert. 1983. *Where Have All the Adjectives Gone?* Amsterdam: Mouton Publishers.

Graham, Laura. 1995. *Performing Dreams: Discourses of Immortality among the Xavante of Central Brazil.* Austin: University of Texas Press.

Greenberg, Joseph. 1972. Numeral Classifiers and Substantival Number: Problems in the Genesis of a Linguistic Type. *Working Papers on Language Universals* 9:1–39.

Hill, Jonathan. 1987. Wakuénai Ceremonial Exchange in the Northwest Amazon Region. *Journal of Latin American Lore* 13(2): 183–224.

———. 1988. The Soft and the Stiff: Ritual Power and Mythic Meaning in a Northern Arawak Classifier System. *Antropológica* 69:55–77.

———. 1992. A Musical Aesthetic of Ritual Curing in the Northwest Amazon. In E. Jean Langdon (ed.), *Portals of Power,* pp. 175–210. Albuquerque: University of New Mexico Press.

———. 1993. *Keepers of the Sacred Chants: The Poetics of Ritual Power in an Amazonian Society.* Tucson: University of Arizona Press.

———. 2009. *Made-from-Bone: Trickster Myths, Music, and History from the Amazon.* Urbana: University of Illinois Press.

Hill, Jonathan, and Susan Staats. 2002. Redelineando el curso de la historia: Estados euroamericanos y las culturas sin pueblos. In Guillaume Boccara (ed.), *Mestizaje, identidades y poder en las Américas,* pp. 13–26. Quito and Lima: Abya Yala and Instituto Francés de Estudios Andinos.

Lakoff, George. 1982. *Categories and Cognitive Models.* Berkeley: Institute of Cognitive Studies, University of California at Berkeley, Berkeley Cognitive Science Report Series.

———. 1987. *Women, Fire, and Dangerous Things: What Categories Reveal about the Mind.* Chicago: University of Chicago Press.

Matos Arvelo, Martín. 1912. *Vida indiana.* Barcelona: Casa Editorial Maucci.

Nimuendajú, Kurt. 1950. Reconhecimento dos Rios Içana, Ayarí, e Uaupés: Relatorio Apresentado ão Serviço de Proteção ãos Indios do Amazonas e Acre, 1927. *Journal de la Société des Américanistes* 39:128–70.

Noll, Richard. 1983. Shamanism and Schizophrenia: A State-Specific Approach to the "Schizophrenia Metaphor" in Shamanic States. *American Ethnologist* 10(3): 443–59.

Santos-Granero, Fernando. 1998. Writing History into the Landscape: Space, Myth, and Ritual in Contemporary Amazonia. *American Ethnologist* 25(2): 128–48.

About the Contributors

Aristóteles Barcelos Neto is lecturer in the Arts of the Americas program at the University of East Anglia. He has gathered ethnographic collections for several museums in Brazil, Portugal, France, and Germany. He is the author of *Visiting the Wauja Indians: Masks and Other Living Objects from an Amazonian Collection* (Museu Nacional de Etnologia, 2004) and *A arte dos sonhos: Una iconografia ameríndia* (Assírio and Alvim, 2002). He has also published various articles and books based on his research on Amazonian and Andean ritual, material culture, and iconography. He is currently working on a film trilogy about sacred objects and miracles in the central Andes of Peru.

Philippe Erikson is lecturer (since 1996) and chairman of the Department of Anthropology (since 2005) at the University of Paris X-Nanterre. He has spent three years doing fieldwork with Panoan peoples, namely the Matis of western Brazil (since 1984), the Chacobo of northeastern Bolivia (since 1991), and the Cashinahua of Peru (since 2007). His research interests include comparative western Amazonian social organization, material culture, cosmology, and body ornamentation. He is the author of *La Griffe des Aïeux: Marquage du corps et démarquages ethniques chez les Matis d'Amazonie* (Editions Peeters, 1996)—also published in Spanish as *El sello de los antepasados: Marcado del cuerpo y demarcación étnica entre los Matis de la Amazonía* (Abya-Yala/IFEA, 1999)—and he has edited *La pirogue ivre: Bières traditionelles en Amazonie* (Musée Français de la Brasserie, 2006). His numerous publications also include contributions in *Amazonía Peruana, Anthropozoologica, Campos, Current Anthropology, Journal de la Société des Américanistes, Journal of Latin American Lore, Journal of the Royal Anthropological Institute, L'Homme, Mana, Natural History, Scripta Etnologica,* and *Techniques and Culture.*

Maria A. Guzmán-Gallegos is writing her PhD dissertation at the University of Oslo. She has spent several seasons doing fieldwork in Amazonian Kichwa communities in Ecuador. Her research focuses on Kichwa notions of personhood and gender and how these intertwine with particular understandings of agency, the nature of objects, and kinship. She is also interested in the relation between notions of personhood and materiality and Kichwa ideas and practices concerning the constitution of space. In relation to the latter, she has placed particular emphasis on the importance that the Amazonian Kichwa ascribe to relations with nonindigenous actors, whether missionaries, nongovernmental organizations, oil companies, or the state. She is the author of *Para que la yuca beba nuestra sangre: Persona, género y parentesco en una comunidad kichwa en la amazonía ecuatoriana* (Abya Yala, 1997).

Jonathan D. Hill is a professor of anthropology at Southern Illinois University, Carbondale, and the editor of the journal *Identities: Global Studies in Culture and Power* (Taylor and Francis, Inc.). He did extensive fieldwork with the Wakuénai (also known as Curripaco) of Venezuela in the 1980s and 1990s and is the editor of *Rethinking History and Myth: Indigenous South American Perspectives on the Past* (University of Illinois Press, 1988), *History, Power, and Identity: Ethnogenesis in the Americas, 1492–1992* (University of Iowa Press, 1996), and (with Fernando Santos-Granero) *Comparative Arawakan Histories: Rethinking Language Family and Culture Area in Amazonia* (University of Illinois Press, 2002). He is the author of *Keepers of the Sacred Chants: The Poetics of Ritual Power in an Amazonian Society* (University of Arizona Press, 1993), *Made-from-Bone: Trickster Myths, Music, and History from the Amazon* (University of Illinois Press, 2008), and numerous articles and chapters on music, myth, and history in lowland South America. In 2007, all his field recordings of Wakuénai music and narratives were digitized and placed on the Web site (www.ailla.utexas.org) of the Archives of Indigenous Languages of Latin America at the University of Texas. He is currently editing (with Jean-Pierre Chaumeil) a volume of essays covering new research on indigenous ritual wind instruments in lowland South America.

Stephen Hugh-Jones is emeritus research associate of the Cambridge University Department of Social Anthropology and a fellow of King's College. He has done long-term field research in the region of the Colombian northwest Amazon. His research and publications have focused on the indigenous peoples of northwest Amazonia. His thematic focus has ranged from ethnobotany and ethnozoology to symbolism, mythology and ritual, kinship and architecture, the cocaine business and the articulation of different economic systems, and alternative systems of education. He is currently engaged in a study of ceremonial objects, visual display, and ceremonial exchange that will form part of a wider study of northwest Amazonia as a regional system. He also has research interests in Tibet and Bhutan and is currently directing a study of the Pad gling traditions in Bhutan. Recent publications include "The Gender of Some Amazonian Gifts: An Experiment with an Experiment" in T. Gregor and D. Tuzin (eds.), *Gender in Amazonia and Melanesia: An Exploration of the Comparative Method* (University of California Press, 2001) and "The Substance of Northwest Amazonian Names" in G. vom Bruch and B. Bodenhorn (eds.), *The Anthropology of Names and Naming* (Cambridge University Press, 2006).

Els Lagrou is senior lecturer at the Graduate Program of Anthropology and Sociology of the Federal University of Rio de Janeiro. Her theoretical interests center on cosmology, ritual, shamanism, aesthetics, gender, and emotions among Amerindian people. Since 1989, she has been conducting field research among the Cashinahua of the Purus River in the Brazilian rain forest (in the state of Acre) near the frontier with Peru, now having done a total of eighteen months of fieldwork in the area. This research led to a PhD degree at the University of St. Andrews and at the University of São Paulo, to a book titled *A fluidez da forma: Arte, alteridade e agência em uma sociedade ameríndia (Kaxinawa)* (Topbooks, 2007), and to several articles and chapters of books published in Brazil and abroad—among them: "Homesickness and the Cashinahua Self: A Reflection on the Embodied Condition of Relatedness," in J. Overing and A. Passes (eds.), *The Anthropology of Love and Hate. The Aesthetics of Conviviality in Native Amazonia* (Routledge, 2000); "Sorcery and Shamanism in Cashinahua Discourse (Purus River, Brazil)," in N. Whitehead and R. Wright (eds.), *In Darkness and Secrecy: The Anthropology of Assault Sorcery and Witchcraft in Amazonia* (Duke University Press, 2004); and "Social Metaphors of Sociality and Personhood in Cashinahua Ritual Song," in U. Demmer and M. Gaenszle (eds.), *The Power of Discourse in Ritual Performance, Rhetoric and Poetics* (LIT-Publishers, 2007).

Joana Miller carried out fieldwork among the Mamaindê, a Nambikwara group from the northwest of the Brazilian state of Mato Grosso, from 2002 to 2005. She obtained her doctorate in 2007 from the Programa de Pós-Graduação em Antropologia Social (PPGAS) at the Museu Nacional/ Universidade Federal do Rio de Janeiro. Her thesis focuses on the relationship between the body ornaments used by the Mamaindê and their theory of the person. She is currently carrying out postdoctoral research at the Laboratoire d'Anthropologie Sociale du Collège de France, where she is studying the Amazonian modalities of objectification and subjectification.

Fernando Santos-Granero is a staff researcher at the Panama-based Smithsonian Tropical Research Institute. He has done extensive ethnographic research in Yanesha and Ashaninka communities of central Peru and historical research on the indigenous societies and economies of the Upper Amazon region. He was director of the Centro de Investigación Antropológica de la Amazonía Peruana (Iquitos, Peru) and research coordinator of the Area of Amazonian Studies of the Facultad Latinoamericana de Ciencias Sociales (Quito, Ecuador). With Frederica Barclay, he is co-author of the books *Selva Central: History, Economy, and Land Use in Peruvian Amazonia* (Smithsonian Institution Press, 1998) and *Tamed Frontiers: Economy, Society, and Civil Rights in Upper Amazonia* (Westview Press, 2000), and co-editor of the six volumes of the *Guía etnográfica de la alta amazonía* (STRI/IFEA, 1994–2007). With Jonathan D. Hill, he has co-edited *Comparative Arawakan Histories: Rethinking Language Family and Culture Area in Amazonia* (University of Illinois Press, 2002). He is the author of *The Power of Love: The Moral Use of Knowledge amongst the Amuesha of Central Peru* (Athlone Press, 1991), *Etnohistoria de la alta amazonía, siglos XV–XVIII* (Abya-Yala, 1992), and *Vital Enemies: Slavery, Predation, and the Amerindian Political Economy of Life* (University of Texas Press, 2009). He has also published numerous articles and book chapters on native Amazonian history, shamanism, sociality, and philosophies of power.

Terence Turner is emeritus professor of anthropology at the University of Chicago and Cornell University and has worked with the Kayapo of central Brazil since 1962. His writings on the Kayapo cover social organization, myth, ritual, history, politics, values, and inter-ethnic relations. He has also published numerous papers on general theoretical topics, including structural analysis and interpretation of ritual and myth; the social construction of the body; emotions and subjectivity; family structures and kinship terminology; the application of aspects of Marxian theory to anthropology; and the theoretical basis of anthropological approaches to human rights, multiculturalism, and activism in support of indigenous causes. He has made a number of ethnographic films about the Kayapo with the British Broadcasting Company and Granada Television International. In 1990, he founded the Kayapo Video Project, through which the Kayapo have become able to shoot and edit videos about their own culture and encounters with Brazilian society.

Harry Walker obtained a bachelor's degree in anthropology from the University of Melbourne and is presently a doctoral candidate at the University of Oxford. Between 2004 and 2006, he conducted sixteen months of fieldwork with the Urarina of the Chambira river basin in Peruvian Amazonia, focusing on kinship and social organization, gender, and ritual language. He has previously worked with rural populations in Cambodia as an applied anthropologist. He has forthcoming publications on humor and male solidarity and the permeation of money and foreign goods into traditional forms of exchange. Current research interests include rhetoric and ritual discourse, subjectivity, modernity, and political economy.

Index